BUSINESS ETHICS

Concepts, Cases, and Canadian Perspectives

Edited by W. Peter Kissick

Lu Zhang

2012
EMOND MONTGOMERY PUBLICATIONS
TORONTO, CANADA

Emond Montgomery Publications Limited
60 Shaftesbury Avenue
Toronto ON M4T 1A3
http://www.emp.ca/highered

Printed in Canada on recycled paper.

We acknowledge the financial support of the Government of Canada
through the Canada Book Fund for our publishing activities.

Acquisitions and development editor: Mike Thompson
Marketing manager: Christine Davidson
Director, sales and marketing, higher education: Kevin Smulan
Supervising editor: Jim Lyons
Copy editor: Gillian Scobie
Production editor: Andrew Gordon
Proofreaders: Paula Pike & David Handelsman
Indexer: Edwin Durbin
Text designer and typesetter: Tara Wells
Cover designers: Stephen Cribbin & Simon Evers
Cover image: *The Encounter*, sculpture by William McElcheran
(photo by R. Dittwald)

Library and Archives Canada Cataloguing in Publication

Kissick, W. Peter (William Peter), 1965-
Business ethics : concepts, cases, and Canadian perspectives / W. Peter Kissick.

Includes index.
ISBN 978-1-55239-319-2

1. Business ethics.   2. Business ethics—Canada.   I. Title.

HF5387.K56 2012   174'.4   C2012-900500-2

Brief Contents

Contents

PART THREE Applying Ethical Principles: Cases and Analysis

APPENDIX Additional Case Exercises

Preface

When my colleagues and I in the Queen's University commerce program recently redesigned our Introductory Business Ethics and Corporate Social Responsibility course, we examined a wide range of text offerings, hoping to properly complement the new course structure we were planning. We wanted a book that would provide sound discussion on the important underlying concepts of business ethics—foundational philosophies, principles of corporate social responsibility (CSR), stakeholder analysis, and the fundamental issues facing key corporate stakeholders. But we also knew that our students would be attracted to, and benefit greatly from, the fascinating cases and controversies inherent in the study of business ethics, and we wanted to make such materials available to them. In the end, we sought out a book that would look a lot like the one in your hand right now.

In *Business Ethics: Concepts, Cases, and Canadian Perspectives*, we have assembled some of the most respected business ethics scholars in Canada. They have written chapters that *explain* core concepts in their areas of expertise, allowing this book to serve as a standard textbook. However, we have also invited the authors to provide their perspectives on the issues and cases common in the field. These insights will challenge students to analyze some of the more controversial elements of business ethics, armed with an understanding of key underlying concepts. A large number of short cases are presented (with each chapter in Part Three beginning with a sector-specific case study, and a dozen wide-ranging case exercises presented in an appendix at the end of the text), all of which will help form the basis of lively classroom debates. I believe that this book can be used as an effective textbook and reader, and also provide a backbone to, and impetus for, invigorating discussions about the many aspects of business ethics.

Acknowledgments

Editing this book was a truly a labour of love. I got to be the first to read the work of these insightful writers, whose drafts were so strong that I often had little actual editing to do. I would like to thank all of the contributors for their efforts and enthusiasm. I would also like to express my gratitude to my colleagues at Queen's School of Business who have helped design the business ethics course on which the structure of this book is based: Jim Ridler, John Phelan, and Christine Coulter, with an honourable mention to Peggy Cunningham, who has had a significant influence on business ethics teaching at Queen's. Finally, I thank the professionals at Emond Montgomery Publications who so skillfully shepherded this project: Mike Thompson, Jim Lyons, Gillian Scobie, and Tara Wells.

—*Peter Kissick*

The author and the publisher wish to thank the contributors for their dedication to this project. They also wish to acknowledge the following people for their suggestions, feedback, and assistance during the various stages of development of this book: Joel Bakan (UBC), John Bishop (Trent University), Michael Cody (Simon Fraser University), Wes Cragg (York University), Peggy Cunningham (Dalhousie University), Richard Dixon (University of Alberta), Diane Girard (McGill University), Jai Goolsarran (Centennial College), Sefa Hayibor (Carleton University), Diane Huberman-Arnold (Carleton University), John Knox (Nipissing University), Bob Korth (SFU), Ian Lee (University of Toronto), Chris MacDonald (Saint Mary's University), Cameron Pyper, Don Waterfall (University of Toronto), Kernaghan Webb (Ryerson University), Jaana Woiceshyn (University of Calgary), and William Woof (York University).

Please also visit the website for this book for more information and additional resources: **www.emp.ca/businessethics**.

About the Authors

Frederick Bird is a research professor in political science and the Balsillie School of International Affairs at the University of Waterloo, and distinguished professor emeritus at Concordia University.

Leonard J. Brooks is a professor of business ethics and accounting at the Rotman School of Management, University of Toronto.

Darren Charters is an instructor in the School of Accounting and Finance at the University of Waterloo.

Michael Cody is an instructor in the Beedie School of Business, Simon Fraser University.

Christine Coulter is an instructor and academic integrity adviser at Queen's University School of Business.

Wesley Cragg is professor emeritus of business ethics at the Schulich School of Business, York University.

Peggy Cunningham is dean and R.A. Jodrey Chair in the Faculty of Management, Dalhousie University.

Richard J. Dixon is executive director of the Centre for Applied Business Research in Energy and the Environment, Alberta School of Business, University of Alberta.

David J. Doorey is an associate professor in the School of Human Resource Management at York University, and director of Osgoode Hall's LLM Program in Labour and Employment Law.

Cathy Driscoll is a professor in the Department of Management, Sobey School of Business, Saint Mary's University.

Diane Girard is an instructor in the Desautels Faculty of Management, McGill University.

W. Peter Kissick is an associate professor of business law and business ethics and distinguished faculty fellow in business law at the Queen's University School of Business, and is director of the Queen's Business Law Clinic, Queen's University Faculty of Law.

Chris MacDonald is an associate professor in the Philosophy Department at Saint Mary's University, and a visiting professor at the Ted Rogers School of Management, Ryerson University.

Margaret McKee is an assistant professor in the Department of Management, Sobey School of Business, Saint Mary's University.

Jordan Mitchell holds an MBA from the Richard Ivey School of Business and has written and published over 100 cases with professors at several business schools, including Harvard, Ivey, IESE, Darden, and Dalhousie.

Pamela Murphy is an assistant professor and E. Marie Shantz Fellow in Accounting, Queen's University School of Business.

Kernaghan Webb is an associate professor in the Department of Law and Business at Ryerson University's Ted Rogers School of Management, and founding director of the Ryerson University Institute for the Study of Corporate Social Responsibility.

David Weitzner is a special assistant professor of strategy/policy at the Schulich School of Business, York University.

William Woof is an instructor at the Schulich School of Business, York University.

PART ONE
Foundations of Business Ethics

What Is Business Ethics, and Why Study It?

Introduction

In recent years, commerce programs have increasingly been requiring their students to take a stand-alone course in business ethics. Initially, students' reactions were mixed: many thought the course long overdue while others wondered aloud why *they* would need a course that would tell them "how to act properly." Happily, most business students nowadays are no longer surprised to find themselves sitting in a class called "Business Ethics and Corporate Social Responsibility" (or "Responsible Leadership," "Business Sustainability," or whatever term is used at their particular school for such a course).

Canadian high school students are aware of the foibles of Bernard Madoff, the government bailouts of automakers and large financial institutions, and the greenhouse gas effect. And, broadly speaking, students have a *sense* of what business ethics (BE) is about, even if they are less sure about what corporate social responsibility (CSR) or stakeholders are. If anything, the notion of ethics has become so ubiquitous in the media over the past decade that some business observers wonder whether perhaps it has lost much of its meaning. Indeed, corporate scandals such as the 2008 financial crisis are discussed in the same terms as Tiger Woods's marital problems.[1] Thus, undergraduate business students arrive in our courses not wanting a rationale as to why they should take the course, but with more practical concerns: what specifically is a BE-CSR course about and what useful skills will I develop?

---

1 In perhaps a telling commentary, a columnist in a popular sports magazine recently declared in a column that he would no longer pass judgment on the morality of athletes, because it had become so common as to be "sport itself."

Consequently, we in the field of BE-CSR no longer have to justify our existence, but we still have to define, in more explicit terms, not just what ethics and CSR *are*, but also how they can be *applied*. In many ways, we face similar issues to those that teachers of introductory accounting or marketing face with a new class—students arrive with a lot of broad knowledge, some misinformation, and little in the way of specific understanding.

In the program I teach (at Queen's University), for several years at the outset of our course we have asked our students questions like: "What do you think business ethics is?" and "What do you expect to gain from this course?" The responses, while unsurprisingly varied, do provide some common themes. Students would like to understand the broader context for business. They've read about various notorious cases, and would like to understand them. They sense that there will be difficult questions ahead in their careers and seek some tools for addressing them. Finally, students want to see a broader picture—and BE-CSR *can* provide the "big picture" view that the traditional business disciplines cannot.

To generalize these sentiments, it seems that students think that BE-CSR helps teach them *why*, when other courses are teaching them *what* and *how*. But beyond philosophical discussion, BE-CSR must enable business students to become better managers or professionals so they can benefit their own careers and meet the expectations of society.

Why Study Business Ethics?

As mentioned, fewer and fewer students are asking this question. That may be simply because they think they already know (or maybe they think *should know*). In my experience, that is not always the case and, consequently, it is still a question worth asking (and answering). Milton Friedman once famously said that the only social responsibility of business is to make a profit. While Friedman has been both lauded and reviled for this comment,[2] business practice in Canada and around the world has rendered this statement remarkably narrow. Friedman and followers of the traditional "theory of the corporation," suggest that corporations are run for the benefit of their owners: the shareholders. Friedman wrote that corporations must operate "within the rules of the game ... without deception or fraud" (Friedman 1970). It follows then, using Friedman's logic, that if a corporate manager (or board of directors) were to consider the interests of any person or group of people beyond the shareholders, it would be akin to the imposition of a tax on those owners, which the executives have no legitimate right to do. And yet

---

2   Much more so than he probably imagined in 1970 when he wrote those words in a short article for the *New York Times Magazine*, I suspect.

business today considers the views of consumers when advertising a new product, the concerns of environmental interest groups when determining how its new factory should be built, and (in what may be the ultimate heresy to Friedman) the interests of its employees when it sets up a philanthropy program. In other words, business today looks beyond the interests of shareholders when making decisions—it considers the perspectives of other *stakeholders*.

Stakeholders are people, or groups of people, who have an interest in a business decision. They have a legitimate desire to see a certain outcome from a business decision, because they would benefit from that decision, or perhaps be threatened by a different outcome. For example, shareholders may wish to see a marginally profitable plant shut down, but employees at that plant would be threatened by such an outcome—they would be losing their jobs and financial security. Both are stakeholders in that business and both views need to be taken into account to make an ethical decision. Businesses have found that they ignore the perspectives of broader stakeholders (employees, customers, interest groups, communities, and yes, shareholders too) at their peril. Consumers "shop with their feet" and will go to another retailer if they don't like one store's policies. Employees have been given (by statute) many more rights than they have ever had, and they assert those rights to affect corporate decision making. Interest groups such as the World Wildlife Foundation, Greenpeace, or People for the Ethical Treatment of Animals (PETA) wield considerable power for swaying public opinion, and by consequence, corporate decisions. (For example, in Chapter 4, we will examine the impact PETA had on McDonald's and its chicken supply policy.) And today's corporations consider the communities in which they operate. Although Friedman said corporations should not be engaged in philanthropic endeavours (it would amount to "stealing" from the shareholders), Canadian corporations routinely make charitable donations.

It is easy to argue that we are more focused on business ethics because newspaper headlines make it unavoidable. Most of us have heard the names Enron, WorldCom, Bernie Madoff, and Conrad Black. But why have these cases received so much publicity? Certainly, the sheer size of the collapse of Enron or Madoff's pyramid scheme would be difficult to ignore, but an elaborate accounting scandal is not a very reader-friendly subject. The fact is, as will be discussed in many chapters in this book, the stakeholders of businesses are now demanding that their concerns be heard. And while this certainly includes shareholders at annual general meetings of public companies, it also includes environmental interest groups, consumers, governments, and employees. The communities affected by modern business are *more aware* than ever before of corporate malfeasance, and are *demanding* more than ever before that they be treated fairly, and that their rights not be trampled by corporate (in)action. So, in essence, business ethics considers the impact of business not just on society broadly, but on the specific groups of stakeholders who may be affected by business decisions.

Most companies now have ethics policies as part of employment agreements; indeed, if a public company would like to list its shares on the Toronto Stock Exchange, it must have a corporate ethics policy that binds its directors. Other companies have external ethics policies that address issues affecting external stakeholders, such as who can be a supplier to that company, or even who can be a customer.[3] Asking "Why business ethics?" seems to have become an antiquated notion.

Before we leave the topic of increased societal expectations, we should also discuss the societal expectations on professionals, because many readers of this book will become accountants, or bankers, or investment advisers, or gain some other professional designation. It has long been thought that the term "professional" did not only mean special expertise, but also connoted a certain degree of trustworthiness and integrity. After all, if everyone knew physiology or the law of contracts, we wouldn't need doctors or lawyers. But these are highly technical areas that take years of study and practice to master; consequently, we place our trust in these experts, who help us make decisions about vital parts of our lives. For that reason, professionals have carved out a sort of monopoly (along with monopoly pricing). Accordingly, society does not condone unethical behaviour by professionals. And professional licensing bodies hold their licensed members to very high standards: a crisis of ethics can cost the modern professional her licence to carry on her practice.

In answering "why study business ethics," we have focused solely on macro reasons—why society demands good BE and why corporate organizations would want to act ethically. But ethics can also be a very personal issue. Simply by being members of a society, we run into ethical dilemmas. For instance, is it acceptable for a professor to tell a student in class that her answer to a question was "good," when he knows that the answer was, in fact, wrong? He does this to encourage the student to participate in class, or to not hurt the student's feelings or embarrass her, but nevertheless the professor has still told a lie. Likewise, the business manager or professional will be constantly confronted by ethical dilemmas. Does the manager promote her friend over another applicant she does not know? Does the manager tell her boss that what he has just proposed may be illegal? Does the professional "hide" the mistake his firm has just made to save a client embarrassment?

---

3   For an interesting example of an "external" ethics policy, consider the Ethical Policy of Vancouver City Savings Credit Union ("VanCity"). https://www.vancity.com/AboutUs/OurValues/EthicalPolicy/.

Thus, we must also study business ethics so that, on an individual level, business people and professionals can identify the ethical issues that may confront them. By studying business ethics, we can also learn skills to identify and analyze choices to resolve these ethical dilemmas.

What Is Business Ethics? What Is CSR?

So far, in making the case for studying business ethics and CSR, we have really been discussing the role of business in modern society. That analysis has assumed that businesses will act ethically, and that they will adhere to some idea of "social responsibility."[4] However, we haven't yet really defined "business ethics" and "corporate social responsibility," and what underlies those concepts.

Ethics is the application of, or acting within, moral principles. In other words, an ethical person has values, and acts in accordance with those values. Those values are perceived as being good, or as representing the best in man or society. In Chapter 2, when Christine Coulter explains some ethical philosophies, you will be introduced to the theories of Immanuel Kant, John Stuart Mill, and John Rawls, each of whom attempted to explain what would constitute what is truly moral. Put in plain language, the ethical manager tries to do what is *right*—in a normative sense. "Normative" means how things *ought* to be. For instance, Canadian society might believe that polluting our waterways is "bad" because we value healthy water ecosystems; an ethical manager would not make a decision that would cause untreated sewage water to be dumped into the St. Lawrence River.

Ethicality is often confused with "legality." *Legality* can be defined succinctly as compliance with legal obligations. Legal obligations might be those imposed by a government, by an industry or professional regulatory body, or even by courts of law. While there can be no doubt that managers must act within the confines of the law, we will see in Chapter 7 that acting in strict compliance with the law does not necessarily mean acting ethically: for the "moral manager," they are two separate obligations.

Moral, Amoral, and Immoral Actions

While the various authors in this book may disagree on various aspects of business ethics and CSR, we all expect the modern manager to aspire to be a "moral manager." A *moral manager* is a businessperson who, while in a position to make corporate decisions, decides in a way that takes into account ethical duties (his own and those of the organization). "Moral," in this context, can be contrasted

---

4 Or put another way, we have assumed that the rational business manager will want to act ethically and fulfill his societal role.

with someone who acts "amorally." An amoral decision is one in which the decision-maker does not consider ethical obligations at all. She may not be "immoral"—that is, intending to do harm to someone or something else to benefit herself—but she may simply only be considering the "bottom line," without regard to the path she would follow to improve it. The moral manager, meanwhile, considers the impact of decisions on broader stakeholders, as well as societal implications.

A simple example will help to illustrate the difference between moral, amoral, and immoral action. Consider a Canadian apparel company that wishes to set up a garment assembly factory "offshore" (that is, outside of Canada). We assume that the modern ethical standard is that child labour is a social ill and should be banned (for example, this is a ban set out in the United Nations Universal Declaration of Human Rights). The immoral manager would *seek out* the country that has the most lax employment laws (and presumably laws that permit employing children), or employment laws that are not enforced, so that he can open a plant and employ child labour (which is considered the cheapest of all). The amoral manager would simply consider which country had the lowest labour costs. He would be sure to comply with the law, but would do no more than that. He is likely to be against child labour personally, but the fact that the laws of the country in which he has chosen to open the plant would permit child labour would not enter his mind. The moral manager would adhere to the principle that the employment of children is always wrong, and therefore would either not set up his factory in that country, or would exceed the labour standards set out in the local laws and be sure not to engage child labour at all.

Corporate Social Responsibility was born from the desire of the modern business to act morally and in congruence with the legitimate wishes of its stakeholders. CSR tends to be considered at a macro level—from the corporation's perspective. Obviously, the company's board of directors and senior executives can have a tremendous influence on the CSR direction of the company. The corporation, understanding the demands placed on it by its broader stakeholders, tries to implement policies that would benefit these stakeholders. It has been suggested by Archie Carroll and others that corporations have four distinct responsibilities: to be financially viable (earn a profit); to comply with legal obligations; to act ethically; and to aspire to "give back" to the community (acting philanthropically). Carroll's pyramid (Figure 1.1) is a visual representation of the levels of responsibilities.

Some critics of CSR have taken issue with the last of the "four levels"— philanthropy. Those critics often conclude that CSR is only about making charitable donations. But the company acting in accordance with its CSR obligations would first ensure that it had met the other three obligations; the company that is losing money and might have to lay off employees would not be acting responsibly if it made a massive financial donation to a local charity. In fact, that company would

Figure 1.1   The Pyramid of Social Responsibility

PHILANTHROPIC RESPONSIBILITIES

Be a good corporate citizen
Contribute resources to the
community; improve quality of life.

ETHICAL RESPONSIBILITIES

Be ethical
Obligation to do what is
right, just, and fair; avoid harm.

LEGAL RESPONSIBILITIES

Obey the law
Law is society's codification of
right and wrong; play by the rules.

ECONOMIC RESPONSIBILITIES

Be profitable
The foundation upon which all others rest.

Carroll's pyramid is a model of how a socially responsible business should work.

At the base of the pyramid is the "economic" level, which refers to the corporation's business success and profitability. Second is the "legal" level, at which the company complies fully with all relevant laws and regulations. At the third, "ethical" level, the corporation must satisfy social demands of justice and fairness. At the fourth level, a corporation must become a good corporate citizen and assume philanthropic responsibilities to improve the communities in which it conduct its business. These could include charitable donations or support of local cultural or athletic programs.

Source: From *Academy of Management Executive: The Thinking Manager's Source* by A.B. Carroll. Copyright © 2004 by The Academy of Management. Reproduced by permission via Copyright Clearance Center.

be harming the community it seeks to serve, by causing many of its employees—and members of that community—to be unemployed.

Consequently, one might wish to define "philanthropy" a little more broadly; in effect, this pillar of the socially responsible business reflects the fact that a business is set in a community, and its decisions should take into account the interests of the broader community. If that means a system of corporate donations to improve the social fabric of a community, so much the better, as long as the corporation is not doing a disservice to its other stakeholders in so doing (Kernaghan Webb will provide a much more complete discussion of CSR in Chapter 6).

How to Engage in Business Ethics and CSR: This Book

Knowing that a manager is expected to act ethically does not necessarily mean the manager will do so, or even that he knows how to make the ethical choice in every case. Many variables make ethical business practice difficult:

- Understanding the issue: Is this an ethical dispute or a factual one?
- Identifying the players: Who are the relevant stakeholders and what do they want?
- Competing stakeholders: Where several stakeholders have competing expectations, who is right?
- Competing ethics: Where there may be diametrically opposed courses of action, each of which can be considered "ethical," how does one make decisions?
- Competing goals: Can I act ethically and also meet the production quotas my boss has set for me?

This book is meant to address these questions, both generally and in specific contexts. The chapters will approach these issues in two ways. First, the book serves as a textbook in the traditional sense, as chapters present approaches to BE and CSR, and some underlying theory and tools for understanding them. However, it should be apparent by now that, like most academic disciplines, these issues are both complex and controversial. Consequently, this book has a second aspect, with contributors providing their perspectives about the analytical tools they have presented. In many cases, the contributors will relate their analyses to specific problems.

The book is divided into three parts. The aim of Part One is to provide the philosophical foundations for BE and CSR. In this part (which includes this opening chapter), we have included chapters that introduce key ethical theories (such as deontology and utilitarianism), and a chapter on critical thinking, especially when addressing a moral dilemma.

In Part Two, we look more specifically at the nature of ethical decisions and CSR strategy. Here we make it clear that BE and CSR are unique areas of study in management academia and are treated like any other discrete area of business study. We consider BE and CSR structurally (stakeholder management and related or alternative theories in Chapters 4 and 5, and a description of CSR broadly in Chapter 6), at an individual level (through the discussions of leadership and how to make ethical decisions in Chapters 8 and 9) and at an organizational level in Chapter 10 (strategic management and CSR). In Chapter 7, we also consider the difference between business ethics and compliance with the law.

Finally, in Part Three, we recognize that while BE and CSR are unique disciplines, they can only be properly understood when seen in action. What do these principles look like when applied to specific business contexts or sectors? To highlight these contexts, each chapter in Part Three begins with a business case that raises issues and questions you should consider as you read. In Part Three, we consider:

- BE and CSR for the small business and entrepreneur (Chapter 11);
- a Canadian company dealing with ethical questions in the context of international business and globalization (Chapter 12);
- the concerns of the modern employee in the workplace (Chapter 13);
- ethical issues inherent in financial reporting and accounting, and especially the incidence of fraud (Chapter 14);
- BE and CSR when companies engage in marketing initiatives (Chapter 15);
- issues of BE in the technology sector (Chapter 16);
- a study of a Canadian industry currently at the heart of a raging BE and CSR debate: the oil-producing sector (Chapter 17); and
- the BE and CSR issues inherent in another uniquely Canadian context, the health-care industry (Chapter 18).

We hope that in reading this book—which features the work of leading Canadian scholars—and (we hope) in using it as the basis for class discussions about business ethics, corporate social responsibility, stakeholders, or the issues presented in the various business contexts, you will not only learn about this area and develop some analytical tools for your future career as a businessperson, manager, or professional, but also that your interest in the area will be piqued. Although in this text we can only begin to address these topics, you will no doubt find this area of study challenging and fascinating. It is our hope that this book, and your introductory courses in business ethics and corporate social responsibility, will act as a springboard for you to become a moral manager or a moral professional, and that your interest in these issues continues to grow.

value conception

REFERENCES

Carroll, A.B. 1991. The pyramid of corporate social responsibility: Toward the moral management of organizational stakeholders. *Business Horizons* (July–August): 39–48.

Friedman, M. 1970. The social responsibility of business is to increase its profits. *New York Times Magazine*, September 13.

DISCUSSION QUESTIONS

1. As you begin your course, what is your preconception of "business ethics"?
2. What do you think you might gain from studying it?

CHAPTER 2 / CHRISTINE M. COULTER

Theories of Ethics: An Introduction for Business Students

Ethic
Living a life is worthy and admirable
"the nature and structure of ethical norms"

Introduction

For some students, reading about ethical theory is not what they thought they would be doing in business school. However, in the pages that follow, this chapter will provide an overview of some of the major traditions of ethical theory, and try to show why understanding them is so useful to the student of commerce. This chapter is not meant to provide an in-depth explanation and analysis of each tradition, but rather to introduce readers to the main ways of thinking about ethical decision making generally. Further chapters will provide opportunities to consider these various theories in the context of real-world business decisions.

CHAPTER OUTLINE

While there are competing theoretical traditions, and specific theories within those traditions that could be included in an introductory chapter, we will limit this discussion to three. These three approaches are mainstays of the field of ethical theory and seem to be approaches that endure over time and across many cultures. These approaches are widely applied, accessible, reflect some shared values, and are useful in practical decision making. First, we will examine *teleological theory*, using John Stuart Mill's conception of utilitarianism as the key illustrative theory of maximizing well-being. Next, our focus will shift to *deontological theories*, drawing on Kant as the prime example of duty-based morality. And finally we will examine *social contract theory,* using John Rawls's work as the key approach to ethics based on a hypothetical social agreement founded upon justice. But first, let us consider theory more generally.

individual - self reflection

A Few Words About Theory

A theory is a system of thought that includes linked principles that seek to explain, guide, and/or predict action or results. A theory is *more* than an idea; it is a conception of something that includes a definition of some end or idea, as well as a way of thinking about the issue at hand, and often a methodology for doing so. A theory attempts to explain and justify a desired state, and provide useful principles of action that lead to that state. An ethical theory, then, includes a coherent conception of a morality (which is the *end,* or *the attainment of good*) and a way of thinking about what is right. The purpose of a theory of ethics, therefore, is to establish and justify the content of a moral life, and to provide principles or guidelines for how to behave morally.

Theories of Ethics: Determining What Is Right

The study of ethics seeks answers to fundamental questions about moral behaviour. Our concern with what is ethical or moral is essentially a concern with what is right. Therefore, to engage in ethical theory is necessarily to be concerned about good action, behaviour, and character. Here are some key points to remember as you begin your study of ethics:

- Determining what is ethical requires concern for others; otherwise "what's right" would always be the self-interested answer.
- The study of ethics appeals to logic rather than instinct; otherwise, "what's right" would be anything we desire.
- Further, the study of ethics seeks integrated and justifiable reasons for *knowing* the right action. Ethical theorists and moral philosophers undertake to create arguments and rational appeals for particular ways of thinking that ought to be accepted by rational individuals. These ways of thinking also create guidelines for appropriate behaviour and decision making to support the espoused belief in what is right.

No theory is perfect. If one were, then there would be no competing theories and decisions would be easy. Ethical theories are particularly tricky because, though rooted in reason, they necessarily appeal to values, and it is challenging in pluralistic societies to achieve consensus on moral values. Much theorizing has been done with the private or public citizen as a subject, rather than the business person per se. Applying traditional ethical and moral philosophies to business is rather new and the fit is not always perfect. But businesses comprise individuals who make decisions in, as members of, and on behalf of their organizations, and these decisions have wide-reaching consequences for other individuals, communities, and sometimes nations beyond the business. Even when acting as agents of business, individuals appeal to some sense of ethics—well-defined or not, principled or not, conscious or not—in their decisions. And so it is important for the student of business to understand basic ethical theory, not only for his or her own decision making, but also for understanding and analyzing the decisions of others.

A Normative Approach to Theory

Throughout much of history, ethics and morality have been firmly rooted in religious belief. What was right was whatever the divine being (that is, God, or gods) dictated. However, since the Age of Enlightenment (a highly influential intellectual movement in 18th-century Europe that advocated reason as a means of reforming society and advancing knowledge), there has been a shift from *religious* authority to a *secular* approach to thinking about the world. Theories of ethics have become secular (that is, related to the natural world and not connected to religion), rooted in worldly definitions of morality, and directed at what individuals should do to achieve a moral life in this life, without reference to an afterlife or divine command. A normative approach to theory is an exploration of what *ought* to be, and what one *should* do, rather than an evaluation or description of what is actually happening in this society or any other. The goal is to establish what the priorities of a moral life should be, and how one ought to behave to achieve these priorities.

This normative approach applies to each of the three key areas of focus for this chapter: teleological, deontological, and social contract theories.

Teleological Theory

Telos is the Greek word for purpose; teleological theory suggests that each thing in the world has some purpose, and what is right is what leads to that ultimate purpose. Therefore, the proper purpose of a thing must be defined before the proper action leading to its fulfillment can be determined. Teleological theories of ethics define the desired moral consequences to be realized, and, often, undesired consequences to be avoided. Right and moral acts, therefore, are those that achieve the desired outcomes. The right act is *instrumental* in that it brings about the preferred outcome. The means to that desired end, as a rule, is not as important a consideration.

Utilitarianism is one of the best-known and widely applied teleological theories. In it, *utility*, or the maximization of human well-being and the absence of pain (where pain is defined as the opposite of happiness) is the desired moral outcome.[1]

---

1   John Stuart Mill explains: "The creed which accepts as the foundation of morals, Utility, or the Greatest Happiness Principle, holds that actions are right in proportion that they tend to promote happiness, wrong as they tend to produce the reverse of happiness. By happiness is intended pleasure, and the absence of pain; by unhappiness, pain and the privation of pleasure" (Mill 2007, 6).

Some Key Definitions

Normative theories explore what *ought* to be, and what one *should* do; they do not describe or evaluate actual states or events. For example, a normative theory of ethics may say that one *should* not commit murder; *actual* commissions of murder would have no bearing on whether this moral principle is correct.

Teleological ethics, also known as *consequentialism*, is concerned with the purpose of things. Thus, the right act is that which achieves the desired outcome. *Utilitarianism*, the best-known teleological theory, states that utility, or the maximizing of human happiness (or minimizing of pain), is the desired moral outcome.

Deontological ethics maintains that one's moral duties or obligations determine right actions in every circumstance, regardless of the consequences. As a result, one must do something because "it is the right thing to do."

Social contract theory is the basis of an approach to ethics that seeks to provide a sufficient amount of social order (laws, political stability, and so on) to allow individuals to pursue their individual goals. Under this "contract," one consents to certain conditions or restrictions, based on the fact that one also benefits from being part of a functioning society.

An **instrumental good** is one that is valuable because it leads to something else. An **intrinsic good**, in contrast, is one that is good in and of itself; it is inherently right and does not depend on anything else. In teleological theories, the good or right act is one that brings about the desired outcome. If the desired outcome is straight teeth for everyone, for example, then the right action is to provide braces for people with crooked teeth. Providing braces is *instrumental* to achieving straight teeth.

Virtue ethics, another important teleological theory with roots in Aristotelian thinking, takes the purpose of human life to be the flourishing and full realization of moral excellence. A fully formed individual is a virtuous one, who achieves the highest levels of human development. One lives life so as to achieve this full humanity and the actualization of human virtues. Therefore, one must define the characteristics of a moral and virtuous person, which may include virtues like honesty, courage, loyalty, compassion, and selflessness. The moral individual behaves in a way that demonstrates these virtues, even if they do not come naturally, so that these behaviours become habit. Once an individual embodies the virtues fully, he or she has achieved the appropriate moral end. (For more on virtue ethics, see Chapter 8 on leadership.)

The central idea is that maximum well-being for everyone is the moral end toward which all persons ought to strive. Individual acts are right insomuch as they lead to this conception of utility.

Roots of Utilitarianism

Utilitarianism is most often associated with the works of Jeremy Bentham and John Stuart Mill. Bentham, writing in the late 18th century, articulated a fully formulated theory of utilitarianism, which espoused the maximization of pleasure and the absence of pain. Bentham argued that pleasure and pain govern human life and that these factors ought to be the basis of a theory of ethics. He argued that ethical acts are those that are instrumental in maximizing pleasure and minimizing pain for everyone. He developed a calculus to help uncover the correct decision, based on the likelihood of the outcome providing the most pleasure for the greatest number of people, and the least pain.

John Stuart Mill, writing in the early 19th century, extended Utilitarian theory to respond to the critique that it simply promoted the maximization of lower-level pleasures and immediate gratification. A strong criticism of Bentham's theory was that it justified short-term indulgence and physical gratification, while sacrificing higher-order pleasures such as intellectual stimulation and appreciation of arts. In response, Mill focused much of his work on defining and defending the primacy of *quality* pleasure, which he referred to as happiness, over the *quantity* of gratification. Mill argued that any person capable of experiencing both higher- and lower-level pleasures would clearly prefer the higher level. Mill was famous for remarking that it "is better to be a human dissatisfied than a pig satisfied; better to be Socrates dissatisfied than a fool satisfied" (Mill 2007, 8). In this comparison, the pig satisfies the lowest-level (usually bodily) pleasures while Socrates pursues higher-level (usually intellectual) pleasures. Mill argued that although Socrates was less likely to succeed in all his endeavours, he was more content and satisfied living a higher-order life than a fool would be achieving instant gratification.

John Stuart Mill

Contemporary Utilitarianism

In its contemporary incarnation, some language has evolved so that the focus of utilitarianism is human well-being but the foundation of utilitarianism remains the same. John R. Boatright adeptly summarizes utilitarian theory as having four main characteristics:

1. Consequentialism: The rightness of an action is determined by its consequences.
2. Hedonism: Utility is the pursuit of well-being and the absence of pain or harm.

3. Maximalism: The focus is on the greatest amount of well-being for the greatest number of people.

4. Universalism: Everyone's happiness must be considered and one's own interests cannot count for more than those of others (Boatright 2009, 33).

Utilitarians fall into two primary camps: *act utilitarians* and *rule utilitarians*. Act utilitarians require one to consider the four characteristics described above when facing a particular situation, and then decide how to act in each particular case. Rule utilitarians ask what the likely outcome would be in all similar situations, and then make decisions based on that calculation. Act utilitarians must therefore make situation-specific decisions each time they face a moral decision, whereas rule utilitarians subscribe to a set of principles founded more generally on utilitarian morality.

Some Shortcomings of Utilitarian Theory

While utilitarianism is an appealing theory, there are some not insignificant shortcomings of this approach to a theory of ethics. Many readers will immediately worry about the focus on the collective evidenced in the universal approach taken in this theory. The theory allows for the possibility of harming one, or a minority, of individuals for the greater overall well-being. An approach prohibiting any pain would render the theory useless in practice because it would be impossible to calculate all possible harm in every individual decision, so the possibility of permitting some harm remains.

A second criticism focuses on the issue of measurement. The critique is twofold. First, there is the problem of being able to categorize and measure well-being or happiness. What makes one individual happy and fulfilled may not satisfy another person. If each person is free to pursue his or her own interests, then how can another person take unknown interests into account in their decision making? Can one really know and measure the pleasure or pain experienced by another? Second, critics point to the issue of critical mass in decision making. How many individuals comprise the "greater" good? Must well-being be equal to be maximized? How much discomfort could one individual endure for the greater good? These questions point to the practical difficulty of applying a utilitarian ethic in some cases.[2]

---

2 As an example of the difficulty of applying the utilitarian ethic, consider an example from the health-care field in a government-run health-care system like Canada's. Decisions are made in conditions of scarcity; not all treatments and medications can be funded because of cost. If treatments are funded in order to maximize well-being, and not every treatment and medication can be funded, how would decision-makers define the critical mass of patients who could be helped to justify paying for a treatment? How many patients could go without treatment? (For more on this example, see the case study on health care in Chapter 18.)

Finally, taken to its extreme, Utilitarianism could be used to justify any actions that lead to an acceptable outcome. Critics point out that the outcome always justifies the means used to achieve it, and that therefore all actions are permissible as long as the outcome is good. For example, lying to achieve personal or non-personal advantage could produce a good outcome without direct harm to anyone, but many argue that lying is unethical because it is intrinsically wrong, regardless of how instrumental it is in achieving a desirable end. Those who sympathize with these criticisms may be drawn to an approach to ethics that appeals to the intrinsic nature of actions, rather than their possible outcomes.

We turn now to the deontological approach to ethical theory.

Deontological Theory

Deos is the Greek word for duty or obligation. Deontological theory argues that the right action in any situation stems from the obligation to behave morally in every circumstance, and that the intention or principles behind actions must be morally pure. In other words, the act itself must be intrinsically moral to be right. Such theories pay no heed to the consequences of actions; in fact, the outcome of the action taken is irrelevant to whether the act is morally correct or not. Deontologists would say that one must do something because it is the right thing to do.

Kantian Ethics

The most widely cited deontologist is probably German philosopher Immanuel Kant. Kant wrote in the late 18th century and his moral philosophy is based on his conception of a good will. For Kant, the ultimate object for humans is a Good Will. Human will provides us with the capacity to reason. Belief in, and pursuit of, the Good Will is also the conclusion that reasoning yields. Kant says reason's "true destination must be to produce a will, not merely good as means to something else, but good in itself, for which reason [is] absolutely necessary" (Kant 2001, 154). Kant uses the term *maxim* to describe the principle on which a decision is made, believing that a principle underlies every

Immanuel Kant

decision, whether one consciously appeals to principle or not. According to Kant, maxims should be judged as moral or not, according to the tenets of morality that all reasonable people would agree to. A moral maxim is good for its own sake, applies universally, is absolutely true in every situation, and is never dependent on context or consequence. An example of a moral maxim is honesty. Kant would never permit a white lie to save face or feelings; on the contrary, he would argue that one must always tell the truth in every situation, because this is the required action based on the maxim of honesty.

The Categorical Imperative

How does one know which maxims are moral and should guide action? Before answering this question, Kant distinguishes hypothetical from categorical imperatives. A *hypothetical imperative* suggests that *if one wants x, one should do y*. For Kant, this type of decision making is permissible in non-ethical decisions, such as what to eat for lunch or when to go to bed. A *categorical imperative*, in contrast, is a command that one must obey in all moral questions, regardless of any other variable: *one must do y*. Kant argues that every individual is capable of determining the right action by understanding the categorical imperative, which he states in a number of formulations.

Kant states the categorical imperative primarily in the following formulation:

> Act only on that maxim whereby thou canst at the same time will that it should become a universal law. (Kant 2001, 178)

In this statement, Kant asks thinkers whether the action is one that the decision-maker would permit everyone in society to take and that would be possible for all to take. *Universalizability* is the key tenet of this formulation; it requires the maxim to be considered in all situations. For example, one cannot endorse lying even in the most complex of circumstances, since we would not endorse lying in similar or different circumstances. Such widespread lying would eliminate trust and prohibit the functioning of society. Therefore, lying cannot be a universal law, and because one has the duty to act only according to a maxim that could be a universal law, one cannot lie in any situation.

A second formulation of the categorical imperative is the following:

> So act as to treat humanity, whether in thine own person or in that of any other, in every case as end withal, never as means only. (Kant 2001, 186)

Here Kant argues that the ultimate human dignity of every individual must always be respected. An individual's worth is not diminished by actions or circumstances, and an individual should never be sacrificed for the collective good. Kant argues that one should never use an individual purely as a means to another end (except when the individual has consented to that relationship). Therefore, although one can, for example, employ the services of an individual for the purposes of one's business (and so use another's labour for one's own gain), one should not trick a customer for the same purpose (and therefore use their ignorance for one's own gain). In the first case, the employee has consented to the use of their labour in exchange for a wage; in the second instance the customer has not consented and is thus treated purely as a means to one's own end.

For Kant, ethics is essentially an exercise in reason. Reason directs us to the development of a Good Will. Kant asserts that by going through the intellectual process of the categorical imperative, any rational person can determine the ethical action to be taken. The ethical action is one that we would apply to everyone and it is one that respects the ultimate dignity of all individuals. This seems simple enough, but there are also some important challenges to Kantian theory.

Challenges to Kantian Ethics

A number of criticisms can be raised against the Kantian approach to ethics, including the inflexibility of Kantian moral theory: absolute and universal in language and intent, it never allows for context, outcome, consequence, emotion, or any other variable to play a role in decision making. While a universal theory is one appeal of Kant's approach, it can also make it difficult to apply in ambiguous or complex situations. In Kant's conviction to always tell the truth, for example, one is unable to tell any level of lie even if more harm comes about as a result of the truth. Many would agree that telling a mother her son died bravely in battle rather than as a coward who fled the battle, for example, seems a more humane and morally permissible approach.

The Kantian approach also raises the difficulty of conflicting duties and rights. In complex ethical dilemmas, there could be competing duties at play and the categorical imperative might not provide the right answer in practice. For example, many people would agree that lying to save one or many lives is not only morally permissible, but perhaps even morally required. Kant, however, would argue that the duty to tell the truth takes precedence because possible consequences are not part of the categorical imperative and the decision-making process. This disregard for consequences and impacts on persons are strong criticisms of the theory.

Social Contract Theory

A third approach to ethical theory is based on social contract theory. The idea of a social contract dates back to thinkers such as Thomas Hobbes and Jean-Jacques Rousseau, and through contemporary philosophers such as John Rawls and T.M. Scanlon. In this approach, it is understood that individuals in a society live together to achieve mutual benefit and a quality of life that would not be achievable without cooperation. In such a condition, individuals consent, at least in principle, to the conditions and terms of social order, to the basic laws and institutions that govern action, and, indeed, to the sacrifice of some individual freedoms in exchange for the functioning of the society. In this section, the philosophy of John Rawls will provide the framework for thinking about what behaviours are right and how one ought to know what is right.

Why a Social Contract?

The idea of a social contract might conjure up images of socialism and redistribution of wealth for some, and though some social contract approaches could justify such an interpretation, that is not the intention of many social contractarians. Instead, the focus, or end good, to be achieved is respect for the moral equality of persons. Such thinkers ask how to set up the conditions and institutions in a society so that they fundamentally respect the inherent dignity and equal moral value of persons. According to Rousseau (1987, 153):

> [I]nstead of destroying natural equality, the fundamental compact, on the contrary, substitutes a moral and legitimate equality to whatever physical inequality nature may have been able to impose upon men, and that, however, unequal in force or intelligence they may be, men all become equal by convention and by right.[3]

A social contract approach does not require that all citizens have similar interests or equal outcomes, but rather that the institutions of a society (political, social, legal, and economic) be designed to safeguard equal liberties and opportunities. Institutions should afford all persons respect and dignity based on the fact that individuals are of equal value morally speaking (and their worth is not based on the talents, wealth, or other attributes they come to possess by good fortune or other means). Persons' individuality is to be respected, and individual interests should not be aggregated into overall well-being. This is important not only to respect the moral equality of persons, but also because the structure of a society plays a role in determining the choices available to individuals. A democratic society shapes political choices; a pluralist society shapes individual possibilities; a capitalist society shapes work, consumption, and life possibilities. Because the structure of society plays such a big role, it is imperative that society be based on principles that treat individuals fairly so that all persons have maximum life possibilities.

Methodology for a Social Contract

Different social contract approaches consider individuals to be differently motivated by self-interest and willing to cooperate with others, but most theorists agree on an intellectual exercise whereby individuals in some "state of nature" (a state prior to the existence of social, political, and economic institutions) are required to decide on the rules of cooperation in the society. Individuals may have different levels of knowledge about their own abilities, talents, interests, values, and prospects. In John Rawls's conception of this state of nature (which he termed the *original position*), individuals have no knowledge of their personal situations or

---

3   Jean-Jacques Rousseau wrote *On the Social Contract* in 1762 and is widely considered to be a founder of social contract theory. The term "fundamental compact" in this quotation is akin to social contract.

dispositions, and are thus behind a *veil of ignorance* concerning their own circumstances. In this way, Rawls attempts to compensate for what he considers morally arbitrary advantages—or the advantages enjoyed because of things beyond one's control, such as natural intellect, talent, family circumstance, gender, wealth, and other possible advantages. All persons are required to imagine themselves in a position of equality, and of not knowing where they would end up in the society they design. Rawls argues that a rational individual would seek to design a society that provides for the least well-off; one would want to ensure fair treatment and minimal provisions for those at the bottom of the social order in case one were to end up in that position.

Rawls's theory of justice is complex and cannot be fully examined here. But to summarize, Rawls asserts that the social contract ought to ensure the primacy of justice in all political, social, and economic agreements. In Rawls's theory, the principles of justice are more important than the details and rules for setting up such institutions. He says that principles of justice

> are the principles that free and rational persons concerned to further their own interests would accept in an initial position of equality as defining the fundamental terms of their association. These principles are to regulate all further agreement. (Rawls 1999, 10)

Rawls further asserts that rational people would agree on two fundamental principles of justice. The first principle requires that each person have maximum basic liberties to the extent that they do not conflict with the liberties of others. This principle is meant to apply to the development of the political constitution and government. The second principle asserts that inequalities are permitted in social and economic spheres but that they must be justified in the following way: (1) inequality is permissible only where it is to the benefit of the least well-off and (2) the inequality is attached to positions and offices open to all. The first part of this principle,

John Rawls

called the *difference principle*, asserts that all individuals must be better off despite the inequality than they would be if all things were equal; in other words, the least well-off benefit from decisions as do the most well-off. For example, in a market system, presumably the least wealthy are better off than they would be in a subsistence system, even though the most well-off fare much better. The second part of the principle argues for equality of opportunity, not only for offices and positions, but also for acquiring the skills necessary to be qualified for such positions.

Rawls's theory of justice is concerned with the distribution of advantages and disadvantages, or of benefits and burdens, in a fair society. It does not call for equality of outcome, but rather for founding principles to be based on respect for the moral, equal worth of individuals and that any inequalities be justified as advantageous to all, in principle. Rawls is primarily concerned with political and social institutions, but he also argues that justice in political economy establishes certain limits that "follow from the priority of justice over efficiency and the priority of liberty over social and economic advantages" (Rawls 1999, 230). This means that there will be some limits on the free-market system to comply with the principles of justice.[4] In taking decisions or actions, one must respect the two principles of justice—respect for individual liberties and rights and the moral equality of persons.

Critiques of the Social Contract Approach

While the social contract approach has an appealing emphasis on justice and respect for persons, the theory has important shortcomings. First, some critics argue that Rawls's theory of justice is too encompassing and others that it is too narrow. Some assert that in the original position, rational individuals would take a greater risk in the hopes that they would end up in an advantaged position and therefore the requirements of justice would be less demanding. Others argue that Rawls's thinking should lead us to a requirement for equality of outcome, or a totally even distribution of benefits and burdens in society. There are questions about what an individual is to do when others do not fulfill the requirements of the social contract, when there is corruption in the system, or when others act immorally. Some argue as well that a social contract theory of business is too big a stretch of the purpose of contract theory, which is meant to justify social and political institutions.

Conclusion

This chapter has attempted to introduce students of business to the vast and interesting arena of ethical theory. The goal has been to simplify and summarize the objectives and principles of three major traditions in theory: teleology (illustrated through Mill's utilitarianism), deontology (illustrated through Kantian ethics), and the social contract (illustrated through Rawlsian justice). There are certainly other approaches to ethics, and to making good decisions in business. The traditions chosen for this chapter were based on the following logic: they are widely applied, they are accessible, they have informed the establishment of many of our

---

4 The Rawlsian approach would require any decision-maker to consider *justice* to be the moral imperative, and all decisions would have to respect the principles of justice. In a business case, when deciding whether to accept a bribe in a foreign market, the decision-maker would ask whether such an act would respect the maximum liberties of individuals. Would it make everyone better off, and would the least well off benefit as well as those who benefit from the bribe?

institutions, they reflect widely shared values (well-being, universal dignity, moral equality), and they are certainly useful in practical "real-world" decision making.

It is not the goal of this chapter to apply the theories to test cases—that will follow in subsequent chapters. Our goal has been to introduce students to the theories that are widely practised and to help them identify where the application of those theories is evident, both in their own actions and in those of others. Students will also identify the values that underlie institutional policies and ends. In making decisions that affect other citizens, organizations appeal to some concept of what is right. Understanding different approaches to ethics reveals what those priorities are. Further, through reflecting on their own values, students may find an approach that speaks to them and guides their behaviour and character development. And finally, it is hoped that some of the logic and reasoning shown in this chapter will be useful in developing students' own decision-making and persuasive-reasoning skills.

DISCUSSION QUESTIONS

1. The theories described above are generally considered to be competing theories; that is, one cannot employ one theory in some decisions and another theory in other decisions. Is this understanding of the theories as exclusive correct, and do you think it is practical?

2. In the increasingly global business environment, which is characterized by diversity of background, religious belief, values, and approaches to business, is it possible to achieve agreement on an ethical approach to decision making? Is it necessary?

3. Consider this scenario: a manager has just learned that as a result of delays in the supply chain, she will not be able to ship her product to the customer on time. The customer has just called asking for a status report because he is anxious for the product. This customer represents a very small piece of business to the manager. Apply each ethical lens described above to the situation to advise the manager on how to respond to the customer. Do the theories lead to different answers? Which do you think is correct?

SUGGESTED READINGS AND ONLINE RESOURCES

Canadian Centre for Ethics and Corporate Policy: http://www.ethicscentre.ca/EN/ index.cfm (the resource section includes many articles about business ethics topics).

Caux Round Table—Moral Capitalism at Work: http://www.cauxroundtable.org (network of business leaders including business networks, international organizations, and academic institutions with a focus on prosperity, sustainability, and fairness).

Stanford Encyclopedia of Philosophy: http://plato.stanford.edu/ (short explanations of philosophical concepts and theories).

United National Global Compact: http://www.unglobalcompact.org/ (international initiative for universal standards of human rights, labour, environment, and anti-corruption).

REFERENCES

Boatright, J.R. 2009. *Ethics and the conduct of business*. 6th ed. New Jersey: Pearson Education.

Kant, I. 2001. *The basic writings of Kant*. Trans. A. Wood. New York: The Modern Library.

Mill, J.S. 2007 (1863). *Utilitarianism*. New York: Dover Publications.

Rawls, J. 1999. *A theory of justice*. Rev. ed. Cambridge: The Belknap Press of Harvard University Press.

Rousseau, J.-J. 1987. *The basic political writings*. Trans. D.A. Cress. Indianapolis: Hackett Publishing Company.

Critical Thinking for Business Ethics

Introduction

This chapter will explore the application of critical thinking skills to the study of business ethics. We will begin by defining critical thinking. Students will learn that critical thinking is a systematic approach to evaluating and formulating good arguments in defence of specific beliefs or claims. Next, we will ask why critical thinking is essential to ethics. This involves illustrating how mistaken ethical beliefs can be rooted in either (1) faulty premises or (2) faulty logic. Faulty premises will be further subdivided into unacceptable factual foundations and unacceptable ethical principles.

We will then provide students with a handful of key critical thinking skills that they can apply to analyzing and resolving ethical challenges. First, students will learn about argument structure and the key components of arguments—namely, *premises* and *conclusions*. Next, students will learn about the ingredients of good ethical arguments, and will be given tools for examining both the acceptability of premises and the relevance of particular premises to specific conclusions. Finally, the chapter will include a brief discussion of various well-known pitfalls in ethical reasoning, including logical fallacies (such as the argument from tradition, false dilemma, and the argument from popularity) as well as cognitive biases (such as the framing effect).

What Is Critical Thinking?

The study of critical thinking is the study of what you should believe and why. It is about learning how to sort out which points of view are well supported, and which ones are not.

Good critical thinking skills are vital to an organization. The ability to determine which arguments, claims, and opinions are worth considering is essential if a business hopes to make sound, ethical decisions.

Critical Thinking and Ethics

Critical thinking is absolutely essential for making good ethical decisions. We all have ethical opinions—points of view on various issues. We have opinions on various social issues, such as free speech, or abortion, or the rights of Aboriginal peoples. Within the world of business, we may have views on things like the rights of shareholders, corporate environmental responsibilities, and what constitutes a "safe enough" workplace.

But how do we know which of those points of view are worth keeping? Clearly, not all ethical opinions are equally worthy. So we need an approach to help us sort out which of our current views should be kept, and which we would be better off without. Critical thinking is just the thing we need. Critical thinking provides us with a set of tools for evaluating claims and opinions, by asking whether those claims and opinions are supported by good *arguments*. (For additional coverage of ethical arguments, see Chapter 2, "Theories of Ethics: An Introduction for Business Students," and Chapter 9, "Making Ethical Decisions.")

What Is an Argument?

As the term is used by critical thinkers, an "argument" is an interrelated set of claims designed to convince the speaker's or writer's audience to accept some claim or point of view. All arguments have two basic components:

- A *conclusion*—the claim or point of view that the writer or speaker is trying to get his or her audience to accept;

- One or more *premises*—the reasons that the speaker or writer provides to attempt to convince his or her audience to accept the argument's conclusion.

Here is a simple example of an argument that tries to convince its audience of a simple factual claim:[1]

Apple is set to become a leader in the home computer industry. After all, the company has a tradition of producing beautiful consumer products like the iPod and iPad, and the OS X operating system is winning more and more converts.

The arguer here is trying to convince us of a simple conclusion, a prediction about the future of the home computer industry:

Conclusion: Apple is set to become a leader in the home computer industry.

Further, the arguer gives us two reasons, or premises, in support of that conclusion:

Premise 1: Apple has a tradition of producing beautiful consumer products like the iPod and iPad.

Premise 2: The OS X operating system is winning more and more converts.

Whether those two premises are true, and whether they add up to a convincing case for the arguer's conclusion, are separate matters, ones we will return to later. For now, it is enough to see that what this arguer is attempting to do is to provide two reasons in support of a conclusion.

Here is another simple example, but this time the argument tries to convince its audience of a particular ethical claim:

Bribery involves an attempt to get someone—usually a government official—to turn their back on their sworn duty. Bribery also distorts markets, allowing second-rate companies to beat out ones that make better products. So, bribery is wrong.

Again, the arguer is trying to provide support for a fairly straightforward point of view:

Conclusion: Bribery is wrong.

And again, the arguer has provided two premises in support of that point of view:

Premise 1: Bribery involves an attempt to get someone—usually a government official—to turn their back on their sworn duty.

---

1   Note: a "factual" claim is simply a claim that the speaker intends as a statement of fact. To call it "factual" does not mean it is true. It just means the speaker intends it to be taken as truth.

Premise 2: Bribery also distorts markets, allowing second-rate companies to beat out ones that make better products.

Again, we won't worry about whether this is a strong argument or a weak one. We'll get back to that later. For now, it is enough to begin to see the basic parts that make up the underlying structure of every argument.

Notice that the two examples above each have two premises. But, in principle, there's no limit to how many premises an argument may have.

What Makes a Good Ethical Argument?

To be strong, an ethical argument needs to possess three crucial characteristics:

- It must have premises—starting points—that are *plausible*.
- It must have premises that are *relevant* to the question at hand.
- It must have premises that provide *sufficient support* for its conclusion.

Plausible premises. First and foremost, a good ethical argument must have premises that are plausible. That is, they must be starting points that your audience considers reasonable. If your audience doesn't even think that your *starting* points are reasonable, your argument will simply never get off the ground. For ethical arguments, you will typically need two different kinds of premises. First, you will usually need some *factual premises*—that is, premises that explain the facts of the case you are considering. Second, you will need some *ethical premises*—premises that bring some ethical rule or principle or value to bear.

For example, here is a simple ethical argument:

Factual premise: Our training materials encourage our salespeople to lie to customers.

Ethical premise: Lying is unethical.

Conclusion: Therefore, our training materials encourage unethical behaviour.

For this to be a strong argument, *both* the factual premise and the ethical premise need to be ones that our audience is likely to see as reasonable. Consider, in contrast, the following example:

Ethical premise: People should be free to try to satisfy their own needs.

Factual premise: Shoplifting doesn't hurt anyone at all.

Conclusion: So, there's nothing wrong with shoplifting if you need something.

In the example above, there is a weakness in the argument's factual premise. The claim that "shoplifting doesn't hurt anyone" is clearly false—shoplifting hurts whomever owns the merchandise involved. That may be the owner of a small store or the shareholders in a large chain of stores. Thus, as an attempt at a statement of fact, that factual premise looks pretty bad. The fact that the argument above is based on such an implausible factual claim renders the entire argument suspect.

Next, take a look at this example:

Ethical premise: All pollution is unethical.

Factual premise: Manufacturing steel causes pollution.

Conclusion: Therefore, manufacturing steel is unethical.

In this example, the factual premise provided is clearly true: the process of manufacturing steel does cause many kinds of pollution. That fact is widely known, and if you're not sure, you can look it up to verify it. But look at the ethical premise. While we all agree that pollution is problematic, to say that all pollution is unethical is far too bold a claim. After all, *all* production processes—even ones that try very hard to reduce waste—produce at least *some* pollution. If all pollution were unethical, that would make all manufacturing of any kind unethical, and that simply isn't plausible. So, the ethical premise offered in this argument is not one that very many audiences would be willing to accept if they thought it through. The result is that this is a very weak argument.

Relevant premises. The premises of an argument need to be not just plausible, but also relevant to the topic at hand. Premises that are true, but off-topic, won't do anything to support your conclusion. Consider this example:

Ethical premise: Polluting our nation's waterways is unethical.

Factual premise 1: The mining industry has done little to reduce the amount of pollution it produces.

Factual premise 2: Besides, the mining industry has historically made use of child labour.

Conclusion: Therefore, the mining industry needs to clean up its act and do a better job at reducing pollution.

In the argument above, factual premise 2 is problematic, because it isn't clearly relevant to the *conclusion* being presented, and the conclusion is what indicates the topic of the argument as a whole. The problem is not that factual premise 2 is untrue—it is, in fact, entirely true that the mining industry once used child labour. The problem is that the premise is irrelevant to the issue at hand. This argument's conclusion is about pollution, so any premise that isn't about pollution is merely a distraction. Now, it may well be that this argument's *other* premises are true and relevant, and they might even be enough to support the conclusion on their own.

But we need to be careful to watch for irrelevant premises, because in some cases they may tilt our thinking on a topic and make a weak argument seem stronger. For example, if we have a strong negative reaction to the very idea of child labour, then we may immediately jump to accept this arguer's conclusion, without thinking critically about whether the other premises presented are true and relevant and support the conclusion.

Sufficient support. Finally, even if the premises offered are reasonable and relevant, we need to ask whether they add up to sufficient support for the conclusion being offered. The question whether a particular set of premises provides *sufficient* support to establish the truth of a particular conclusion is a very complex question indeed. The most we can do here is to provide a few examples that will illustrate what good and bad arguments look like in this regard.

Here is an example of an argument with premises that provide very strong support for the argument's conclusion.

Premise 1: All sweatshop labour is a form of slavery.

Premise 2: All slavery is unethical.

Conclusion: Therefore, all sweatshop labour is unethical.

The premises here provide *very* strong support for the argument's conclusion. In fact, if these premises are true, it is *logically impossible* for the conclusion to be false. But, of course, we need to remember that *the only thing* we are determining at this stage is whether the premises provide sufficient support for the conclusion. We could still see other problems with an argument like this. We might, for example, object that one or more of these premises is, in fact, not reasonable—but that is a separate issue. Even if we have doubts about one or more of the premises, it is still useful to be able to determine that, yes, *if* these premises are true, then they *do* provide sufficient support for the argument's conclusion.

For contrast, here's an example of an argument in which the premises do not provide such strong support:

Premise 1: *Some* sweatshops use slave labour.

Premise 2: Slave labour is unethical.

Conclusion: Therefore, all sweatshop labour is unethical.

Here, the premises provide only weak support for the argument's conclusion. After all, premise 1 makes only the very modest claim that *some* sweatshops use slave labour. To use that as the basis for the conclusion that all sweatshop labour is unethical is clearly a bit of a stretch. There might, of course, be *other* reasons to think that sweatshops are unethical, but the argument given here doesn't provide very strong support for that conclusion. Here is another example:

Premise 1: I have a friend whose boss used to read her emails.

Premise 2: I read about a case where a company hired private investigators to spy on employees.

Conclusion: Employers don't respect employees' right to privacy.

What can we say about this argument? Notice that the conclusion here amounts to a very broad generalization: it implies that all employers, everywhere, are unethical in this particular way. And the only evidence supplied consists of stories about two particular employers. Clearly, that's not enough evidence to provide anything remotely like *sufficient support* for such a broad generalization. A couple of instances are seldom enough to provide good support for any broad claim.

But, in some instances, data about specific cases can provide very good support for a broad conclusion, as long as there are enough such cases. Compare the argument above to this one:

Premise 1: We surveyed 100 major corporations, and 87 of them admitted that they had experienced security breaches involving customer data over the last 12 months.

Premise 2: Another survey of more than 1,000 smaller companies revealed that a large majority of them don't have formal privacy policies to ensure that customer data are kept secure.

Conclusion: It seems like protection of customer privacy is a major problem in corporate Canada today.

This is a pretty strong argument, for a couple of different reasons. First, the conclusion of this argument is moderate. It doesn't say that all companies have this problem; it merely says that it is a "major problem." The second—and most important—strength of this argument lies in the large amount of evidence that it brings to bear. A large amount of evidence can easily provide *sufficient support* for a reasonably modest conclusion.

In a full course on critical thinking, you would learn to categorize arguments as either *inductive* arguments or *deductive* arguments, and would learn that different kinds of arguments can fail or succeed in very different ways. Some arguments are so constructed that, if they work as planned, they will provide sufficient support— in fact, they will guarantee their conclusion. Other arguments are constructed in such a way that, even if they work as planned, providing *strong* and perhaps even *compelling* evidence, they can never *fully guarantee* the truth of their conclusion. Unfortunately, getting into such distinctions in any detail is beyond the scope of this short chapter. (See the suggested websites at the end of this chapter for useful links.) But, for our purposes, the key question to ask yourself about any particular argument is this: if these premises are in fact true, *how likely* do they make it that the conclusion of this argument is also true? If the argument's premises, taken together, make it *very* likely that the argument's conclusion is true, then the argument is a *strong argument*. If the premises, taken together, provide little or no support for the conclusion, then the argument is a *weak argument*.

Sources of Trouble

In the section above, we discussed the basic ingredients required for a strong argument—that is, the ingredients that an argument needs if it is going to provide good support for its conclusion. The *lack* of one or more of those ingredients gives us very strong grounds for criticizing an argument. But there are a couple of particular kinds of problems that we will deal with in greater detail below.

Fallacies

Reasoning can go astray in many, many different kinds of ways. Some errors in reasoning are so common that, over the years, they've been given names. Learning about these faulty arguments, or *fallacies*, will help you spot these errors in other people's reasoning, and help you avoid making them yourself. Once you know about them, you'll immediately start spotting them all over the place. You may be wondering why these kinds of arguments are so common when they are so clearly faulty. The sad truth is that experience shows that these kinds of arguments can be psychologically attractive. In some cases, we are drawn to them because they look superficially like other, better, kinds of arguments. In other cases, we may be drawn to them because they seem simple, and support conclusions that fit with our own biases or objectives.

Straw Man

- Definition: A "straw man" is any argument in which the arguer criticizes a weakened or distorted version of his or her opponent's point of view, rather than dealing directly with that point of view.
- Example: "I don't see why you're opposed to raising the tax on corporate profits. It's stupid to think that corporations shouldn't pay their fair share."
- Example: "Lawyers say that corporations are legally treated as 'persons,' so that they can own property and sign contracts. But that's ridiculous! Anyone who thinks that corporations have all the rights of people like you and me must be crazy."
- Why it's a fallacy: A *straw man argument* is a fallacy because it relies on premises that are typically entirely irrelevant to the issue at hand. Criticizing something that your opponent actually *didn't* say and *doesn't* believe may make you look clever to uninformed onlookers, but won't ultimately convince anyone who is capable of thinking critically.

Ad Hominem ("Appeal to Person")

- Definition: An *ad hominem* argument is another form of argument that is often used in debates; it is one that focuses on criticizing a person, rather than focusing on the strength of that person's reasoning. (*Ad hominem* is Latin for "to the person," which is why this fallacy is sometimes called "appeal to person.")
- Example: "There's no way this new ad campaign is going to work. I mean, c'mon, Johnson is an idiot!"
- Example: "Dilraj says that leading market indicators suggest that the economy is on the verge of recovery. But you can't rely on his word—after all, Dilraj is gay!"
- Why it's a fallacy: An *ad hominem* argument is a fallacy because, typically, the identity or character of the person making a claim is not relevant to deciding whether that claim is true or not. A fool or liar making a strong argument is still making a strong argument, and a brilliant person saying something foolish is still saying something foolish. We should focus on the quality of the person's argument, rather than on the person.

Argument from Tradition

- Definition: An argument from tradition argues that we should believe or do something simply because some group we belong to has believed or done that thing for a long time.
- Example: "Of course we should let our sales staff set their own sales targets. We've always done it that way."
- Example: "Our company has always paid men more than women. Why should we change now?"
- Why it's a fallacy: In most cases of argumentation, history is irrelevant. The fact that a belief has a long history doesn't make it true, and the fact that some practice has gone on for years doesn't mean make it the right way to do things.

Argument from Popularity

- Definition: An *argument from popularity* involves arguing that we should believe or do something simply because believing it or doing it is popular.
- Example: "We should go with the ad campaign featuring the girl in the bikini. Everyone knows that sex sells."
- Example: "All of our competitors lure customers with low advertised prices and then 'up-sell' them. So there's no reason why we shouldn't do it, too."
- Why it's a fallacy: The fact that a lot of people believe something is very poor evidence that it is true. There are lots of matters of fact about which most

people are very poorly informed. Consider, for example, that once upon a time "everybody knew" that the Earth was flat. But that was, of course, false. Similarly, once upon a time it was widely believed among CEOs that a corporate board of directors was mere "window dressing." Thirty years ago, plenty of people would have said that "everyone knows" that having a board of directors was a mere formality, but that didn't make it true. Today, it is widely acknowledged that a talented and conscientious board of directors brings considerable value.

False Dilemma

- Definition: A *false dilemma* is any argument that tries to convince you that you only have two options, and must choose one, when that is not really the case.
- Example: "Look, either you support my proposal to expand our sales force, or you're not a loyal employee. And you don't want me to think you're a disloyal employee, do you!?"
- Example: "Either we say no to the union's demand for improved safety equipment, or we're going to have to roll over and play dead every time they ask for something! So we have to say no!"
- Why it's a fallacy: In a true *dilemma*, you have only two options, and must make a hard choice between them. In some cases, the two options may both be ones you like. But more often, we use the word *dilemma* to describe a situation in which we must choose between two alternatives we don't like. A false dilemma tries to portray a more complicated situation *as if* it only presented two options, to make the audience feel as if they must choose one.

Cognitive Biases

Another source of problems in trying to make good arguments is what are known as *cognitive biases*. Cognitive biases are well-researched patterns of faulty reasoning to which human beings are subject.

We would all like to believe that we are rational decision-makers, able to assess information in an unbiased way to make the choices that are well-suited to getting the things we want. It is comforting for us to believe that our thinking is clear and unbiased. But there is considerable psychological evidence that that is simply not the case. We are all subject, to a greater or lesser degree, to the *cognitive biases* discussed briefly below (as well as many others). These biases are all the more dangerous because the arguers are typically not aware of the ways in which the biases are affecting their reasoning. Below, we outline several key cognitive biases, and propose strategies for thinking critically in the face of such biases. Note: the word "bias" here doesn't indicate *racial* bias. It simply refers to the way our thinking can be *slanted* or *pulled* in a certain direction, despite our best intentions.

The Framing Effect

In the *framing effect*, the way we describe, or *frame*, a question has an enormous and unjustifiable effect on how we answer that question. Here's an example: imagine that every year about 1,000 people contract a particular disease—a disease that kills 100 percent of those who contract it. Next, imagine that two new drugs are developed to treat that disease. If Drug A is given to all 1,000 patients, it will save 800 of the 1,000. On the other hand, if Drug B is given to all 1,000 patients, the result will be that 200 of the 1,000 die. Which drug would you choose? The catch, of course, is that the effect of the two drugs is exactly the same: either way, 800 will live and 200 will die. But a large number of experiments have found that people will respond differently depending on whether the issue is framed in terms of *lives saved*—which of course generates a positive response—instead of being framed more negatively, in terms of *lives lost*. The framing effect may be useful in marketing, but it is dangerous for critical thinking.

Confirmation Bias

Confirmation bias is the natural tendency we all have to seek out and remember information that confirms our own prior points of view, and to avoid or forget information that might change our minds. For example, a manager contemplating an ethically controversial decision may have a subconscious tendency to seek input from those employees most likely to agree with her, and to avoid input from employees who are likely to challenge her. In fact, she would be much better off talking to employees who are most likely to challenge her; after all, if her decision can withstand *critical* evaluation, she can be all the more confident that it is a good one. The same is true when seeking feedback from customers. Confirmation bias can result in overconfidence, which can in turn lead to poor decision making.

False Consensus Effect

The *false consensus effect* is the name given to the tendency people have to overestimate the extent to which others agree with their points of view. In situations requiring ethical judgment, the false consensus effect may make us more certain than we ought to be that other people share the same ethical beliefs that we do, which may make us more confident than we ought to be in the ethical premises we use in our arguments. This is especially likely to be a problem for managers in hierarchical organizations—people below them in the hierarchy may have a tendency to express agreement with, or at least to keep quiet when they disagree with, the boss's point of view.

Ingroup Bias

Ingroup bias is the tendency people have to think well of, to trust, and to give preferential treatment to, members of their own group. In some situations, *ingroup*

SIDEBAR

Thinking Critically About Wikipedia

The Internet is a fantastic source of information, but it's also a source of *mis*information. One of the most exceptional—and controversial—sites on the Internet is Wikipedia, "The Free Encyclopedia." The English-language version of Wikipedia includes nearly four million articles on a huge range of topics. But Wikipedia should always be used carefully.

Anyone with a computer and an Internet connection can write and edit Wikipedia articles. That is both the key strength and the key weakness of Wikipedia. On the plus side, this means that a huge number of volunteers have contributed to the evolution of Wikipedia, contributing countless hours to writing and editing articles, and bringing to the project an enormous range and depth of expertise. On the minus side, the fact that anyone can contribute means that some articles and edits are likely to be done by people who lack the relevant expertise. It also means that people with less honourable intentions—pranksters, as well as those out to promote some agenda—are able to edit Wikipedia articles anonymously in a way that serves their own interests.

But a critical thinker will realize that some types of Wikipedia articles are likely to be more reliable than others. Some articles, for example, are on highly contentious topics, such as the BP oil spill (titled the "*Deepwater Horizon* oil spill" in Wikipedia). You should approach the contents of such articles with caution, because they are apt to be modified from time to time by individuals whose interests lie in promoting a particular point of view, rather than in providing clear, unbiased information. At any given moment, it is entirely possible for such an article to contain biased comments, misinformation, or even outright lies. (Lies can of course be reversed, and Wikipedia does have a dispute resolution mechanism, but still, there are no guarantees.)

Other kinds of Wikipedia articles are much less risky. For example, most technical articles on physics or basic economic theory are reasonably safe sources of information. It is unlikely that there is anyone out there trying to use a Wikipedia article to fool you into thinking that the charge on an electron is positive (when it is actually negative) or that the law of demand says that consumers buy less of a good when prices fall (when it actually says the opposite).

The best advice, of course, is never to rely on just one source of information for anything really important. For academic essays, you might begin your background research by skimming a few relevant Wikipedia articles to gain a broad perspective on a few subtopics; but you should quickly move toward more authoritative sources written by experts in their field, who are accountable for the accuracy of their work.

Want to know more about the strengths and weaknesses of Wikipedia? There is, of course, a Wikipedia page about that! (See http://en.wikipedia.org/wiki/Wikipedia:Researching _with_Wikipedia.) But also remember to think critically about what you read there.

bias may take such familiar and vicious forms as racism or sexism. But in some cases the effect is more subtle: people have a natural tendency to cluster into groups and to treat each other differently on that basis. (In business, of course, we often encourage a form of ingroup bias: team spirit, including the belief that *our* company is the best and that we *will* beat the competition, is an important part of competitiveness in business.)

Moral Luck

The term *moral luck* refers to the tendency to attribute moral credit and blame to individuals as a result of events that are not, strictly speaking, within their control. For example, imagine two factories, both of which use unsafe machinery. If the unsafe conditions result in the death of a worker in one of those factories, the managers of *that* factory may well be labelled highly unethical, perhaps criminal; whereas the managers of the other factory—with the same dangerous conditions but no worker deaths—may avoid blame altogether. Both sets of managers are engaged in the same behaviour, putting workers at the same risk, but we have a tendency to judge one group much more harshly, as a result of *luck alone*.

Combatting Cognitive Bias

The cognitive biases discussed above are very common, and very hard to combat. There is no secret recipe for avoiding such biases to make rational decisions, but the following rules of thumb may help:

- Be aware that cognitive biases are a pervasive feature of all human reasoning, and that you, too, are susceptible to them.
- Seek out a range of points of view. Many cognitive biases are the result of relying on too few sources of information.
- When possible, avoid relying on intuition. That's not to say that intuition isn't important sometimes. But sometimes relying on intuition is just an excuse for lazy thinking. This is especially true where numbers are involved. If you have access to numbers, write them down and do the math, rather than going with your gut.

Conclusion

Critical thinking is an essential element of ethical decision making. At heart, it is a systematic approach to evaluating and formulating good arguments in defence of specific beliefs or claims. All of us have beliefs and intuitions about ethical issues in the world of business. The challenge is to apply the tools of critical thinking so that we can determine, through conversation, which of those beliefs and intuitions can be well-supported by reasons that are acceptable to all involved.

DISCUSSION QUESTIONS

1. Open up an issue of your local newspaper, and turn to or click on the "Editorial" or "Opinions" page. Can you find, among the arguments put forward there, examples of one or more of the fallacies and cognitive biases discussed above?

2. Which of the fallacies and cognitive biases discussed in this chapter have you seen in the reasoning patterns of your own friends and family?

3. Choose an important ethical issue in the world of business, one about which you have a strong opinion. Write that opinion down. What premises would you offer in support of that opinion? Do those premises amount to what an impartial audience would agree is "sufficient support" for that conclusion?

SUGGESTED READINGS AND ONLINE RESOURCES

For a concise explanation of *deductive* and *inductive* arguments: http://www.iep.utm.edu/ded-ind/.

Bazerman, M.H., and D.A. Moore. 2009. *Judgment in managerial decision making.* 7th ed. Hoboken, NJ: John Wiley & Sons.

n.a. Cognitive bias. In *Wikipedia.* http://en.wikipedia.org/wiki/Cognitive_bias.

n.a. Fallacy. In *Wikipedia.* http://en.wikipedia.org/wiki/Fallacies.

Vaughn, L., and C. MacDonald. 2012. *The power of critical thinking.* 3rd Cdn. ed. Toronto: Oxford University Press.

PART TWO
Making Ethical Business Decisions

An Introduction to Stakeholder Analysis

Introduction: The Context for Stakeholder Analysis

In an enormously famous (and, some would say, enormously influential) article, Milton Friedman wrote in 1970 that the sole motive for the corporate manager was to increase the profits of the corporation, so as to maximize the return to the shareholders. He said that the corporate executive—or director—could not be motivated by anything else because he was the agent of the corporation's owners—his principal, to whom he owed all fidelity.

> In a free-enterprise, private property system, a corporate executive is an employee of the owners of the business. He has the direct responsibility to his employers. That responsibility is to conduct the business in accordance with their desires, which generally will be to make as much money as possible while conforming to the basic rules of the society, both those embodied in law and those embodied in ethical custom (Friedman 1970, 4).[1]

Friedman's view, alternatively referred to as shareholder capitalism or agency theory, reflects the orthodox approach to the "theory of the corporation" prevalent throughout most of the 20th century, especially in North America. By the

---

1 While not relevant to the discussion in this chapter, it is amusing that both proponents and opponents of the corporate social responsibility movement have latched onto this passage, citing the influential economist as an ally.

1980s, however, some sociologists and others who studied the corporation as a social vehicle began to question whether the world had moved beyond shareholder capitalism as the defining paradigm of business. Some wondered whether the corporation should have a purpose beyond profit maximization. Notably, Charles Handy (2002) suggested that a corporation should have a purpose beyond profits—that making a profit was fine, but that it should be a means to a nobler end. That end could be innovation or the improvement of society. Handy therefore suggested that the interests of shareholders were but one concern of a corporation's board of directors.

In recent years, and especially in the past two or three decades, corporate scandal has received greater attention in the media. While it would be hard to argue that business managers were becoming more dishonest than their forerunners, it has *seemed* that there is a crisis in business ethics. Public opinion polls taken in the United States over the past decade or so have suggested that the American public believes business to be more responsible for the drop in quality of life than any other actor, including the various levels of government. Corporate executives, these polls have suggested, have among the lowest ethical standards of all professionals.

This increasingly negative perception of business and business people can be explained in several ways. It could be that ethical standards of business have, in fact, declined. However, this would be extremely difficult to prove. As ethical standards are to some degree a reflection of society, it is difficult to compare business ethics from the early 20th century with those in 1985 or 2011. But the fact that the expectations of society change might explain the perception that business is now less ethical. North American society has grown increasingly more affluent, better educated, and more interconnected than ever before. When coupled with a strong sense of individual rights (as contained in the Canadian Constitution, which in its current form was proclaimed in 1982), we can observe that North American society is more demanding than ever before. Employees are more empowered and consumers are more sophisticated. Add to that the rise of the environmental rights movement in recent years, and it is easy to understand why there are greater demands on the dominant service organizations in our society: business and government. It could be argued, therefore, that business is not necessarily less ethical, but that the various players in North American society *expect them to be more ethical.* And the modern-day North American expects the good corporation to consider the impact of its decisions on him, whether he is an employee, consumer, or environmentalist.

Given this context, writers like Edward Freeman began to suggest that the shareholder capitalism model espoused by Friedman was outdated. These writers suggested that the stakeholders of a corporation were not just its shareholders, but also its employees, customers, the government, communities, and the environment. It is this new *paradigm*[2] of business that will be the subject of this chapter. In it, we will explain stakeholder theory, and what it seeks to accomplish. We will then set out the reasons for using a stakeholder analysis in business decision making. In the largest section of this chapter, we will explain *how* to engage in stakeholder analysis to arrive at a business decision. Finally, the last section will briefly discuss some of the difficulties with this paradigm.[3]

What Is Stakeholder Analysis?

Many credit Edward Freeman with developing the stakeholder model of business, in his writings in the 1980s (e.g., Freeman 1984). One can look at stakeholder management in two different ways: as an approach to the ongoing management of a business and as a way to make business decisions when specific issues arise for managers. We label the latter context "stakeholder analysis." In either context, the business—or the manager—must try to understand the perspectives of the various stakeholders on the business or transactional problem, and then make business decisions that take those stakeholder views into account. In a sense, it is akin to looking at a business context or issue through a prism, with each turn of the prism revealing the issue or context is a slightly different way.

Engaging in stakeholder management or stakeholder analysis does not mean that every stakeholder is given the exact outcome they seek. A corporation's stakeholders often have perspectives or desires that conflict with those of other stakeholders. Shareholders, for instance, may believe that management should lay off a number of employees to keep costs down; the union representing those employees would naturally have a very different view. Through stakeholder analysis, the manager, after identifying the stakeholders and stakes (the stakeholders' desired outcome, as more expressly defined below), can assess those stakes and fashion a response that takes those competing views into account.

It is a fallacy to suggest that stakeholder management ignores the wishes of the shareholders. It is difficult to conceive of many large issues a corporation would face that would either not have an impact on the shareholders, or in which the shareholders would have no interest. These shareholder interests (or stakes) would be legitimate to varying degrees, depending on the issue, and the manager would ignore them at his peril.

---

2   A "paradigm" is a model—in this case, a model or exemplary way of thinking about how to carry on business.

3   In the next chapter, William Woof discusses challenges to stakeholder theory and cites other possible models.

SIDEBAR

Typical Stakeholders in a Business

In this chapter, we have defined a stakeholder as a person or a group of people who has something at risk or who legitimately expects an outcome in a business decision. This definition assumes that the relevant stakeholders could vary from issue to issue for the corporate decision-maker. Depending on the context, it may be necessary to define the stakeholder groups more specifically (for example, *shareholders* might be common shareholders, *employees* might be unionized workers, and *customers* might be female customers for a women's health product, or young children whose parents have been sold a potentially hazardous toy).

The descriptions below are intended to show the "typical stakes." They are not exhaustive of each stakeholder group, and could vary from context to context. But these are the groups that are most often seen as legitimate stakeholders in most of the company's ongoing business:

- **Shareholders** Shareholders have an expectation of a return on their investment (that is, a *financial* expectation); they expect that their *legal* rights will be respected.
- **Employees** These important internal stakeholders hope for the continued *financial* success of the company as it means continued employment; they have a *right* to safety and welfare on the job; employees maintain an *interest* in the direction and policies of their employer; and, finally, most employees have *legal* rights under contracts or labour laws.
- **Customers** Customers or clients most typically have an *interest* in the quality, innovation, and price of products being offered.
- **Suppliers** A business's suppliers typically have *financial* stakes in the company's decisions, often reflected in *legal* stakes (in the form of a supply contract).
- **Governments** Given governments' law-making function, they hold a *legal* interest in ensuring that companies adhere to laws and regulations for that business; governments also have a *financial* interest in continued tax revenue (corporate and individual), and interest in the continued employment of their citizens by companies.
- **Community and interest groups** Beyond customers or governments, others in the community may be affected by corporate decisions, and hold *interest* or *moral* stakes in corporate decisions. For example, a community group may organize to protect a historic building from being purchased and renovated by a fast-food restaurant.
- **Environment** While there is still some debate whether the natural environment can be considered a stakeholder, those who say it should be would suggest that there is a *moral* stake, in terms of the continued sustainability of the natural environment.

In the end, stakeholder management is employed to address the needs of broader categories of individuals or groups that are affected by the business, or who themselves affect the business on an ongoing basis. Stakeholder analysis is a strategy used on an issue-by-issue (transactional) basis to arrive at the best possible outcome when making a business decision.

Why Stakeholder Management and Analysis?

There are at least four broad reasons why stakeholder management can be considered a better management strategy than one focused solely on shareholders: it responds to the demands of modern society; it accords with the emerging legal reality; it is morally superior; and it may be a more effective business strategy in this century.

Let us first discuss the reality of modern society. The stakeholder theorist will argue that if a corporation pursues a stakeholder-focused strategy, ultimately all legitimate stakeholders, *including* shareholders, will benefit to a greater degree than if a shareholder model is pursued. If we return to the discussion of the evolution of society in the introduction to this chapter, we observe a better educated, better-informed, and more interconnected society than ever before. In 2012, if there is a product liability issue at a plant that makes toys in China, we learn about it in North America almost immediately, and parents demand to know what Canadian or American toy manufacturers are doing about it. That manufacturer had better consider the needs of the North American consumer now, rather than wait to hear what the shareholders think at an annual meeting several months away. In other words, stakeholders learn about corporate actions—especially corporate malfeasance—more quickly than ever before; additionally, societal stakeholders take a greater interest in corporate action for the reasons mentioned above. This means that stakeholder-focused management is not simply *preferable* on a moral level, but it may simply *be* the modern societal (and business) reality.

The demands of a modern society aside, it may be that Canadian law now requires corporations to consider stakeholders more broadly than just shareholders. In a 2008 decision, the Supreme Court of Canada (SCC) held that in making corporate decisions, the board of directors of a public company must bear in mind the interests of stakeholders beyond the common (or voting) shareholders that elect the board. In that case, at issue was an offer to the common shareholders of the publicly held Canadian telecommunications giant, BCE, so that the public company could be "taken private" (pursuant to a takeover bid), and the board of directors, called upon to advise on the bid, considered only the effect of the bid on the shareholders. The holders of corporate bonds (debt-holders) argued that the deal was unfair to the creditors of BCE (or, more specifically, the debt-holders of BCE's subsidiary, Bell Canada). The SCC ruled that when considering what was in the "best interests of the corporation," the directors had a duty to consider the interests of all stakeholders, including the debt-holders. The court did not specifically define who a stakeholder could be, but the decision suggests that management would need to consider someone other than the owners of the company, and that would include creditors and employees.

Third, some argue in favour of stakeholder management by suggesting that it is the most moral way to conduct business. This philosophical argument suggests that because a business needs, and exploits, its employees and the natural environment to produce its goods and services, and requires consumers to ultimately purchase those goods, care should be taken to preserve these disparate interests. Kantian ethics would suggest that an action that uses people as a means to an end is unethical; likewise, profiting from employee work without considering employee needs is considered unethical.[4] Businesses also benefit from being located in a specific community—from a ready supply of skilled labour, to government incentives such as tax breaks or subsidies, to a well-developed infrastructure. Businesses are therefore morally required to consider the interest of the community when making strategic decisions. Thus, it follows that a stakeholder model must be implemented because business is morally obligated to consider the environment in which it carries on business and the community in which the business thrives.

Finally, stakeholder management may simply be a good business strategy—for two very diverse reasons. First, an understanding of the community, including existing customers and potential customers, may position the business to take advantage of opportunities that might not be readily apparent to a company focusing solely on the bottom line and shareholder return. Consider the vision of the late Steve Jobs at Apple: he looked at technological products from the consumer's point of view, and was seen as "revolutionary" in the technology industry.

Additionally, stakeholder management can help avert business disaster. Understanding stakeholders can help businesses understand not only what they want, but also what they do not want. An interesting case in point is McDonald's, in its dealings with PETA (People for the Ethical Treatment of Animals) in the early 2000s. Had McDonald's looked more broadly at the context in which its suppliers operated, and if it had considered PETA's views in a longer-term perspective, it might not have taken the public relations hit it did.

Finally, on the point of stakeholder management as a sound business strategy, while not every crisis can be avoided, well-implemented stakeholder management

---

4   Refer also to Leonard Brooks's discussion of the balance now demanded of employer and employee interests in the modern workplace in Chapter 13.

SIDEBAR

McDonald's vs. PETA

In the late 1990s and early 2000s, McDonald's Corporation ran into a formidable and perhaps surprising stakeholder in the form of the interest group PETA (People for the Ethical Treatment of Animals). It began after McDonald's launched a lawsuit against environmental activists in the United Kingdom, alleging that they had defamed McDonald's by distributing erroneous information outside their restaurants. McDonald's successfully argued in court that five such pamphlets were inaccurate and libellous, but the chief justice in the trial found that McDonald's did in fact allow cruel treatment of pigs and chickens.

PETA, spurred on by the corporation's apparent unwillingness to talk, and its perceived "win" in court, began a public relations campaign using billboards and other media in major North American cities in order to pressure McDonald's into improving its practices. By 2000, after many public demonstrations had helped put this issue in the news, McDonald's said that it would implement changes to its supply policies, and would adopt several of the recommendations PETA had made in its original criticisms of the fast-food giant. On its website, PETA took full credit for these changes and continued to work with McDonald's to modernize the company's animal welfare standards. However, in February 2009, PETA re-launched its "McCruelty" campaign in an effort to get McDonald's to adopt more humane chicken slaughter methods.

One could conclude that McDonald's underestimated PETA—in this case, the corporation had failed to see the interest group as a stakeholder.

PETA has made McDonald's one of the prime targets of its campaigns, and is often credited with forcing the restaurant giant to change its practices and the standards of its suppliers.

Source: PETA. www.peta.org. Reprinted by permission.

can help a business to respond quickly and effectively to that crisis. Consider the "Tylenol scare" experienced by Johnson & Johnson in the early 1980s, when several consumers of Tylenol capsules died from arsenical poisoning after a small number of Tylenol bottles were tampered with. J&J's response, considered today the "gold standard" in responding to a crisis, is an excellent example of how putting the interests of consumers and the broader community ahead of the short-term profits of the company and shareholder return can result in longer-term success. At the time, some industry observers felt that J&J had "over-responded" by voluntarily pulling all bottles of Tylenol off store shelves.[5] Yet, within two years, Tylenol was again the dominant "pain-reliever" brand, and is still a market force today. In the end, employees and shareholders were rewarded with the continued financial viability of J&J, and consumers were satisfied with the company's due diligence in implementing tamper-proof packaging (which is the industry standard today).

Consequently, we can see the benefits of implementing a stakeholder-focused approach to management. It enjoys legal and moral advantages, and can help businesses identify both new opportunities and potential challenges (or even crises). Finally, it is a better reflection of modern society's expectations. All of which is good *in theory*, but how does this work in practice?

How to Engage in Stakeholder Analysis

In this section, we will outline briefly how stakeholder management—and more specifically, the transactional stakeholder analysis—can be implemented: that is, how it works. We will discuss who could be considered a stakeholder, what stakes are, how to deal with competing stakes, and, finally, how to use this analysis to arrive at a response to an issue. This section will close with a paragraph about ongoing stakeholder management.

What Is a Stakeholder?

In the context of a business decision, a stakeholder is someone (or a group of people) with either something at risk in the decision, or who legitimately expect(s) a specific outcome. In many business decisions, we find that the following groups of people are the *typical* stakeholders with an interest in the outcome (although the context may dictate that there are others): shareholders, employees, customers, suppliers, the government, interest groups, and the broader community. Despite these convenient groupings, it is important to identify stakeholders as specifically

---

5   Both bottles of capsules (which had been tampered with) and tablets (which had not) were recalled. Interestingly, it was considered almost impossible for the tablets to have been sabotaged, and yet new tamper-proof bottles for both types of products were introduced by J&J.

as possible. For instance, unionized employees may have a very different perspective than salaried management; male consumers may perceive an issue differently from female consumers;[6] even different classes of investors may have concerns that are distinct from one another (as in the *BCE* case).

This is not a subjective exercise—because someone decides he is interested in an issue affecting a company does not necessarily mean that person is a stakeholder with whom the business manager should be concerned. The manager would have to assess, as objectively as she can, whether that stakeholder has enough legitimacy, power, or urgency to be considered a stakeholder who is entitled to an outcome. Consequently, who may be a stakeholder in any given situation can vary. Business students learn that one of the fundamental principles of the capitalist system is the attraction of capital from private investors—so they are quick to suggest that shareholders should always be considered a stakeholder. Indeed, shareholders should be considered a stakeholder in most large corporate decisions; however, we can think of some corporate decisions where the shareholder view is only minimally relevant. Consider J&J's reaction in the Tylenol scare—in a case where consumers had died, it would have been inappropriate to put the interests of shareholders first. Likewise, in the case of the hiring or firing of an officer (other than the CEO, perhaps), shareholder concerns are likely to be less important. However, where the issue being discussed is the CEO's compensation package, one would think the shareholders' views would be of pre-eminent importance.

To help illustrate the notion of stakeholders, let's consider a simple fictional example. Assume that a large North American car manufacturer called ABC Motors emerged from the 2008–2009 recession in dire financial straits, having survived primarily with the help of financial assistance from the governments of Ontario and Canada. It must now decide the fate of its car assembly plant in Smallville, Ontario, where ABC employs 25 percent of the workforce. In this decision, who are the stakeholders? Certainly the shareholders are concerned with continued financial losses. The employees are clearly concerned with their continued employment and livelihood. The broader citizenry (and city council) of Smallville will be dramatically affected by any decision to close the plant, considering the plant's economic spinoff effect on the town. Finally, the provincial and federal governments will be concerned with this decision on several levels, from the need to provide social assistance to displaced workers, to lost tax revenue, to the terms

---

6   Consider Unilever's marketing campaigns for two health and beauty products: Dove and its "Real Beauty" campaign for women, and the seeming objectification of women in the campaign for Axe, a men's product.

imposed in their financial bailouts of ABC. To solve this problem, we can turn the prism different ways and arrive at different answers.

Some commentators speak of "primary and secondary" stakeholders, or "core and environmental" stakeholders (Karakowsky, Carroll, and Buchholtz 2005, 68–72). This sort of "grouping" assumes that there are de facto "more important" stakeholders and "less important" stakeholders in every problem. This may not be accurate or advisable. If McDonald's were categorizing stakeholders, it is unlikely that PETA would have been considered a primary or core stakeholder, yet on the issue of the ethical actions by its poultry suppliers, PETA certainly became one of the most powerful, legitimate, and urgent stakeholders. Consequently, in individual decisions, it is best to analyze as specifically as possible which are the relevant stakeholders to that issue, rather than relying on preconceived stakeholder groups and rankings.

What Is a Stake?

Having identified stakeholders, it is then incumbent on the manager to determine the stakes they hold. The stakes of stakeholders are their statuses, costs, or rights that are at risk in the decision, or which are expected or desired by those stakeholders in the outcome. As we can see with the ABC Motors example, to one business issue there can exist several opposing stakes. Once the decision-maker has objectively determined who the stakeholders are, he must then "put himself in the stakeholder's place" to determine that stakeholder's stakes. In other words, stakes are considered from the point of view of the stakeholder. At this point, we need not decide whether the stakes are valid, realistic, or illusory; we are simply seeking to determine what the stakeholder expects as a resolution.

Returning to the example of ABC Motors, among the many stakeholders who have an interest in the decision to close the car assembly plant are the plant employees, the shareholders, and the federal government. The employees obviously have a stake in their continued employment and financial security—they want the plant to stay open. Shareholders, by contrast, want ABC to maintain or improve ROI (return on investment or share price), and if the Smallville plant is inefficient or losing money, they would want the plant shut down. The federal government has entirely different stakes—as ABC's creditor, it wants to be repaid and therefore wants a decision that would put ABC on the firmest financial footing, while at the same time it will worry about the political fallout in the riding of which Smallville is part, should it allow the plant to close.[7]

---

7   Not to mention the possible lost tax revenue should the plant shut down, or the amount of employment insurance it will have to pay out in the event of layoffs.

As with the identification of stakeholders and stakeholder groups, the decision-maker should try to identify stakes as specifically as possible. However, it is sometimes helpful to put disparately held stakes into categories. In essence, there are five broad types of stakes that stakeholders could have in a business decision: *financial, legal, rights-based, moral,* and *interest-based.* What follows is a brief description of each type of stake.

Financial: The stakeholder stands to make money or lose money as a result of the decision on the issue. Shareholders typically have financial stakes in their concern over ROI and stock price; employees have financial stakes in wanting continued employment (and being paid a wage).

Legal: The stakeholder can point to a specific law or legal right (for example, a contract) that would entitle them to a specific outcome. For instance, a bank might refer to a provision in a loan agreement that states that a plant must be closed when the company's debt-to-equity ratio exceeds a certain percentage. The government might point to one of its statutes requiring a plant to clean up any pollution it has released. Usually, it can only be considered a legal stake if the law is upheld (i.e., asserting that a decision should be made so that a stakeholder isn't prosecuted would not be a legitimate legal stake).

Rights-based: Many would consider this sort of stake the most fundamental of all stakes, given the United Nations Declaration of Human Rights, and constitutional protections, such as the ones in the *Canadian Charter of Rights and Freedoms.* In this case, the stakeholder asserts that a human right, such as health, safety, or anti-discrimination, is at risk in this decision. For instance, employees may assert their fundamental right to employee safety where the business decision might involve opening a plant in a war-torn country.

Moral: A moral stake is somewhat more difficult to identify in an abstract sense, because it involves a deeply held, sometimes emotional, response to an issue. A moral stake is a conviction or values-based principle a stakeholder would not want to see violated. For example, members of PETA would feel that the treatment of chickens that would ultimately be supplied to McDonald's would be a moral issue—that it would be immoral for these chickens to be kept in over-crowded pens. As another example, fundamentalist Christians in a community would be morally opposed to the opening of an abortion clinic in that town.

Interest-based: Perhaps the most ubiquitous stakes of all—a stakeholder holds an interest-based stake where he is more likely to be pleased with (or look favour-ably on) the decision-maker if a certain outcome is reached. We most typically associate this sort of stake with consumers. For instance, if many consumers have an interest in protecting the environment, then a fast-food restaurant might be well-advised to reduce its non-recyclable packaging, because those consumers are more likely to go to that restaurant over a competitor that hasn't implemented such a policy. While interest stakes are less "fundamental" than deeply held moral stakes, or "life and death" rights stakes, a manager should be well aware of them, because if (for instance) enough consumers hold an interest in some outcome, then it could very well affect sales.

How Do You Analyze Competing Stakes?

As noted in the previous section, the stakes held by relevant stakeholders are often in opposition to others. What is a manager to do if, when tasked with making a decision, he compiles a list of eight different stakeholders, only to discover that these stakeholders present one, two, or even three sets of stakes, many of which are in conflict? How is the manager any further ahead? Well, first, the manager is on her way to providing the most comprehensive answer to her problem, because she knows who the relevant players are and what they desire. But now, armed with this raw material, she must fashion a resolution to the problem. She must realize that it may be impossible to make all of the stakeholders happy. Where one stakeholder (the employees) wants ABC Motors to keep the plant open and another (the shareholders) wants it closed, at least one stakeholder is not going to be entirely satisfied. To fashion a resolution, the manager must determine which of those stakes are more important or relevant. This stage can be referred to as *analyzing the stakes*, or *prioritizing the stakeholders*.

There is no one method that must be used to determine the relative importance of stakes and therefore the relative priority of stakeholders, although I will briefly set out one useful method below. Before explaining that method, we need to consider some important observations about such an analysis. First, the analysis of the stakes and stakeholders is not a merely academic exercise, but one whose aim is to solve an issue, or provide a corporate direction—the decision-maker should not lose sight of that fundamental goal. Second, having determined the stakes from the perspective of the stakeholders, the decision-maker must now analyze these stakes *objectively, relative to the decision-maker*. Just because an environmental interest group is complaining very loudly that your supplier's offshore labour practices are exploitative does not necessarily mean that they are or that that organization's views on non-environmental issues is entirely relevant. Third, the decision-maker should be very clear about what the issue is and what problem or question she is trying to solve. Shareholders may have very legitimate interests in the ongoing operation of a public company, but their interests may be irrelevant when deciding on the specifics of a CSR (corporate social responsibility) program that will engage the employees of a business. Last, and perhaps most important to keep in mind, stakeholder analysis does not mean that everyone will be made happy when the decision is made. In many cases, stakeholder analysis is able to help fashion solutions that address numerous stakeholder concerns. But where two different stakeholders' stakes cannot be reconciled, the manager will be faced with a dilemma.

One method of determining the relative importance of stakes (and stakeholders) is to assess them in terms of their *legitimacy, power,* and *urgency.* The word "relative" is important—this analysis is necessarily comparative to determine which stakes are more significant than others. Of the three, it can be argued that legitimacy is the most important.

Legitimacy means an objectively clear entitlement to a desired outcome, either the extent of the risk the stakeholder is exposed to, or the strength of commitment to the stake. Generally, stakeholders advancing rights-based stakes have high legitimacy; those whose stakes are interest-based are less intimately affected and therefore are considered to have lower legitimacy. For example, consumers may only care about the price of a product (an interest stake in its price), but the cheapest method of manufacturing the product means sweatshop employment conditions that would violate the employees' rights-based stakes. In this case, the employees' stakes would be more legitimate than those of the consumers.

Power, in the context of competing stakeholders, means the relative influence of the stakeholder over the decision-maker. For example, McDonald's may not have thought PETA was highly legitimate in its concerns over the fast-food company's supply management policies, but it could not deny the interest group's ability to influence public opinion about McDonald's when PETA used the media to get out its message. In that case, PETA was a powerful stakeholder. In another situation, when the decision-maker is the board of directors trying to determine whether or not a dividend will be paid to shareholders, the board should be cognizant of the fact that the shareholders elect directors at each annual meeting; a vote jeopardizing the dividend could result in the "powerful" shareholders voting the directors out of office. While interest stakes held individually may not be the most legitimate or powerful ones, if a large number of consumers have an interest stake in an aspect of your corporate direction or operations, that interest stake should be seen as a powerful stake given the sheer number of interested people who hold it.

Urgency considers how soon this stakeholder needs or wants its stakes to be met. In the Tylenol case—a classic "crisis"—the risk of consumers completely losing confidence in the product meant that Johnson & Johnson had to react immediately and remove the bottles from store shelves. The stake of consumers was therefore more urgent. If a legitimate stakeholder has immediate needs, it is hard for a decision-maker to ignore that stakeholder when fashioning a response.

This analytical structure is not without its shortcomings. For example, what happens when an illegitimate stakeholder has a large amount of power? In that case, the decision-maker may choose not to accept that stakeholder's point of view because of the lack of legitimacy, but would still be well-served to respond to the problem in such a way that the powerful yet illegitimate stakeholder's stakes are addressed (even if negatively). Also, how does the decision-maker keep track of the relative "weightings" for each factor for each stakeholder? Business students are familiar with matrices—and a matrix might be appropriate in this exercise. A numerical value could be given for each stakeholder (or even on every stake) for each of the three criteria (out of 5 or 10, for instance).[8]

As stated at the beginning of this section, this is not a scientific analysis, but rather a comparative one. The point is to determine which stakes are the most important or most pressing, so as to take them into account when responding to an issue. Assessing their relative legitimacy, power, and urgency is only one way of sorting through these issues, but a fairly effective and comprehensive one.

Transactional Responses

The point of undertaking stakeholder analysis in the context of a transactional issue is to come to a response to the issue, and then to implement that decision. Once the decision-maker has determined the relevant stakeholders and their stakes and then prioritized them, she now knows which stakes must be addressed. If the analysis indicates that one stakeholder is far more relevant in the situation than all others, then the response is quite straightforward: she must satisfy that stakeholder's desired outcome before any other stakes can be met. Unfortunately, business decisions are seldom that "clean," and the results of the analysis will very often reveal that there is more than one relevant stakeholder.[9] In that case, the decision-maker may choose to fashion a "compromise" response that best meets the needs of the relevant stakeholders. Alternatively, the decision-maker may choose to satisfy the stakes of one or two of the relevant stakeholders, and not others; in that case, the manager must take care to be able to defend her decision in the face of a legitimate stakeholder. In other words, while that stakeholder's stakes may not have been reflected in the decision, their stakes should be borne in mind when the decision is communicated or implemented.

Ultimately, the decision must address the specific issue, and stakeholder analysis is a tool to help the manager come up with the broadest, most defensible decision, which will likely also be the best decision for the company and the majority of its stakeholders.

---

8   It is my inclination to weight legitimacy somewhat more heavily, because, inevitably, the more legitimate stakeholder cannot be ignored in the response.

9   Although it would be hoped that the analysis will have also shown that there are some stakes that are relatively less important, and the decision-maker can worry less about those stakeholders in her response.

Ongoing Stakeholder Management

Much of this chapter has discussed stakeholder analysis in a transactional context-specific issue by specific issue. However, stakeholder management can also be a useful tool for ongoing management by the moral company. If the business is aware of its most important stakeholders in its ongoing operations, it is less likely to suffer an unexpected crisis; it will also be able to observe opportunities presented by its stakeholders. If a car manufacturer in the early 1990s had known that its consumers were going to become environmentally conscious, it would have invested more of its research and development budget into the development of hybrid-engine cars. Employers who treat employees as stakeholders often find that their employees are more highly engaged in their work and more loyal to the employer.

For ongoing stakeholder management to be effective, it cannot be the sole jurisdiction of one corporate area; all managers and all lines of business need to be cognizant of the stakeholders relevant to their specific areas as part of their day-to-day work lives. Much more could be said about this, but other chapters in this book will discuss organizational integrity and ethics and you can read more in those chapters.

Problems with Stakeholder Management

As argued in this chapter, stakeholder theory can be a powerful and highly effective method of corporate decision making for the responsible business. However, the manager who is following stakeholder theory must be wary of falling into "traps." First, stakeholder management is meant to be a comprehensive decision-making strategy, and to be effective, it should be efficient. As discussed at the end of the last section, stakeholder management should be part of the job responsibilities of all decision-makers in a corporation; however, when stakeholder management is left to a compliance or public affairs department separate from line operations, it becomes cumbersome and inefficient. Additionally, if stakeholder management is not part of everyone's job, but rather is imposed by one corporate department, it will be a strategy that is resented by many employees and managers.

Second, some may be concerned that the structure of the analysis presented in this chapter could give too much influence to the "powerful stakeholder," who might lack the bona fides of other, less powerful, stakeholders. Those critics would say this structure simply codifies the status quo. To guard against this, the decision-maker must be sure to identify all relevant stakeholders (so that the weak and strong are both "on the radar"); then the decision-maker must properly assess the legitimacy of these stakeholders and give vent to the wishes of not the merely powerful stakeholder, but the powerful stakeholder who is *also legitimate.*

John Boatright worries that stakeholder management unduly minimizes the role of the shareholders (Boatright 2006). He suggests that shareholders play a crucial role in ensuring that the corporation is engaged in wealth creation (which benefits all stakeholders), and that the principles of corporate governance bestow on the shareholders a certain importance. However, proper stakeholder management always gives credence to the usually highly legitimate stakes of the shareholders and acknowledges their voting rights over the board of directors of a corporation (Freeman 2009). Indeed, given the numbers of examples where corporate boards of directors have ignored these shareholder rights, it would seem important for shareholders that directors do engage in stakeholder management to ensure that *shareholder stakes* are recognized!

Finally, one might worry about whether stakeholder theory is in fact broad enough to allow the corporation to act in a truly and fully ethical way. The definition of stakeholder, taken narrowly, would seem to assume a *person* or *people*. This begs the question: can something lacking a personality, such as the environment, be a stakeholder? This is, of course, a concern: does this decision-making structure ensure that the environment is "on the radar" because it has no "voice"? Some have sought to personify the natural environment by saying it is the stake of future generations, but that seems both unduly technical, and impractical (who speaks for those not born?). Fortunately, we have seen examples of corporate leaders who have treated the natural environment as a stakeholder in its own right: the late Ray Anderson's transformation of his modular carpet company, Interface Carpets, is an example of a CEO taking a profitable company and completely re-engineering it to be environmentally sustainable for the simple reason that he felt a moral obligation to the environment that his operations affected. Others note that the sustainability of the environment has become a stake in itself of many consumers, employees, and certainly interest groups like Greenpeace or the Sierra Club.

In the next chapter, William Woof presents criticisms of stakeholder theory.

Conclusion

Stakeholder analysis and management may seem complicated. But it has evolved as our society has become more complicated—as consumers and interest groups and employees and, yes, even shareholders, have demanded more accountability from corporate actors. It is therefore a decision-making strategy in keeping with our times. And it does not have to be cumbersome and complex; the enlightened manager will practise stakeholder management on an ongoing basis, so that when issues arise (or worse, a crisis occurs), she understands the perspectives of the people and groups that will be affected by the issue and what outcome they will demand. It is an essential tool that every modern manager should learn and master.

DISCUSSION QUESTIONS

1. Is the corporate manager who needs to make a business decision a stakeholder in her own right? If so, when?
2. Consider a situation in which the father of an applicant to a highly competitive business school offers the school a donation of $500,000 if the school admits his daughter to the program. Assume the daughter's high school grades are 5 percent below the minimum threshold for admission, and there are dozens of applicants who have better grades. Perform a stakeholder analysis to determine what the dean of the school should do.
3. Is the environment a stakeholder? Does the stakeholder model do a disservice to environmental concerns if it is not?

REFERENCES AND SUGGESTED READINGS

BCE Inc. v. 1976 Debentureholders. [2008] 3 S.C.R. 560.

Boatright, J.R. 2006. What's wrong—and what's right—with stakeholder management. *Journal of Private Enterprise* 21 (2): 106–130.

Freeman, R.E. 1984. *Strategic management: A stakeholder approach.* Boston: Pitman.

Freeman, R.E. 2009. Managing for stakeholders. In *Ethical theory and business*, 8th ed., ed. T.L. Beauchamp, N.L. Bowie, and D.G. Arnold. Toronto: Pearson Prentice Hall.

Friedman, M. 1970. The social responsibility of business is to increase its profits. *New York Times Magazine*, September 13.

Handy, C. 2002. What's a business for? Harvard Business School case #R0212C.

Karakowsky, L., A.B. Carroll, and A.K. Buchholtz. 2005. *Business and society: Ethics and stakeholder management.* Toronto: Thomson Nelson.

Critiques of Stakeholder Theory

Introduction: Questions and Debates

After covering the basics of stakeholder theory and corporate relationships with stakeholders in previous chapters, the discussion now moves to the ways in which stakeholder theory itself can be successfully challenged. There are a number of lively debates about this within stakeholder theory. Who should actually count as a stakeholder? How are stakeholders best classified? What are the best ways to manage stakeholder relationships? Moreover, it is clear that stakeholder theory will continue to gain in importance because of how corporate practices have changed over the past 40 to 50 years. We no longer think of corporations as primarily manufacturing products that are sold locally and valued mainly for their utility. Most firms are now global. Over the past quarter century, Western corporations have outsourced most of their manufacturing to developing nations and are now much more concerned with product branding and building the public image of the corporation and its practices than in making their products. As a result, stakeholder relationships with customers, suppliers, and employees have been radically transformed. It is no wonder, then, that stakeholder theory has risen to prominence in line with the rise of globalization. However, our concern here will be with how effective stakeholder theory is and whether it is still applicable. To what degree does stakeholder theory fulfill ethical expectations within a business context? Should we be more broadly concerned instead with issues of corporate social responsibility and sustainability?

Traditionally, the primary approaches to critiques of stakeholder theory have come from the perspective of *shareholder theory*, or the theory of the firm. Corporate managers have fiduciary obligations to their shareholders. These obligations in turn become the basis for corporations' contractual relationships with stakeholder groups. Thus, we need to ask how far management can go beyond these basic contractual duties to establish and manage desirable relationships with stakeholder groups based on their intrinsic value (treating their interests as valuable for their own sake).

Stakeholder theory can also be critiqued from a perspective based on corporate social responsibility and sustainability. This will be addressed in the second half of the chapter. The definition of stakeholder that will be used is that of R. Edward Freeman, the founder of stakeholder theory. The term will thus include anyone or any organization that can be affected by the activities of a given corporation.

SIDEBAR

Fiduciary Duty

Fiduciary responsibilities refer to the duties of corporate executives to maximize the value of the firm through increased earnings, market share, or some other financial standard. Managers thus act as the agents of the shareholders and value this relationship above all others. All other considerations that managers may legitimately have are deemed to be the means to the end of this higher objective.

Shareholder Theory

Historical Background

Shareholder theory emerged from the rise of corporations in the late 19th century. Under the Fourteenth Amendment of the US Constitution, corporations were granted legal personhood and therefore entitlements to basic protections under the law.[1] This was the result of the growing complexity of industrialized development in the West by the early years of the 20th century and the need to ensure that corporations were adequately capitalized. Such financing required an ownership base far beyond the funding that could be provided by a few corporate owners. More broadly based corporate ownership by the public at large then required fundamental legal protections for shareholders. The concept of limited liability was used, ensuring that shareholders could not be held liable for corporate activities and commitments beyond what they had actually invested. Fiduciary responsibility was legally imposed on corporate management to overcome *the principal–agent*

---

1   *Santa Clara County v. Southern Pacific Railroad* (118 U.S. 394) was the 1886 landmark ruling by the US Supreme Court that extended the equal protections clause of the Fourteenth Amendment to cover corporations.

problem—that is, agents, such as lawyers and managers, having more knowledge and power than the principals who engage their services. Given that managers had very significant advantages over owners through their day-to-day knowledge of the operations of the company, they were charged with maximizing profits for shareholders to prevent them from exploiting these asymmetries to their own advantage. For example, in the case of Adelphia, the US cable operator, executives were able to borrow corporate funds to finance personal business projects without full disclosure to shareholders. Adelphia had been a family-owned and -managed corporation, and its owner-managers continued to think of the company as a family firm even after it went public. They considered it acceptable to borrow company funds to finance family business ventures because they regarded themselves as the principal owners of the company and thus not bound to disclose these other ventures to the shareholders. They failed to appreciate that as managers they had explicit responsibilities to all of the owners of the firm, including themselves. The principal–agent relationship required them to discharge such responsibilities impartially. Under theories of the firm developed by Adolf Berle and others during the 1930s and 1940s, the considerable power vested in management was a cause for social concern and regulatory oversight and we can see a clear manifestation of this power in the Adelphia case (Berle and Means 1932).

The Nexus-of-Contracts View

These legal restrictions made it difficult for stakeholder theory to get off the ground. Any concern corporate management exhibited for stakeholder relations over and above mere contractual requirements would look like a violation of management's essential fiduciary responsibilities to shareholders. This strict reading of managerial responsibilities was supported by the concept of the corporation as a "nexus of contracts," an idea that has since been strongly endorsed by free-market advocates.[2] In this reading, a corporation's responsibilities are strictly defined by law according to the contractual obligations undertaken with all of their primary stakeholder groups: employees, suppliers, and customers. It has fulfilled its fiduciary responsibilities by negotiating these contracts to the best advantage of its own shareholders.[3] Any stakeholders that do not have a contractual relationship to the corporation ("non-voluntary stakeholders," such as homeowners living downstream from a polluting factory) have no legitimate claims in the corporation's activities.

---

2   The nexus-of-contracts theory originates with Jenson and Meckling (1976).

3   Boatright (2006) argues that stakeholder theory is not compatible with corporate governance theory but can be used as a procedure for managing stakeholder concerns.

The nexus-of-contracts view spelled out the mutual obligations of corporations and their stakeholders in fairly minute detail. Failure to comply with the terms and conditions of the contracts had legal remedies, such as lawsuits or bankruptcy court. In contrast, stakeholder theory required corporations to take a longer-term view of the relationships between a corporation and its stakeholders, beyond ensuring strict compliance with contractual terms and conditions.

The Rise of Stakeholder Theory

What brought stakeholder theory to life was the realization by corporate managers that managing these long-term stakeholder relationships successfully actually worked to the shareholders' benefit. We can readily find historical examples to demonstrate this.

In the late 1930s, US labour relations, especially in the auto industry, were plagued by violent strikes as corporate managers sought to maximize gains to shareholders by resisting the power of unions to organize. By the end of the 1940s, more entrenched labour laws had given unions an advantage, and corporate managers realized that, to ensure labour peace, it was better to manage these relationships over the long term. Prosperous workers had more disposable income to purchase consumer goods such as automobiles, and a wide range of corporations and their owners benefited as a result. In the 1990s, increasing public concern over sweatshop operations in some countries led US apparel manufacturers to manage their supplier relationships more closely with respect to their factory operations in the developing world.[4]

As we have noted, globalization led to an increasing focus on stakeholder relationships. The traditional nexus-of-contracts model was built on the idea that the value of a corporation was vested in its "book value"—roughly the net worth of a corporation's plant and equipment. With globalization, and the growing phenomenon of mergers and acquisitions in the US business world throughout the 1980s, it was quickly realized that corporate value far surpassed mere book value and encompassed a great deal of goodwill and wealth vested in intangible assets, such as the recognition value of a corporate logo. For example, a pair of Nike shoes cost very little to manufacture once production had been outsourced from the United States, with its high-cost unionized labour, to low-cost developing nations. However, the shoes could still be sold for a high markup in the United States because of the endorsement value of a high-profile athlete like Michael Jordan or Tiger Woods. The

---

4 More recently, stakeholder management has been made a legal requirement. The 2006 *Companies Act* passed by Parliament in the United Kingdom places legal burdens on corporate directors to consider the interests of employees, as well as the effect of corporate decisions on communities and the environment.

"brand value" of a product was suddenly more important than its utility value—the value emphasized under the traditional nexus-of-contracts model. In the new world based on brand value, managers spent more time massaging the corporate image and how that image would be perceived by customers over the long term.

The development of stakeholder theory by R. Edward Freeman and others in the mid-1980s was thus certainly very well timed to address the changing circumstances in the new globalized business world, and the theory's success is well-deserved. These circumstances have compelled corporate managers to take a long-term view of stakeholder relationships that goes far beyond mere contractual compliance. This long-term view is ethically valuable in itself, given the strong propensity of corporate mangers to focus on short-term profit issues. Corporate managers can set forth "win–win" scenarios that effectively align corporate and stakeholder interests over the long run. However, this long-term view also assumes long-term beliefs in the strength and stability of markets and their supporting institutions (government agencies, courts of law, and so on). Whether these assumptions can be successfully defended in our current era of credit crises, climate change, and resource depletion will be considered below. For now, though, the debatable claim that "win–win" scenarios successfully align the interests of corporations and stakeholders over the long term presents a new line of criticism of stakeholder theory.

Business Ethics or Business Strategy?

Although management concern for stakeholder interests fosters a long-term management perspective—in itself an ethical benefit—the nature of that concern must be questioned. Are stakeholder interests only *instrumentally* valuable, that is, as a means to the end of corporate profits? If so, why not treat the relationship purely in strategic terms—that is, as just one element in an overall plan for expanding revenues, profits, market share, etc.? Why do ethics have to be brought into the equation at all? If this criticism holds, then stakeholder theory functions as little more than a cover for corporate opportunism (Marcoux 2000). It must be demonstrated, then, that stakeholder interests have intrinsic worth—that they are valuable for their own sake. Stakeholder theorists like Freeman defend their positions by denying that stakeholder relationships are instrumentally valuable, claiming that ethics and value creation are deeply embedded in corporate strategies. Thomas Donaldson and Lee Preston (1995) have defended stakeholder theory on the normative grounds (conditions that ought to exist) that stakeholder interests must be considered intrinsically valuable. In this reading, stakeholders have legitimate interests in the corporation that must be respected and valued independently of the interests the corporation has in its stakeholders. Each stakeholder group must thus be valued for its own sake and not as a means for promoting the ends of the corporation. The "Brand Ambassadors" case below brings these issues into focus.

CASE STUDY

Brand Ambassadors at Universities

Using "brand ambassadors" at major universities in North America represents an important new marketing strategy used by corporations as diverse as Target, Hewlett-Packard, American Eagle, Red Bull, and Microsoft. Brand ambassadors are established, influential students hired by the companies to wear or use corporate products and to promote their use among new students. The ambassadors earn good money and perks, while corporations can establish lifelong relationships with the new students who are the targets of these campaigns and who have ample funds to spend on new clothes, computer equipment, and other staples of university life.

The tactic of using product placements or staged "customer" testimonials is now well established in business practice. Corporations willingly pay to have their products mentioned, displayed, or showcased in movies. Celebrities are paid to go on TV talk shows and discuss their use of designated products and their satisfaction with them. The objective in both cases is to break the consumer's association of a product with the formal presentation of an advertisement. In the first case, the consumer makes a false association of the product with its placement, assuming the product's use in a film or a television show represents its commonly accepted use rather than its deliberate insertion on the basis of payment. Celebrity endorsements, on the other hand, work through the substitution of stakeholder roles. A celebrity paid by a corporation to be a pitchman poses as a satisfied customer.

The brand ambassador strategy combines elements of both product placement and celebrity endorsement. The product placement occurs on a university campus and the "celebrity endorsement" comes from brand ambassadors who are hired on the basis of their success in university life as senior students (their membership in fraternities or sororities, or their positions in successful university sports teams or clubs). This combination creates a number of ethical issues for stakeholder theory.

American Eagle brand ambassadors on campus. Which companies have a presence on your campus? How subtle, or obvious, are they in their marketing?

Source: Jeremy M. Lange.

First, universities themselves can become non-voluntary stakeholders in this process. While corporate agents do take steps to keep university officials fully informed of the activities of brand ambassadors, many activities organized on campus by brand ambassadors are informal (such as helping new students arriving on campus unload personal belongings and move them to dorm rooms) or involve solicitations on Facebook or Twitter that use the university's name or logo. Such activities don't usually require setting up a kiosk, which would entail the payment of fees to the university. School officials worry that informal endorsements of this nature may conflict with established contracts with corporations already doing business on campus (for example, Pepsi might have an exclusive contract for soft drink distribution on campus). Some organized activities align well with established university programs. Ambassadors for Target stores have organized late-night shopping trips that take students away from binge drinking parties. However, many educators also worry about what they describe as "the commercialization of the education experience and everyday college life."

An important ethical justification of stakeholder theory is the claim that managers treat stakeholder interests as intrinsically valuable, not as the means to the end of corporate profits. As Donaldson and Preston (1995) state: "The descriptive accuracy of the theory presumes that managers and other agents act *as if* all stakeholders' interests have intrinsic value." Is that the case here? Do marketing activities aimed at branding—establishing lifelong consumer loyalty to particular products—retain the same respect for this intrinsic value or is that value better served by restricting marketing activity to the utility value of products? Is a university campus an appropriate venue for brand ambassador marketing strategies, given that most universities are keen to market their own brand logos? Is "the commercialization of everyday college life" an appropriately ethical commercial objective for a university?

Sources: Donaldson and Preston (1995) and Singer (2011).

To sum up, then, sound markets supported by strong institutions facilitate the possibility of long-term planning. That in turn guarantees the viability and effectiveness of stakeholder theory, both from an ethical and business perspective. Corporate managers can set forth "win–win" scenarios that effectively align corporate and stakeholder interests over the long run, but this must be accomplished on the basis of the intrinsic value of stakeholder interests. Conversely, the viability of stakeholder theory is threatened if or when markets and institutions lack this strength and soundness. Corporate managers might well be accused then of attending to stakeholder concerns when the interests of their own shareholders come under threat as a result of some form of market failure. Stakeholders, for their part, might well discover that their own interests in the relationship with a given corporation had been suddenly changed or undercut by some change in market conditions. Which of these two visions will prevail?

Beyond Shareholder Theory

Corporate Social Responsibility Theory

The question about which vision will prevail takes us beyond the tight relationship between shareholder theory and stakeholder theory. Shareholder theory focuses only on the interests of shareholders and stakeholders. It assumes that markets will be sound, permanent, and viable, and that ethical issues and concerns are largely resolved by attending to the interests of shareholders or stakeholders. If markets and their supporting institutions are truly strong and resilient, then we have no ethical concerns beyond these networks of relationships, we are all free to expand economic wealth through the creation of value, and a minimum set of laws enforced by government is sufficient to guarantee beneficial outcomes. Theories of corporate social responsibility, however, take us beyond this narrow domain of allied interests. Corporate social responsibility (CSR) theory asserts that corporations have much broader obligations toward the social problems or externalities they create. For example, oil companies would be the organizations most aware of declining oil production in many parts of the world. The externality in this case is the loss of a crucial and non-renewable global resource that must be sustained in amounts that are plentiful and cheap enough to provide the impetus for global economic growth. The oil companies could take the lead in influencing governments around the world to adopt alternative forms of "green energy" as a substitute for oil. The guiding assumption in both shareholder and stakeholder theory is that such problems or issues can instead be successfully managed or resolved by society. What is at stake, regardless of which path is chosen—CSR or stakeholder theory—are the interests of society at large.

With a CSR approach, there is a shift in focus—from internal stakeholders, such as employees, suppliers, and customers, toward issues that are primarily the concern of government and of civil society. Stakeholder theory expands to include both government and civil society as stakeholders in corporate operations, but this presents a new set of problems and difficulties. Governments have a fundamental mandate to make and enforce regulations and laws and have an obligation to do so impartially. However, in a globalized world, governments also have a duty to promote the success of their own corporations as they expand their overseas operations. This opens the door to potential conflicts of interest in governments' responsibility to protect the interests of their own citizens. In a globalized world, governments can exercise significant influence over large networks of stakeholder relationships, as evidenced by the following example.

The Case of Genetically Modified Organisms

In 2001, the Royal Society of Canada produced a commissioned report on the government's process for approving the use of genetically modified organisms (GMO) in food products. The issue was highly sensitive because, on the one hand, Industry Canada, the federal government agency responsible for promoting Canadian corporations and products globally, was committed to supporting GMO manufacturers like Monsanto. On the other hand, a different federal government agency, Health Canada, was responsible for regulating the safety of genetically modified (GM) foods. The Royal Society report was highly critical of the government's approval process, arguing that companies like Monsanto did not make all of their product testing reports available to government agencies for independent review and that safety standards for the classification of GM foods were deficient. Nonetheless, the report caused a huge backlash of criticism from government, industry, and media sources. Part of the problem can be traced to the large influence that corporations like Monsanto can exercise over the political process through lobbying and campaign contributions. Although the Canadian government's primary responsibility is to its citizens—in this case to use its regulatory authority to ensure the safety of food products—at the same time globalization has also made the government an important stakeholder in the success of corporations like Monsanto.

The lesson to be taken away from this example is important. The ethical integrity of stakeholder theory very much depends on upholding the intrinsic value of stakeholder interests. In this case, that value can only be upheld by taking seriously the objective assessments of the Royal Society report, a report that had the benefit of strong input from independent scientists with no private interest in Monsanto's success. Clearly, the intrinsic value of the interests of Canadian consumers, who depend on their government to ensure high standards of food safety, was compromised in this case. Prompt identification and effective resolution of externalities and potential conflicts of interest that can emerge in stakeholder relationships are very important objectives. If this process is not prompt and effective, then long-term issues will result that have to be resolved by companies like Monsanto exercising corporate social responsibility. This is especially true in a globalized world where there is considerable pressure to standardize regulatory practices. Not only Canadian consumers but consumers around the world may have their interests compromised if there is no process to identify and resolve conflicts of interest. As an example, the increased use of genetically modified crops has led to a corresponding growth in the use of herbicides, which are also manufactured by corporations, like Monsanto, that specialize in GM technology. As weeds develop an increasing resistance to herbicides, farmers have to make use of stronger defoliants, which are also manufactured by Monsanto (the creator of Agent Orange).[5] Governments thus have an increasing responsibility to oversee these environmental developments and to provide regulation as necessary. However, this is a difficult undertaking when the Canadian government also has an interest in promoting Monsanto's business success. It is thus up to Monsanto to take the initiative and assume the responsibility for these kinds of problems and issues.

Tackling Major Global Problems

Social Contract Theory

Not only do governments around the world have to deal with issues related to genetically modified organisms, they also have to face other severe problems related to sustainability. Climate change is probably the most serious. The current scientific consensus shows that focused, well-coordinated government activity will have to be undertaken on a global basis over the next decade to counteract climate change's most serious effects. Global oil production from existing sources now appears to be in a permanent decline because of the peak oil phenomenon. Global food production also faces potential shortfalls, as does the availability of and access to clean water. Finally, the after-effects of the global credit crisis that began in 2008 have still not been addressed.

What all of these issues and concerns show is that the idealized world under which stakeholder theory thrives—a world of stable markets and robust institutional support—is becoming increasingly less viable. We can't merely attend to the interests of shareholders and other stakeholders and assume that all ethical responsibilities related to business have been discharged. We can no longer assume that addressing all the duties and obligations we owe each other regarding our social responsibilities (corporate and otherwise) is enough. We have to get back to the basics of social contract theory and engage the full set of relationships among civil society, government, and business. (See the discussion of social contract theory in Chapter 2.) Given the globalized nature of business, we have to take a worldwide perspective on these social-contract relationships. By developing extraordinary innovations like GM food, corporations like Monsanto could make significant contributions to global food security by facilitating agricultural production that

---

5   "Agent Orange" is the code name of an extremely toxic herbicide used by the US military to deforest the jungles and rural lands of Vietnam, Laos, and Cambodia during the Vietnam War.

would not otherwise be possible. (GM crops grow in poor soils that are not conducive to standard crops.) However, GM crops also contaminate standard crops through cross-pollination and thus could severely undermine the very food security they were designed to enhance. If we are to achieve an acceptable global level of economic, social, and environmental sustainability, we need to be more proactive and attentive to the possibilities of unforeseen externalities or unanticipated issues that could emerge in the future. For example, trace amounts of the insecticides used in GM corn have now been detected in humans, even though this was not supposed to be possible.

New Paradigms? The Stakeholder Economy

Some stakeholder theorists have therefore proposed a new model called the "stakeholder economy" in which the direct one-on-one relationship of corporation to stakeholder is extended into larger networks of relationships that encompass the globe (Barnett 1997). For example, the failure of Lehman Brothers (the New York investment bank and broker-dealer) in September 2008 triggered a global chain reaction of market failures that brought together numerous organizations and agents who almost certainly had no idea that they had a stake in the success or failure of a New York bank with which they had no direct relationship.

Proponents of traditional stakeholder theory reject this stakeholder economy model because it transforms a theory of organizational strategy and ethics into a theory of political economy, thereby depleting it of much of what they consider to be its viability and effectiveness. (Notice how this traditional account assumes the sound functioning of markets and the effective support of political institutions. That soundness and effectiveness was lacking in the Royal Society example, when a national context of regulatory oversight was transformed into one of globalized corporate promotion.) For traditionalists like R. Edward Freeman, this rejection of the stakeholder economy in light of deteriorating circumstances means that corporations and their stakeholders will have to increase their level of vigilance. In his words, "these same conditions [of globalized expansion] imply a greater need for *organizational-level* policies and individual responsibility and recognition of stakeholder obligations" (Freeman, Phillips, and Wicks 2003, 492), but this immediately raises the question whether such elevated levels of corporate vigilance are even possible in a globalized context. While the collapse of Lehman Brothers was, in fact, anticipated, its devastating consequences were not. If financial experts cannot foresee dire threats to the sustainability of the global financial system, how can the agents and corporations caught up in these global webs of stakeholder relationships do so?

Corporations have a crucial role to play in this project of global sustainability, but their approach to corporate social responsibility will have to be more extensive.

It will no longer be sufficient for corporations to follow the rubric of Archie Carroll's CSR pyramid—that is, compliance with law, attention to ethical duties, and provision for corporate philanthropy (Carroll 1991).[6] Corporations have crucial expertise in climate change, peak oil, and other forms of resource depletion. Corporate managers, shareholders, and other stakeholders may well have to collaborate in finding solutions to these problems and, in the process, agree to significantly curtail profits. A new paradigm for corporate citizenship may well have to emerge, one by which corporations agree to assume significant responsibilities under the social contract model, rather than the traditional models of corporate social responsibility, shareholder, or stakeholder theory.[7]

Conclusion

In this chapter, we examined the traditional critique of stakeholder theories, which is tied to shareholder theory. Stakeholder theorists like R. Edward Freeman strongly emphasized this relationship because a mutually beneficial relationship between shareholders and stakeholders is, in their view, the best way to maximize value creation for society. In fact, Freeman sees a close association between his views and those of the famous free-market economist Milton Friedman. In R. Edward Freeman's view, it is prudent for corporate managers to attend to the interests of their key stakeholders far beyond mere compliance with contractual terms and conditions. Managers who adopt such long-term strategies will be rewarded by the market. As Freeman et al. (2010, 77) note:

> Anecdotal evidence supports the idea that firms that do not attend to the interests of key stakeholders over time tend to suffer in the marketplace. If a firm is not attending to its interests and there is more value to be created with another set of stakeholders, it only makes sense that stakeholders would defect and take their resources elsewhere.

The problem, as we have seen, is that a high level of stability in markets and their supporting institutions is needed to make the stakeholder model work, and the problems that we have noted in a globalized world—finance, climate change, resource depletion, and other challenges—suggest that this is not the case. Moreover, these are not problems that can be addressed merely by corporate social

---

6   Carroll's pyramid is a four-stage model for understanding the components of corporate social responsibility. For details, see the illustration of the pyramid in Chapter 1.

7   One possibility in this regard is sustainability innovation. Through collaboration with competitors within a single industry (usually under the control of government supervision), corporations can pool resources to devise effective solutions to serious problems such as climate change or peak oil (Belz 2011).

responsibilities. They require serious thinking at the level of the social contract model if they are to adequately address the full range of issues pertaining to social, economic, and environmental sustainability.

It should be noted that while stakeholder theory requires this idealized set of conditions, shareholder theory does not. No matter how severe the problems with global finance or trade turn out to be, the shareholder model of managers attempting to maximize returns for the owners of an enterprise will not be replaced any time soon. Governance problems may demand that the model be reformed from time to time, and we will always have to be mindful of aligning the interests of managers and shareholders over the long term, but the shareholder model itself is extremely robust.

Nor should criticisms of the stakeholder model be interpreted as refutations. This model is very important in the world of product branding, public relations, and corporate image building. What critiques of stakeholder theory seek to uncover are its limitations.

There is no shortage of ideas for keeping stakeholder theory vibrant and relevant. Jeffrey Frooman (2010) of the University of New Brunswick has suggested shifting the focus away from stakeholders as organizations toward the issues that create "networks of organizational interests." When firms collaborate on common concerns and problems, management becomes more flexible. That makes it easier for firms to respond to fast-moving events in global business and the corporate alliances those events can create or quickly change. Others have argued that we can and should find ways to legally compel corporations to attend to stakeholder interests while fully maintaining the force of fiduciary responsibilities. These ideas are likely to continue to provoke lively debates about stakeholder theory well into the future.

DISCUSSION QUESTIONS

1. Why is it important for corporate managers to consider stakeholder interests as having intrinsic value? Wouldn't it be sufficient for managers to simply take a strategic approach to stakeholder interests and ensure that they are aligned with overall corporate/shareholder objectives?

2. Is it better to think of stakeholder relationships in terms of immediate and direct relationships with customers, suppliers, employees, etc., or should we pay more attention to the larger networks of relationships required by the stakeholder economy? Is it possible to consider the stakeholder economy from both a global and a national perspective?

3. Given the nature of stakeholder relationships with government, how should corporations manage these relationships so that all important

social problems and externalities are effectively addressed? How should Monsanto's management have addressed the issues raised by the Royal Society report?

SUGGESTED READINGS AND ONLINE RESOURCES

Donaldson, T., and L.E. Preston. 1995. The stakeholder theory of the corporation: Concepts, evidence and implications. *The Academy of Management Review* 20 (1): 65–91.

Freeman, R.E., R. Phillips, and A.C. Wicks. 2003. What stakeholder theory is not. *Business Ethics Quarterly* 13 (4): 479–502.

REFERENCES

Barnett, A. 1997. Towards a stakeholder democracy. In *Stakeholder capitalism*, ed. G. Kelly, D. Kelly, and A. Gamble, 82–98. London: Macmillan.

Belz, F.M. 2011 (September 20). Open sustainability innovation gives companies a competitive advantage. *Business Week*.

Berle, A., and G. Means. 1932. *The modern corporation and private property*. Piscataway, NJ: Transaction Publishers.

Boatright, J.R. 2006. What's wrong—and what's right—with stakeholder management. *Journal of Private Enterprise* 21 (2): 106–130.

Carroll, A.B. 1991. The pyramid of corporate social responsibility: Toward the moral management of organizational stakeholders. *Business Horizons* (July–August): 39–48.

Donaldson, T., and L.E. Preston. 1995. The stakeholder theory of the corporation: Concepts, evidence and implications. *The Academy of Management Review* 20 (1): 65–91.

Freeman, R.E., K.E. Martin, P.H. Werhane, and A.C. Wicks. 2010. *Business ethics: A managerial approach*. New York: Prentice Hall.

Freeman, R.E., R. Phillips, and A.C. Wicks. 2003. What stakeholder theory is not. *Business Ethics Quarterly* 13 (4): 479–502.

Frooman, J. 2010. The issue network: Reshaping the stakeholder model. *Canadian Journal of Administrative Sciences* 27: 161–173.

Jenson, M.C., and W.H. Meckling. 1976. Theory of the firm: Managerial behavior, agency costs and ownership structure. *Journal of Financial Economics* 3 (4): 305–360.

Marcoux, A.M. 2000. Balancing act. In *Contemporary issues in business ethics*, ed. J.R. Desjardins and J.J. McCall, 92–100. New York: Wadsworth.

Quinn, D.P., and T.M. Jones. 1995. An agent morality view of business policy. *The Academy of Management Review* 20 (1): 22–42.

Singer, N. 2011 (September 11). On campus, it's one big commercial. *New York Times*, B1.

Corporate Social Responsibility: The Canadian Experience

Introduction

Corporate social responsibility (CSR) as understood and practised in Canada reflects the influence of a variety of factors and conditions unique to Canada, but is also strongly affected by the broader global environment in which Canadian firms operate. As we will see in this chapter, Canadian history and geography, our political and legal system, and economic factors all play roles in shaping the Canadian approach to CSR. The global context for Canadian CSR is also explored in this chapter. In diverse ways, a range of global actors, instruments, institutions, and processes affect the definition and practice of CSR as carried out in Canada.

We begin by exploring definitions of CSR that have been developed or used in Canada, as well as linking Canadian understandings of CSR to the broader global environment, to business ethics, and to law. We also identify some of the unique features of the Canadian context that have influenced CSR practice in Canada. We then explore some important CSR contributions and initiatives of the Canadian government, the private sector, and civil society. We will see that one of the unique characteristics of Canadian CSR initiatives and practices has been a number of cooperative efforts involving those three sectors. The chapter closes with a brief discussion of possible future developments in Canadian CSR, and three discussion questions for your consideration.

Defining CSR

In recent years, the government of Canada and other key stakeholders have publicly supported two definitions of social responsibility. The first definition is contained in the 2006 federal government publication, *Corporate Social Responsibility: An*

Implementation Guide for Canadian Business (Industry Canada 2006). This definition, and the guide itself, were the product of a multistakeholder process, involving representatives from government, the private sector, non-governmental organizations (NGOs), and academics. We will return to the guide's definition of CSR below. The second definition of social responsibility is found in the ISO 26000: 2010 *Guidance on Social Responsibility*, an international standard published in 2010 (ISO 2010). It was developed with the participation of Canadian stakeholders as well as a wide range of governmental, private sector, consumer, academic, NGO, and other actors from other countries and international organizations. The ISO 26000 standard represents an international consensus view of the meaning of social responsibility. By comparing the Canadian and ISO 26000 definitions of social responsibility, we have a point of departure for understanding Canadian and international interpretations of the term "corporate social responsibility."

According to the Canadian guide, CSR is an evolving concept, and also goes by other names, such as corporate accountability, corporate ethics, corporate citizenship, sustainability, stewardship, the "triple bottom line," and responsible business. Key elements of the Canadian guide's definition of CSR include:

- the idea that CSR supports firms pursuing a "triple bottom line" of environmental, social, and economic (ESE) objectives, moving beyond a purely economic focus;

SIDEBAR

A Canadian Definition of CSR

In *Corporate Social Responsibility: An Implementation Guide for Canadian Business*, CSR is understood as "the way firms integrate social, environmental and economic concerns into their values, culture, decision making, strategy and operations in a transparent and accountable manner and thereby establish better practices within the firm, create wealth and improve society" (Industry Canada 2006, 5). The guide goes on to say that CSR builds on a base of compliance with legislation and regulations, and typically includes "beyond law" commitments and activities. These relate to corporate governance and ethics, health and safety, environmental stewardship, human rights (including core labour rights), human resource management, community involvement, development and investment, involvement of and respect for Aboriginal peoples, corporate philanthropy and employee volunteering, customer satisfaction and adherence to principles of fair competition, anti-bribery and anti-corruption measures, accountability, transparency and performance reporting, and supplier relations, for both domestic and international supply chains.

- the emphasis on engaging with and addressing the expectations of *stakeholders* (i.e., the views of all those potentially affected by a firm's actions), not just *shareholders* (who tend to be preoccupied with enhanced short-term share value);
- the notion that *compliance with law is a base* that is then built on by a range of corporate commitments *going beyond law* that address a wide variety of ESE issues;
- the importance of *transparency and accountability* in CSR performance. In other words, providing the stakeholders and the general public with an account of CSR activities is an important part of CSR; and
- the need to consider *supply-chain relationships*. Thus, for example, it is not enough to focus solely on those who are directly employed by a business. Instead, it is expected that the workers of companies who provide products and services to a business are also important dimensions of CSR.

SIDEBAR

International Definition of CSR

Social responsibility is defined in the International Standard ISO 26000 as the responsibility an organization has for the impacts of its decisions and activities on society and the environment, through transparent and ethical behaviour that

- contributes to sustainable development, health, and the welfare of society;
- takes into account the expectations of stakeholders;
- complies with applicable law and is consistent with international norms of behaviour; and
- is integrated throughout the organization and practised in its relationships.

The standard offers a framework of seven core social responsibility subjects and issues (see Figure 6.1 on page 78):

- organizational governance,
- human rights,
- labour practices,
- the environment,
- fair operating practices,
- consumer issues, and
- community involvement and development.

We can see that both definitions emphasize that firms need to address the environmental and social impacts of their activities, to comply with law, and to

Figure 6.1   ISO 26000, Social Responsibility: Seven Core Subjects

Launched in 2010, ISO 26000 was designed as a holistic approach to social responsibility, emphasizing the interdependence of seven key factors shown in the figure above.

Source: Copyright International Organization for Standardization. www.iso.org. Reprinted with permission.

make commitments to address norms that go beyond law; and that it is important for firms to consider the expectations of stakeholders, to be socially responsible in their relationships with others, and to be transparent and accountable in their CSR approaches and activities. Thus, on the whole, the Canadian and international definitions are quite compatible.

These two "practice-oriented" CSR definitions used in Canada are also consistent with leading academic conceptions of CSR. For instance, a Canadian business ethics professor (with an American co-author) has described CSR as having overlapping *economic, legal,* and *ethical dimensions* (Schwartz and Carroll 2003). In this conception of CSR, the *economic dimension* refers to activities intended to have a direct positive impact on the corporation (e.g., by maximizing profit or shareholder value). The *ethical dimension* includes activities undertaken to meet societal and stakeholder expectations (e.g., as evidenced through compliance with industry standards) while at the same time taking into account societal consequences (the utilitarian approach), as well as one's duties or obligations (the deontological approach). The *legal dimension* refers to a firm's responsiveness to legal expectations, such as regulations or legal principles. It includes activities undertaken to ensure legal compliance, to avoid civil litigation, and to anticipate new laws. The CSR definitions contained in the Canadian guide and the ISO 26000 standard align well with this academic definition, although the terminology and emphasis vary. The next paragraph shows that they also align well with a summary of academic research on CSR.

Academic Understandings of CSR

In 2006, Alexander Dahlsrud, a PhD fellow, reviewed 37 definitions of CSR described by 27 different authors from around the world, in publications from 1980 to 2003 (Dahlsrud 2008). He identified five common dimensions in these definitions: (1) an environmental component; (2) a social component; (3) an economic component; (4) a voluntary dimension; and (5) a stakeholder dimension. Because they give prominent attention to these five dimensions, the Canadian and ISO 26000 definitions discussed above are roughly consistent with Dahlsrud's analysis.

Historical Roots of CSR in Canada

Although "corporate social responsibility" is a modern concept that has only really existed for a few decades, it is possible to identify early examples from Canadian history that show corporations playing a "social" role that involved a range of stakeholders and that went beyond their fundamental function as a business. The Hudson's Bay Company (HBC) was incorporated by royal charter in 1670 and is the oldest commercial corporation in North America. While conducting fur trading was its primary function in the early years, HBC also acted as a de facto government, operating in the territory that is now Canada, in some cases resolving disputes among inhabitants of those territories (Foster 1994). Its traders and trappers forged significant relationships with many Aboriginal groups, and its network of trading posts formed the nucleus of future governments in areas that became the Dominion of Canada, areas where HBC was the largest private landowner. Thus, in addition to pursuing conventional commercial objectives, the HBC took on broader "social" functions involving a range of stakeholders. Obviously, the socio-economic circumstances of the 21st century are vastly different from those in Canada's formative years, and we would not describe this as CSR. However, it does provide an early Canadian example of a business being defined as something more than simply an economic enterprise.

Today, many Canadian firms are significant CSR innovators. On environmental and social issues associated with natural resource extraction and in relations with Aboriginal communities (e.g., in the forestry, mining and oil and gas, and hydroelectric sectors), there have been many new business initiatives, although considerable debate remains concerning the societal benefit of corporations operating in the resource sector. The CSR approach of Suncor (see sidebar) illustrates how a present-day Canadian extractive sector company is addressing its environmental, social, and economic impacts and responsibilities.

CSR and the Stakeholder Approach

A key point emerging from the analysis of CSR definitions is the significance of firms taking into consideration the impacts on and concerns of stakeholders. Successful firms develop strong relationships with customers, workers, suppliers, shareholders, lenders, and investors. CSR also suggests the importance of firms building relationships beyond the commercial sphere, with communities, governments, and citizens. This is why some commentators say that firms in the 21st century need to obtain not only a "legal licence" to operate, but also a "social licence" (a term coined by Jim Cooney, a Canadian mining executive). However, while it is comparatively straightforward to obtain a legal licence (e.g., comply with all the terms of relevant laws), it is much more challenging to secure a social licence: who "speaks for" each set of stakeholders? Luckily, there are many ways this question can be answered.

SIDEBAR

Suncor and CSR

Suncor is a Canadian oil and gas firm that extracts oil from the tar sands in northern Alberta near several First Nations communities. On its website, Suncor says that it "pursues a triple bottom line vision of sustainable development—energy development should occur in a way that provides economic prosperity, promotes social well-being and preserves a healthy environment" (Suncor 2011). While investment in the oil sands has resulted in many jobs, considerable tax revenue, and related economic activity, the extraction process is also energy intensive. It produces significant amounts of greenhouse gases linked to climate change, causes air pollution and large-scale alteration of the physical environment, and consumes large amounts of water (with the potential for water pollution). To address the impact it has on the economy, society, and the environment, Suncor has put in place extensive programs to provide jobs and economic opportunities for First Nations communities; developed innovative carbon-capture technology, tailings reclamation, and zero-discharge water programs; and implemented worker health and safety initiatives. Suncor describes its CSR policies and activities in considerable detail on its website, and publishes an annual sustainability report.

The CSR "Toolbox"

Firms can draw on a wide variety of tools to address their ESE impacts. Often, firms put in place a CSR policy or code, which sets out its ESE approach and commitments. In addition, there are a wide variety of third-party standards that firms can "sign on" to (see sidebar on the following page). Often, a firm can hire third-party auditors to "certify" that they are in compliance, and to identify problems. Industry associations can play a key role in creating CSR standards and programs for a particular sector, as is discussed later in this chapter. Firms may establish anonymous "whistleblower" programs so that they can receive tips on, and be alerted to, problematic activities. Firms may also establish stakeholder advisory groups, and create agreements with affected communities to address monitoring, economic opportunities, and other issues, and to hold regular meetings with communities. The following is an example of how one company has made CSR an integral part of their operations.

CSR and Supply Chains

In 2009, Loblaw Companies Limited (Loblaw) made a commitment to source 100 percent of all the wild and farmed fish sold in its stores from sustainable sources by the end of 2013 (Loblaw Companies 2009). This commitment covers more than 2,500 products and 250 vendors. Loblaw is focusing its seafood sustainability efforts on increasing the availability of Marine Stewardship Council (MSC)-certified wild-caught seafood products; establishing more responsibly sourced farmed Atlantic salmon; and introducing International Seafood Sustainability Foundation (ISSF) canned tuna in its stores.

Major Canadian grocery chain Loblaw has tied its seafood supply chain to MSC-certified sources, and other internationally recognized standards.

Source: Eco-opportunity Consulting Inc.

SIDEBAR

CSR Standards Used by Canadian Firms

- ISO 9001: Quality Management Standard
- ISO 14001: Environmental Management Standard
- OHSAS 18001: Occupational Health and Safety Management
- CSA Z-1000: Occupational Health and Safety Management
- ISO 26000: Guidance on Social Responsibility
- SA 8000: Social Accountability Standard
- Fair Labor Association
- Forest Stewardship Council Sustainable Forestry Standard
- Marine Stewardship Council Sustainable Seafood Standard
- United Nations Global Compact
- Global Reporting Initiative

CSR and the Investment Community

The Canadian investment community is a potentially important driver for Canadian firms' CSR activity. In 2008, Canadian assets that were invested using socially responsible guidelines were estimated at around $609.2 billion (Kropp 2009). Large national pension plans such as the Canada Pension Plan Investment Board (CPPIB) have adopted socially responsible criteria in their investment strategies. The CPPIB manages $152.3 billion in assets, representing the pensions of 17 million Canadians. Associated with the investment community are CSR-oriented agencies (institutional intermediaries) that track and rate companies' CSR performance. Recent studies indicate that institutional intermediaries, such as the Dow Jones Sustainability Indexes and CSR ranking agencies, influence market assessments of a firm's social responsibility (Doh et al. 2010). The research suggests that deletions by CSR ranking agencies can result in a significant decline in stock prices, and that investing in CSR may protect firms from a negative CSR event. At the same time, a positive CSR event can help redeem past poor CSR performance. We now turn to an examination of how the law helps firms develop CSR.

CSR and the Law

We have seen that in practising CSR, firms comply with the law as well as making and meeting commitments that go beyond the law. Thus, for example, a firm might commit (through its CSR code or policy) to creating economic opportunities for First Nations communities, or to meeting environmental standards, or to ensuring that third-party suppliers in developing countries meet environmental or labour requirements, even though the firm is not required by law to make or meet these requirements.

SIDEBAR

Talisman Divests from Sudan

In 2003, Talisman Energy Ltd. decided to divest itself of its operations in Sudan, following allegations that it was supporting genocidal activities in that country that were negatively affecting the value of its shares. The actions against Talisman included shareholder resolutions calling for an independently verified report of its activities in Sudan and a lawsuit launched in the United States (the lawsuit was later dismissed). Talisman is now a member of the United Nations Global Compact and several other CSR initiatives. Talisman's vice-president of corporate responsibility and government affairs, Reg Manhas, is reported as saying that the value of good corporate citizenship, while hard to measure, is "like an insurance policy, how do you quantify the benefits?" (Manhas 2007).

Law helps in three ways: to constrain, to facilitate, and to prescribe the CSR activities of firms. Law *constrains* firms through regulatory laws pertaining to such issues as worker health and safety, consumer protection, and pollution control. These laws are mandatory requirements, and a firm cannot be considered socially responsible if it does not meet these laws. As the Lululemon example provided later in this chapter suggests, a product said by a firm to have certain environmental attributes, when it does not, contravenes consumer protection laws that prohibit misleading advertising.

On the other hand, contract law is a good example of a type of law that *facilitates* CSR. Contracts are legal agreements between parties, where one party agrees to do one thing in exchange for another party agreeing to do another thing. When a Canadian firm requires its third-party suppliers in developing countries to meet certain environmental or social conditions if they wish to remain clients of the firm, contract law is thereby used as a legal mechanism to facilitate CSR behaviour. Examples of laws that *prescribe* CSR include reporting requirements whereby firms must publicly disclose what they are doing to improve communities or the environment (see examples of the public accountability statements required of large banks and insurance companies, described below).

CSR, Corporate Governance, and the Canadian Courts

In 2010, the Supreme Court of Canada in the *BCE* decision said that directors of corporations registered under the *Canada Business Corporations Act* have a fiduciary obligation to act in the best interests of the corporation, viewed as a "good corporate citizen," and in the course of their duties, directors may consider the concerns of a wide variety of stakeholders, including shareholders, communities, governments, consumers, the environment, and others. The significance of this judgment stems from its repudiation of the idea that directors owe a duty to exclusively protect the interests of *shareholders*. Instead, a broader *stakeholder* approach is appropriate.

Criticisms of CSR

While the CSR concept has gained considerable momentum and profile in Canada and around the world, there are good reasons to be skeptical of the idea. For one thing, if a for-profit company were to simply devote itself to good causes, it would probably go out of business. If a company does not reliably make good products that are wanted by consumers, and sell them at competitive prices, while providing good customer service, then, no matter how environmentally and socially responsible it might be, it will not be in business for long. The challenge for a company, then, is to integrate social and environmental factors into its day to day decision making, so that it is both making a profit and addressing CSR in a meaningful way.

A second criticism is that some firms engage in CSR "window dressing"—that is, they "talk the talk" but do not necessarily "walk the walk." While there is always this possibility, as we have seen there are laws in place that prevent firms from not living up to their promises. For example, in 2007, after the federal government agency responsible for enforcing the law concerning misleading claims by businesses intervened, Lululemon removed claims suggesting there were therapeutic benefits from a line of clothing products made with seaweed, which had been marketed throughout its 40-retail-store national network (Competition Bureau 2007). In the United States, Nike settled out of court after a consumer brought a legal action against it, challenging statements Nike had made about the treatment of its workers in developing-country supplier factories (Brown 2003).

A third criticism of CSR is that companies assume responsibilities that rightfully belong to governments. As is perhaps evident from the Lululemon example, governments continue to play a central role in regulating the conduct of businesses. The government role vis-à-vis CSR is explored in greater detail below.

The Canadian Government and CSR

All levels of government in Canada use various instruments, processes, and institutions to address CSR by Canadian businesses. As was discussed in our earlier description of CSR and the law, a primary way in which governments affect the CSR activities of firms is by enforcing regulatory laws that protect consumers, workers, and the environment. But the role of government extends beyond enforcement. Starting in the early 1990s, Canadian governments worked with the mining sector, labour unions, Aboriginals, and the environmental community, through a process referred to as the Whitehorse Initiative, to support mining activity that is conducted in a socially, environmentally, and economically responsible manner (Fitzpatrick et al. 2011).

Corporate Social Responsibility: An Implementation Guide for Canadian Business, discussed earlier, is an example of a guidance document developed by the federal government to assist firms in developing robust approaches to CSR. In 2006, following hearings by a parliamentary committee concerning the social and environmental impacts of the Canadian extractive sector overseas, the Government of Canada organized a multistakeholder national round table process on CSR and the Canadian extractive sector in developing countries. In 2009, this led to the government announcing its "Building the Canadian Advantage" CSR Strategy for the Canadian extractive sector operating abroad. This includes four main pillars: (1) support for initiatives to help developing countries manage their resource development; (2) endorsement and promotion of widely recognized international CSR instruments (see the sidebar below for a list of government-supported instruments); (3) support for the development of a CSR Centre of Excellence; and (4) the creation of the Office of the Extractive Sector CSR Counsellor (Foreign Affairs and International Trade Canada 2009).

Another approach is for governments to provide financial support to Canadian firms on the condition that the firms meet certain environmental or social criteria. For example, Export Development Canada is a federal Crown corporation that provides financial assistance to Canadian firms in their overseas activities if those firms agree to comply with the government's certain environmental and social conditions.

SIDEBAR

Federal Support for International CSR Instruments

The federal government has expressed support for the following international CSR instruments:

- the OECD Guidelines for Multinational Enterprises;
- the International Finance Corporation Performance Standards on Social and Environmental Sustainability;
- the Voluntary Principles on Security and Human Rights for projects involving private or public security forces;
- the Global Reporting Initiative (GRI) for CSR performance reporting;
- the ISO 26000 International Standard, providing guidance on social responsibility;
- the UN Principles of Business and Human Rights; and
- the Extractive Industries Transparency Initiative.

The Canadian Private Sector and CSR

Canadian businesses have engaged in a wide variety of CSR activities. We have seen that individual firms may make specific commitments as part of their CSR code or policy. In addition, industry associations for particular sectors can play key roles in promoting CSR for their members. A pioneering example of this is the Responsible Care program of the Chemistry Industry Association of Canada (CIAC), which has since been emulated by other Canadian industry associations and followed at the international level (CIAC 2011). The Responsible Care initiative was established in 1985 to address public concerns about the manufacture, distribution, and use of chemicals following the chemical spill in Bhopal, India in December 1984. The CIAC describes Responsible Care as the chemistry industry's commitment to sustainability, which it describes as the betterment of society, the environment, and the economy. Its principles help companies create safer and more environmentally friendly products and processes, as well as identify and eliminate harm throughout the entire life cycle of their products.

The program covers all aspects of a member company's business. These include environmental protection, resource conservation, occupational health and safety, process safety, research and development, transportation, product stewardship, purchasing, security, and social responsibility. It requires engagement with plant-site neighbours, communities along transportation corridors, emergency responders, critics and advocates, as well as with governments at all levels, to advance laws and regulations in support of sustainability. The Responsible Care program includes:

- ethics and principles for sustainability, which the most senior executive of every CIAC member company recommits to annually;
- codes of practice covering the entire life cycle of chemical products and processes—from their inception in the lab and through their manufacture, transportation, use, and disposal;
- a requirement that member companies have a robust "plan-do-check-act" management system in place to drive continuous improvement in meeting the intent of the codes;
- a suite of support documents and collective processes to assist companies in understanding and meeting the intent of the codes, including minimum standards; guidelines and checklists; tracking, analysis, and reporting of performance (e.g., safety and health, process safety, transportation safety, emissions, and wastes); and a continuously updated database of successful practices;
- a national advisory panel made up of 12 to 16 activists, advocates, and academics covering the range of society's concerns, that advises the association on how to understand and exceed the public's expectations; and

- a verification process with verification teams consisting of advocates, industry experts, and neighbours who visit all companies every three years to ensure that the ethics and management systems are in place to ensure compliance with the intent of the codes and that performance is continuously improving to meet peer and public expectations. The teams' verification reports are publicly shared by the companies and are posted on the CIAC's public website.

The CIAC Responsible Care program has become the basis for an international chemical industry Responsible Care program, now operating in over 50 countries around the world.

Similar programs have since been developed by a number of other industry associations, including the Mining Association of Canada (Towards Sustainable Mining program), the Prospectors and Developers Association of Canada (the e3 Plus program), the Canadian Association of Petroleum Producers (Responsible Canadian Energy program), the Forest Products Association of Canada (with all members signatories to the Canadian Boreal Forest Agreement), and the Canadian Electricity Association (the Sustainable Electricity program). One large group has not yet been discussed: what can individual Canadians do to spread CSR and make sure corporations are living up to their CSR ideals?

Canadian Civil Society and CSR

In Canada, it is not uncommon for members of civil society to form groups, called non-governmental organizations (NGOs), to address the economic, social, and environmental impacts of the private sector. Some work collaboratively with the private sector and governments. For example, the Canadian Parks and Wilderness Society and the David Suzuki Foundation, along with seven other environment-oriented NGOs, have worked closely with the Forest Products Association of Canada to create the Canadian Boreal Forest Agreement, which, among other things, has suspended logging activity on close to 29 million hectares of land to protect caribou (FPAC 2010). In 2009, the Assembly of First Nations (AFN) signed a memorandum of understanding with the Mining Association of Canada to strengthen the mining industry's engagement with First Nations economies, by creating employment and business (Canadian Newswire 2009). Earlier in this chapter, the mining industry's Whitehorse Initiative was described, involving a range of NGOs (among other parties). The federal CSR Extractive Sector round table involved NGOs as well as industry and governments. NGOs may also adopt critical stances toward corporate environmental and social practices, as we saw in the Talisman Energy example. In these ways, NGOs can be effective in bringing issues to public attention.

Conclusions

In this chapter, we reviewed Canadian and international definitions of CSR and noted the particularly important role for CSR in the Canadian resource extraction and Aboriginal communities. We have been introduced to a number of CSR tools and standards Canadian firms use to address their environmental, economic, and social challenges. We examined the legal dimensions of CSR and explored the nature and merits of criticisms of CSR, and we analyzed the roles of Canadian governments, the private sector, and civil society. What is clear is that CSR is an evolving and challenging concept. It offers many opportunities for innovation by Canadian businesses willing to address their economic, social, and environmental impacts in an integrated way—and considerable risks for those who fail to act to address those impacts proactively.

DISCUSSION QUESTIONS

1. A corporation has been convicted of violating environmental protection laws, but it also provides more than one million dollars each year in support of the arts. Based on your understanding of CSR as discussed in this chapter, can the corporation be considered "socially responsible"?
2. How can businesses "engage" with stakeholders while continuing to make a profit for shareholders? When and how do such stakeholders "approve" of a firm's practices? If they disapprove, then what?
3. What are the similarities and what are the differences in the process for firms obtaining *a social licence* to operate, as opposed to *a legal licence* to operate?

SUGGESTED READINGS AND ONLINE RESOURCES

Foreign Affairs and International Trade Canada. 2009. *Building the Canadian advantage: A corporate social responsibility (CSR) strategy for the Canadian international extractive sector*. http://www.international.gc.ca/trade-agreements-accords -commerciaux/ds/csr-strategy-rse-stategie.aspx?view=d.

Industry Canada. 2006. *Corporate social responsibility: An implementation guide for Canadian business*. http://www.ic.gc.ca/eic/site/csr-rse.nsf/vwapj/CSR_mar2006.pdf/ $FILE/CSR_mar2006.pdf.

Maclean's Magazine. 2010. Good for business: Corporate social responsibility report 2010 (annual survey of companies). http://www2.macleans.ca/2010/06/14/ jantzi-macleans-csr-report-2010/.

REFERENCES

Brown, S. 2003. Nike, Kasky reach settlement. http://www.adweek.com/news/advertising/nike-kasky-reach-settlement-67001.

Canadian Newswire. 2009. Assembly of First Nations (AFN) and Mining Association of Canada (MAC) join forces to work on improving First Nations economies with signing of MoU at INTES 2009. http://www.newswire.ca/en/story/509757/assembly-of-first-nations-afn-and-mining-association-of-canada-mac-join-forces-to-work-on-improving-first-nations-economies-with-signing-of-mou-at-int.

Chemistry Industry Association of Canada (CIAC). 2011. Responsible care. http://www.canadianchemistry.ca/ResponsibleCareHome.aspx.

Competition Bureau. 2007. Lululemon VitaSea Clothing: Competition Bureau takes action to ensure unsubstantiated claims removed from Lululemon clothing. http://www.competitionbureau.gc.ca/eic/site/cb-bc.nsf/eng/02517.html.

Dahlsrud, A. 2008. How corporate social responsibility is defined: An analysis of 37 definitions. *Corporate Social Responsibility and Environmental Management* 15: 1–13.

Doh, J.P., et al. 2010. Does the market respond to an endorsement of social responsibility? The role of institutions, information, and legitimacy. *Journal of Management* 36 (6): 1461–1485.

Fitzpatrick, P., et al. 2011. From the Whitehorse Mining Initiative towards sustainable mining: Lessons learned. *Journal of Cleaner Production* 19 (4): 376–384.

Foreign Affairs and International Trade Canada. 2009. *Building the Canadian advantage: A corporate social responsibility (CSR) strategy for the Canadian international extractive sector.* http://www.international.gc.ca/trade-agreements-accords-commerciaux/ds/csr-strategy-rse-stategie.aspx?view=d.

Forest Products Association of Canada (FPAC). 2010. The Canadian boreal forest agreement. http://www.fpac.ca/index.php/en/cbfa/.

Foster, H. 1994. "The Queen's law is better than yours": International homicide in early British Columbia. In J. Phillips et al., *Essays in the history of Canadian law, Volume 5: Crime and criminal justice*, 41–111. Toronto: University of Toronto Press.

Industry Canada. 2006. *Corporate social responsibility: An implementation guide for Canadian business.* http://www.ic.gc.ca/eic/site/csr-rse.nsf/vwapj/CSR_mar2006.pdf/$FILE/CSR_mar2006.pdf.

International Organization for Standardization (ISO). 2010. *ISO 26000: Guidance on social responsibility.* http://www.iso.org/iso/social_responsibility.

Kropp, R. 2009. Canadian SRI assets increased to $609 billion in 2008. *Social Funds.* http://www.socialfunds.com/news/print.cgi?sfArticleId=2691.

Loblaw Companies Limited. 2009. Loblaw sustainable seafood commitment. http://www.loblaw.ca/Theme/Loblaw/files/LoblawSustainableSeafoodCommitment2011.pdf.

Manhas, R. 2007. Talisman in Sudan: Impacts of divestment. http://www.enewsbuilder.net/globalcompact/e_article000775162.cfm?x=b11,0,w.

Schwartz, M., and A. Carroll. 2003. Corporate social responsibility: A three domain approach. *Business Ethics Quarterly* 13 (4): 503–530.

Suncor. 2011. http://www.suncor.com.

Law, Morality, and Business

Introduction

Any instructor who has taught both business ethics and business law courses has likely been asked at some point by students why courses in business ethics (BE) are typically compulsory, whereas business law courses are often elective (meaning everyone must take a BE course in the business education program, but people may *choose* to take business law). Perhaps those who pose this question are really asking why there needs to be a BE course at all, when a course in business law would suffice. In fact, most students believe that law is important to the business person, because we need to know the rules of the game if we are to play the game at all—

that is, to participate in the economy of a society. Then, in BE class, these students are introduced to Archie Carroll's pyramid of corporate obligations (1991), where legal obligations and ethical obligations occupy separate rungs of responsibility. "Aren't they the same thing?" ask these students (who henceforth will be referred to as the "Redundancy Camp"). This sentiment flows from an assumption of many business students—and many business people too—that if a business wants to act "properly," it must simply obey its legal obligations. After all, law is about social control and the adjustment of human behaviour, and, similarly, to behave ethically is to adjust your behaviour to meet social norms. Put simply, the members of the Redundancy Camp ask: "*If I obey the law, then haven't I met my ethical obligations?*"

Questions About the Purpose of Law and Ethics

In response, one might suggest first that the issue is not as simple as that question supposes. Don't we have to determine the purposes of both law and ethics in society before we compare them? Second, even if that question does go to the heart of the issue of the social regulation of business people, it still begs several other questions. What are these legal obligations? What does it mean to "obey the law"? Are legal obligations synonymous with moral obligations?

This chapter will try to answer the first "big" question mentioned above, as well as the other questions raised. To do so, we will first discuss the nature of legal obligations. We will then contrast the nature of law and morality and discuss how effective the law is as a social regulator (and more specifically, how effectively it regulates business). Finally, we will argue that law and morality regulate us in crucially different ways, and thus the enlightened business manager would be well advised to consider both the legal and ethical nature of the decisions they make and the implications of their actions.

Before discussing these three topics, it will be helpful to get some important underlying definitions and assumptions out of the way. While much of this chapter will be about defining "law," we will be *contrasting* law and morality (or legal obligations and moral obligations). Morality can be defined as principles concerning the distinction between the rightness and wrongness of an action. Ethics, by extension, is the application of moral principles—or to act or decide in accordance with morals.

In presenting this chapter, we chose to contrast law and "morality" instead of "ethics," despite the fact that one more often hears of "legal decisions" and "ethical decisions." This is because we want to get to the heart of what these obligations are—why do we adhere to these obligations? We do not refer to a law providing for capital punishment as being ethical or unethical, but rather moral or immoral. Elsewhere in this text, the making of ethical decisions is discussed (see Chapter 9).

Finally, we will be referring to the Canadian legal system, specifically the common-law system of law found in all provinces except Quebec. The Quebec system of civil law is predominantly set out in the *Civil Code of Quebec*; by contrast, common law is, to put it simply, "judge-made law," and is the predominant law system in the English-speaking world. The fundamental difference between the two is that in a civil code system, disputes between parties are resolved with reference to rules set out in a large piece of legislation called a civil code. In a common-law system, disputes are settled by judges, who apply principles that have evolved from previously decided cases.

The Nature and Purpose of Law

So why do we have laws in society? To ensure justice? To codify morality? To create a more efficient society? In truth, all three of these answers are reflected in Canadian law and can be approached in two different ways.

One way would be to look at law pragmatically: from the perspective of a citizen in a given jurisdiction, what is it that law does? This approach would consider how law attempts to regulate us and affect our conduct. In this way, we see law as a regulator. Another way is to look at this question more philosophically (or perhaps from a societal perspective) and consider the very nature or essence of law, asking why we have law at all, or what its purpose is at a societal level.

Law's Broader (Societal) Purposes

Philosophers have disagreed about law's central purpose for centuries. Civilizations have attempted to write down rules since ancient Babylonia; King Hammurabi, in the 18th century BCE, is widely considered the creator of the first "law code" (often called Hammurabi's Code). Emperor Justinian, at the end of the Roman Empire in the 6th century CE, created what has been credited as the first civil code (on which the civil laws of most European countries and the province of Quebec are broadly based). It is fair to say that in those times, a sovereign, or ruler, had much greater law-making power than any politician, bureaucrat, or judge. Consequently, early law codes amounted to the publication of the sovereign's word.

Historically, there has been a school of thought that says that law is really nothing more than an expression of the will of the sovereign. This is typically considered the basis for the *positivist* approach. Positivists see a clear distinction between what is and what ought to be—that is, law should be looked at as separate from morality. By the 19th century, an English philosopher, John Austin, had further distilled the positivist notion of law as being the "command of the sovereign," with "sovereign" being defined as more than simply a ruler; it also included an elected parliament.

It is probably fair, however, to suggest that ancient law codes were based almost entirely on the normative values of the sovereign (or ruler): or put simply, the ruler's morality. Modern positivists would suggest that law and morality are distinct (and should remain distinct). Positivism is often considered to be a reaction to a school of thought in the 17th and 18th centuries known as *natural law theory*. To natural law theorists, law and morality cannot be separated; law must be about fundamental and immutable moral principles. Initially, natural law theorists saw law as facilitating the fulfillment of man's natural purposes—or what man was created to do.[1] Natural law theory was born out of the so-called Age of Enlightenment (also known as the Age of Reason) in 18th-century Europe, when philosophers argued that man could achieve a better society through *reason* (rationality). Consequently, the more secular natural law writers saw law as representing man's rational pursuit of truth. Other, more religious, natural law theorists saw legal principles as inherently divine—that is, as being commands from God. Whichever

---

1   Note that here we are using the term "man" in the generic sense, as indicative of "humanity" generally.

natural law stream is pursued, laws cannot be forsaken, because they represent fundamental human truths and therefore fundamental human values.

The debate between positivists and natural law theorists is a constant of legal philosophy. Natural law theorists would consider positivism far too narrow, rendering law as almost trivial. For instance, natural law theorists would argue that a positivist must concede that the laws passed by Germany's Third Reich in the 1930s were effective laws, despite later being judged as immoral and allowing for genocide. Positivists, on the other hand, would note that the premise of natural law theories—which states that law should reflect what amounts to an immutable truth—can have a dark side: in the 20th century alone, natural law was used to justify several acts of genocide. For example, Adolf Hitler believed in the "truth" that the Aryan race was supreme, and on that basis justified his systematic extermination of other races of people in Europe.

Most 21st-century Canadians would argue that neither of these legal philosophies entirely captures the essence of our law. For example, consider the laws underlying posted highway speed limits. These are laws written by our provincial governments. While we may disobey the posted speed limits when we are driving, we nevertheless seldom question the law's legitimacy if we are caught speeding and get a ticket. Why is that? Do we think this law is legitimate because following highway traffic laws is the morally "right" thing to do? Or are we simply being realistic: the government wrote the law and can (and will) use its agents to enforce it, and thus if we are given a ticket, we shouldn't really be surprised? The answer for most of us lies somewhere in between. We obey some laws because we don't want to be punished (the law is what it is, whether we like it or not), whereas we obey other laws because at a deeper level we believe the law is about proper social conduct. In the end, legal philosophy only gets us so far in determining the purposes of law.

The Specific Purposes of Law

Now let us answer the question about law's purposes in a more pragmatic way. Admittedly, trying to define "law" could be a life's work, and could open its own intellectual debate. However, a short-form definition of law could be: *a set of rules of general application that govern conduct or situations, that are enforceable through a recognizable means, and that bind members of a society.* Laws are the express rules we agree to abide by in exchange for the benefits of being part of a society, the society as defined by a specific geo-political area (i.e., country or province). Laws in Canada are created by governments (federal, provincial, or municipal), their subordinate agencies, and the courts.

When we think of laws, most of us think of a statute created and enforced by our governments, such as the *Highway Traffic Act* and speeding. But law is broader

The Nuremberg Trials

The laws of Adolf Hitler's Third Reich in 1930s and 1940s Germany provide an interesting test for the principles of positivism. Indeed, those laws were indirectly put "on trial" after the Second World War in the famous Nuremberg Trials (1945–1947). After attaining victory over Germany in 1945, the four main Allied powers (the United States, the Soviet Union, Great Britain, and France) convened military tribunals at the Judicial Palace in the Bavarian  town of Nuremberg. The most famous of those trials was the International Military Tribunal (or IMT), in which 24 high-ranking German politicians, military officers, and influential members of society were tried on charges of crimes against peace, crimes against humanity, and war crimes. The charges related to the defendants' actions during the war, including their involvement in the Holocaust, which saw millions of Europeans killed because of their ethnicity (most notably, Jews). A common theme raised in defence was that the defendants were simply obeying the German laws of the time. They argued they should not be found guilty of a crime when they were obeying the law, and their actions should not be viewed through a retrospective lens, or judged by the morality of the victors. These arguments were not very successful; of the 24 defendants, 12 were sentenced to death, and only 3 were acquitted. However, this defence was somewhat more effective in the later trials of lower-ranking German military officials.

Discussion Questions

1. Consider how the positivists and natural law theorists would each analyze the Nuremberg Trials.

2. Were those convicted at the IMT found guilty because they acted illegally, immorally, or both? Is there a difference?

than that. As Smyth, Soberman, and Easson suggest (2006), consider the requirement in Canada that we drive on the right side of the road. We don't drive down the left side of the road because we fear getting a ticket—we fear the resulting traffic chaos and possible personal injury that would ensue. Nor do we drive on the right side because it is somehow morally superior to driving on the left side (as in the

United Kingdom). In other words, that law was put in place for the purposes of societal efficiency.

Law has two main functions: *to regulate the behaviour of societal actors* and *to address societal questions*. And law is only effective if it *can* influence behaviour or adequately answer societal questions because we as members of society *accept it* and if it is *enforceable*. For example, Canadian law once made it legal to discriminate on the basis of race and sex; over time, such laws grew out of favour with the public as Canadian society evolved (and were eventually abolished by the Constitution and human rights legislation). Alternatively, if a government does not enforce a law, out of active disinterest or neglect, then people will act as if that law were not in force at all.

To meet these two purposes, we see four different broad types of laws:

- criminal laws, which *punish*;
- civil laws, which *compensate*;
- regulatory laws, which *regulate* in accordance with governmental policy; and
- constitutional laws, which *structure*.

Let us briefly look at each of these types of laws and examine how they reflect the two broad reasons for law in Canada.

Criminal laws: These are the most *moral* of all laws in that they relate to fundamental questions of right and wrong behaviour. Indeed, criminal laws are the type of law most people think of first. In Canada, most criminal laws are found in a government-made statute called the *Criminal Code*. The *Criminal Code* lists activities that our federal government considers to be anti-social; generally speaking, they reflect Christian morals, and include homicide, theft, treason, and narcotics-related offences. Criminal laws are said to be "penal," meaning that if the government can prove with a relative certainty that an actor was guilty of a crime, then the transgressor will be punished, often through imprisonment. Criminal laws affect behaviour through the notion of deterrence—I do not want to be punished or go to jail, therefore I do not steal.

Civil laws: Civil law is the broad title for laws that govern the relationship between private actors in society. Civil laws relate to matters such as contracts, property laws, personal injury, product liability, and intellectual property. The underlying premise of civil law in Western societies is that private actors (individuals, or collectives such as corporations or partnerships) are free to enter into relationships; if, however, there is a breakdown in the relationship, or a dispute between the private actors, civil laws will provide a solution. Indeed, most civil laws apply when one party has been harmed by another and seeks compensation for its loss. For example, if ABC Co. breaks its contract with DEF Ltd. and does not pay for goods that have been delivered, DEF will sue ABC for the cost of the goods. Likewise, if Joe suffers a personal injury when the brakes of his new car fail, he will seek compensation for his injuries from the car manufacturer. Civil law therefore affects behaviour—typically, we don't want to be sued and have to pay compensation, so we uphold our contractual obligations, and ensure that the products we make are safe.

While civil laws are usually enforced in the context of a dispute between parties (and therefore as a result of a civil lawsuit), their purpose need not be solely about compensation (or acting so as to avoid paying compensation). Civil law also helps to address societal questions. Intellectual property laws determine which person may exploit a patentable invention or copyrighted idea and who owns what land and to what extent.

In English Canada, civil laws are primarily found in the judge-made common law. (As mentioned, in Quebec, as in most of Europe and elsewhere in the world, civil laws are found in a government-created civil code.) As a result, our civil laws do not necessarily reflect a governmental policy (or even a coordinated societal policy), but rather have been created out of the need for judges to resolve disputes between two parties.

Regulatory law: Regulatory law is a somewhat vague term for laws that stand at the border of criminal law and civil law. These laws are created by governments and their delegated agents, never by courts. They impose a procedure on how an activity should be carried out, usually by granting a licence to an actor, as long as the licensee adheres to certain rules. These rules are often about what the government (or its agent) feels are the best practices to engage in the activity in question. As in the case of criminal laws, the government or agency enforces regulatory laws, and being found in violation could result in a penalty. However, it is there that the similarity with criminal law ends—the rules of enforcement generally follow civil procedure and the penalties are civil in nature. That is, violating a regulatory law does not result in imprisonment, but, more likely, the loss of a licence or the right to engage in a certain type of business or activity. Consequently, regulatory laws affect behaviour too—for example, if a restaurant in Ontario wants to keep its licence to sell alcohol, it will comply with the rules of the Liquor Licensing Board of Ontario, and not sell alcohol to persons under the age of majority.

Constitutional laws: Said to be the most important of all of our laws, constitutional laws are laws created by countries to "govern their governors." In Canada, we have the *Constitution Act*, which was passed in 1982 to update the *British North America Act*, a statute of the English Parliament that had stood as our constitution or basic law since Canada's birth in 1867. The *Constitution Act* sets out the structure for our three levels of lawmakers: the federal government, the provincial governments, and the superior courts in each province. It states the powers, and the extent of those powers, that may be wielded by each of these levels of government. Our Constitution, since its repatriation from the United Kingdom in 1982, also includes the *Charter of Rights and Freedoms*, which sets out the rights Canadians have against their governments and governmental actors. The Constitution is, in effect, a *structural* law, and serves the function of answering the most basic societal questions. While Canadians may assert their constitutional rights against governments, the Constitution does not really affect Canadians on a day-to-day basis (unless you happen to be a police officer, perhaps, who must undertake his or her duties on behalf of the government without violating individual rights).

Law and Morality

What role does morality play in the law? Or perhaps it is the other way around—does law, in fact, shape our morality? If we return to the debate between the positivists and the natural law theorists, we see two starkly opposing views: positivists say that morality and law are separate things; natural law theorists say that law must be grounded in morality. The previous discussion of the four different types of law at work in our society showed that sometimes law is entirely consistent with morality, whereas at other times the law, though not necessarily *immoral*, really has little connection to morality. As discussed earlier, though it is true that most Canadian criminal laws are based on moral principles found in Christianity, many civil and regulatory laws are based to a greater extent on principles of efficiency rather than morality. For example, it may not be ethical for me to break a contract with you, but if you do not actually suffer any harm, you will not be able to receive compensation from me. This is because the laws of contract require a real loss before an order for damages will be made. And I will never be thrown in jail for breaching a contract. Finally, there are laws, like the highway speed limits discussed above, that might be seen as moral in some contexts, and entirely *amoral* (unconcerned with moral principles) in others. So immediately we can see that our law is not always based on or reflective of our society's underlying morals.

The Significance of an Apology

Despite these fairly clear examples, the question lingers today (especially in the Redundancy Camp) as to whether law and morality actually pose broadly different obligations. Let us consider a more controversial piece of legislation, the Ontario *Apology Act, 2009*. In 2009, the Ontario government, following in the footsteps of several other jurisdictions (including British Columbia, Saskatchewan, Manitoba, and many US states) enacted legislation that reduced the legal significance of an apology. The statute states that where a party has allegedly engaged in some sort of civil wrongdoing (most typically medical malpractice or negligence) and has made an apology to the injured party, that apology "does not, in law, constitute an express or implied admission of fault or liability by the person in connection with that matter."[2] An "apology" in that statute is defined as we might expect: "an expression of sympathy or regret, a statement that a person is sorry." Leaving aside the problematic technical issues with this legislation (for instance, what specific- ally constitutes an apology?), it does seem striking that governments have opted to codify into a law something that amounts to a social nicety or custom. We teach children to say "I'm sorry" when they bump into someone or cause unintended injury. This is considered good manners—or an exercise of ethical behaviour. There is no law that says that Ontarians must say sorry when they bump into someone or they will be punished. Indeed, the proponents of the *Apology Act* argue that a simple apology is what many injured people really want (as opposed to monetary damages) and the giving of an apology can have the effect of reduc- ing the number of lawsuits. In other words, *the law* is trying to make our society more civil by adopting the moral customs we learned as children.

While the Redundancy Camp (those who believe that there is no difference between legal and moral obligations) might argue that this is a good example of why we need only worry about laws (until the law came into force, the moral custom itself did not prevent lawsuits), ethicists might argue that this legislation shows the effectiveness of a moral custom for dealing with a legal problem. Regard- less, this example highlights the fact that legal conduct and moral conduct are not necessarily synonymous. For example, prior to the enactment of the *Apology Act, 2009*, the "moral act" of saying "I'm sorry" to defuse a problem or dispel a feeling of ill will could actually give rise to a legal fight: the act of apologizing had a dif- ferent legal impact because it could unfairly imply fault or intention. In the case of a medical procedure that went awry, for example, doctors, and especially hospitals, were reluctant to express regret to a patient—or to give an apology—for fear that it would be considered an admission of liability in a future lawsuit.

Questions of Legal Obligation and Moral Obligation

The divide between the role of law and the role of morality in our society can be seen in other ways. The premise of the Redundancy Camp is that adhering to legal obligations is enough to satisfy moral obligations. What if the law is not just *amoral* but contrary to a society's accepted moral principles—that is, *immoral*? Consider a situation in which a father watches his daughter suffer through a painful and incurable disease, and finally acts to accelerate her death so that she need not suffer anymore. Did the father commit murder? According to the Canadian *Crim- inal Code*, he did. However, the father is not likely to have considered complying

---

2   *Apology Act, 2009*, S.O. 2009, c. 3, s. 2(3).

with the law to be as important as doing right by his daughter—he would think his act was morally justified.

Likewise with the Canadian company that wishes to set up a factory in another country. It seeks the jurisdiction with the lowest employment standards so that it can keep its labour costs down. In contrast to Canadian labour laws, the foreign country's laws are substandard. However, the Canadian employer adheres exactly to that country's laws. It can say that it has expressly obeyed its legal obligations, but should it be surprised if it is criticized for operating a "sweatshop"?

Finally, is it enough to comply merely with "the letter of the law"? If a firm treats the law like a checklist, ensuring minimal compliance, has it actually addressed the concerns of its relevant stakeholders? Consider the publicly traded manufacturing firm that discovers a defect in one of its consumer products being sold in Canada, and chooses to quietly stop shipping it to stores. It doesn't report the defect to the government because it does not feel the defect is harmful. It further opts not to disclose this information publicly for fear of damaging its stock price. Technically, it could argue that it has complied with the law—the defective product is no longer on the shelves. However, consider the impact to consumers of defective products already purchased. Also, investors and shareholders may be interested in the potential liability arising from the defective products. In other words, because the firm was more concerned with doing as little as it could to comply with the law (and therefore avoiding the expense, inconvenience, and bad publicity of regulatory liability), it failed to realize that disclosure would have been the more appropriate response for consumers and shareholders.

In the end, we can see that legal principles and moral principles are not the same. They seek to achieve different purposes. Sometimes, they do converge—especially when we consider criminal laws. However, it is also fair to say that there are many laws that are amoral either in purpose or in application: these laws are as much about societal efficiency as they are about "right and wrong." Finally, the ethical business is expected to comply with its legal obligations, but mere compliance with laws may not satisfy a firm's moral obligations. Both are important in the modern Canadian business context, but Archie Carroll was correct to suggest that they are separate obligations.

Law as a Social Regulator

We have discussed the functions of law in our society, noting that we have laws to regulate behaviour and to answer societal questions. To a large degree, it can be said that as long as laws are created through an acceptable process (for example, pursuant to constitutional rules) and are enforceable in some way, then law can fulfill these obligations quite well. Indeed, there has been no civilization since medieval times that has not had *some* sort of system of law.

We next discussed the relativity of law and morality and it was argued that the two terms are not synonymous. Moreover, while many of our laws are based on morality (criminal laws being the clearest example) as the natural law theorists would suggest, many of our laws—especially those that answer societal questions, such as our election laws or the laws that create and give power to our municipalities—are amoral. Indeed, in some cases, one could argue that we obey a law not because of its moral tone, but simply because we don't want to be punished for violating it (it is more convenient if we are not punished or sued). This latter point seems to support the positivist point of view: that the law is what it is, not what it ought to be. This begs one final question for us: do we always know what the law is in any given circumstance?

Many in the Redundancy Camp would argue that law must be the pre-eminent social regulator, because it is easily definable. Indeed, where the law has been written down, we can point to it and say with certainty: "See? There it is. *That* is the law." Those in the Redundancy Camp would argue that the law is therefore objective, unlike moral principles, which are uncertain, variable, and almost never written down. It follows for those in the Redundancy Camp that even after conceding that legal and moral principles are not the same, law is the most important social regulator.

The fallacy in this argument is that law is *not* such a clear social regulator. It is not always definable in every given situation, and it is not black and white, as positivists would suggest. Ronald Dworkin, an American legal philosopher, attempted to put positivism to the test in his 1986 treatise, *Law's Empire*. As the title of his book suggests, Dworkin feels that law (as he defines it) is of paramount importance to society. However, he chided positivists not only for defining law so narrowly as to deprive it of its power to act as an effective social regulator, but also for defining it inaccurately. Dworkin used the concept of "hard cases" to show the weaknesses in the positivist position.

Dworkin suggested that in many cases the law is predictable and easily applied. In many of those cases, Dworkin would see the law lining up squarely with moral principles. In those cases, law is a clear social regulator—the black-and-white concept that so many business students and business people believe it to be. However, according to Dworkin, there are also *hard cases*, cases where the law or its application is not readily or easily determined. What causes hard cases? They arise in three situations:

- situations where two or more laws could apply, in different ways;
- situations where a law applies broadly, but its specific application in a given case is uncertain; and
- situations where a dispute has arisen for which no law has (yet) been written, passed, or created—what judges call "cases of first instance."

Dworkin rightly points out that in any legal system, and especially in a common-law jurisdiction, judges cannot avoid hard cases—they must decide as between two litigants, whether it is a civil case between private parties, or a criminal, regulatory, or constitutional case involving the government and a private party. As a result, judges must do their best to interpret the law or laws as they apply. In doing so, Dworkin urges judges to give the law the "best interpretation" it can have. To Dworkin, this means that judges should apply moral reasoning in their deliberations. He argues that it cannot be otherwise—judges cannot decide hard cases without having recourse to moral arguments applied to the "raw ingredients" or bare legal principles.

Consequently, we can see Dworkin providing a bridge between the natural law theories and the positivists: in "easy cases," the law is predictable and can be applied. In those cases, the law is a clear social regulator. In "hard cases," the law must be interpreted; its predictability is less certain. This is how Dworkin sees law as having an empire—law is interpreted in the best way possible to produce the best social regulation. Decisions in hard cases become, in turn, good precedents, and the law grows. Dworkin therefore frowns on narrow legal interpretations, and mere adherence to the letter of the law. But he cautions us that there will always be "hard cases." He illustrates his theory by comparing law to a flame: in the centre of the flame, the light is bright, sharp, and well defined—these are the "easy cases," where the law, and how it applies, is clear. However, at the outer edge of the flame, the light is dimmer and more diffuse, analogous to the hard cases.

If Dworkin is correct, then in a great number of cases the law may be no clearer a predictive regulator than moral principles are. Indeed, we can point to examples where the moral standard is clearer and better known than the law. For example, picture yourself in an elevator where you overhear the two women beside you discussing a brilliant business idea that one has developed over the past year. She laments the fact that she "just needs an investor to bring this to market." You happen to have access to capital, and without saying a word to her, take the woman's idea and begin to develop it yourself. Did you just violate intellectual property laws? Possibly, but it is by no means certain you did. An impartial observer, however, would say that you have "stolen an idea"; this is unethical.

Conclusion

In the end, we can agree that law is not only a significant social regulator, but an important constraint on business and professionals. Just as Archie Carroll (1991) exhorted business to adhere to legal obligations in his pyramid of obligations for the socially responsible business, few would argue that a business or professional should not obey the law. However, this is not as simple as it seems. For one thing, Carroll was right to separate ethical obligations from legal obligations—the law and morality are *not* synonymous. A firm has not met its ethical obligations simply by obeying the law; the firm that engages in "jurisdiction shopping" for lax environmental or labour laws—and then complies with those laws—will still be criticized for exploiting its employees or the environment. Likewise, the professional who chooses to stand by a moral principle may still be found guilty of a crime, or in breach of contract.

Additionally, the law is not a static, easy-to-define construct. Life is messy and social interactions sometimes make it almost impossible to obtain an easy answer. For example, does an oral conversation give rise to an enforceable contract? Just as it may be debated what the correct ethical approach would be in a given situation, sometimes it is just as difficult to predict how a law will apply, such as the case of the stolen business idea discussed above where the moral principle is clearer than the "applicable law."

Law is an important social regulator and without it, our society would lack structure. No civilization has survived without a set of laws. But we are mistaken if we think that laws are the sole and most perfect regulator of our behaviour. As noted, the law is not always as easy to predict as we would like to think. Nor *should* law be static; it should be flexible enough to adapt to changing societal contexts and emerging problems. But business people and professionals would be wise to remember that a solution that seems *legal* may not be the most *moral*. Legality and morality are two different social regulators, and both should be respected.

DISCUSSION QUESTIONS

1. Judges in Canada are appointed, not elected by "the people," and these judges remain on the bench until retirement. Does it bother you that judges have so much law-making power?
2. Is an immoral law still a law?
3. If you break a law, there is usually a specific punishment. What is the punishment if you act unethically? Does the fact that there are specifically defined consequences for breaking a law make law a more important regulator of our behaviour than moral principles?

REFERENCES AND SUGGESTED READINGS

Apology Act, 2009. S.O. 2009, c. 3.

Canadian Charter of Rights and Freedoms. Part I of the *Constitution Act, 1982*, being Schedule B to the *Canada Act 1982* (UK), 1982, c. 11.

Carroll, A.B. 1991. The pyramid of corporate social responsibility: Toward the moral management of organizational stakeholders. *Business Horizons* (July–August): 39–48.

Dworkin, R. 1986. *Law's empire*. Cambridge, MA: Harvard University Press.

Hart, H.L.A. 1961. *The concept of law*. London: Clarendon Press.

Raz, J. 1980. *The concept of a legal system*. 2nd ed. Oxford: Oxford University Press.

Smyth, J.E., D.A. Soberman, and A.J. Easson. 2010. *The law and business administration in Canada*. 12th ed. Toronto: Pearson Prentice Hall.

United States Holocaust Memorial Museum. Holocaust encyclopedia. http://www.ushmm.org/wlc/en/.

Ethics and Leadership

Introduction

When we read about successful organizations, we often hear about the important role played by the men and women in positions of leadership. We hear about the leaders' ability to develop a shared mission and vision for their organization, to recruit and retain talented people, and then inspire and motivate them to work hard to attain key goals. We hear about their ability to foster a work environment where creativity and innovation are promoted, and employees are encouraged to take risks and feel empowered to tackle challenging problems on their own. More and more, we also hear about the personal, moral character of these leaders, and their ability (or in some cases *in*ability) to develop an organizational climate and culture that promotes ethical and socially responsible conduct.

In this chapter, we will touch on these key abilities of organizational leaders, but we will focus specifically on this last aspect of leadership; the importance of the leaders' personal, moral character, and their power and influence in shaping the ethical climate and culture of their organizations. We think it's important to discuss these particular links in more detail for a number of reasons. First, similar to the ethical crises of the early 2000s involving firms such as Enron and WorldCom, the 2008 financial crisis has brought intense scrutiny to the role played by organizational leaders in promoting, or at least allowing, unethical behaviour that has caused immense harm to many organizational stakeholders. It is important therefore to understand the nature and extent of these influences. Research is also suggesting that firms perceived as unethical may find their longer term success compromised as they struggle to compete for talented employees, satisfied customers, loyal investors, and government support. As tomorrow's leaders, you may well be expected to develop effective strategies for dealing with these new realities, and you must be equipped with the knowledge and understanding to do this work. To help with this, our chapter will accomplish the following:

- define leadership and in particular leadership styles that have been shown to promote ethical behaviour in organizations;
- discuss the importance of leader character and integrity, and the traits and virtues that contribute to a moral character;
- explore the dark side of leadership and ways to avoid fostering negative and unethical work environments; and
- review some of the findings about the role of leaders in shaping organizational culture and climate, and in particular in promoting ethical cultures and climates.

We'll begin by defining our key concepts.

Leadership Defined

We have been studying leaders and leadership for a very long time, and today leadership remains one of the most researched concepts in business. For example, in the 20 years between 1990 and 2010, more than 18,000 journal articles were written on the topic of leadership. Not surprisingly, bookstore shelves are also usually well stocked with titles that incorporate some aspect of leadership. An online search of the Chapters Indigo website in 2011 turned up just under 10,000 titles with the word "leaders," including *The Leader in Me* by US business writer Stephen Covey and *The Opposable Mind: How Successful Leaders Win Through Integrative Thinking* by Rotman School of Management dean Roger Martin. These articles and books showcase what we've learned about the impact of both good and bad leadership on individual and organizational outcomes. Before we start discussing some of these specifics, let's first review what we mean by the term leadership.

Defining leadership is not as easy a task as you might expect. One reason is that there are now many different theories of leadership. Reading some of the articles and books mentioned earlier, you'll come across many different theories, including authentic leadership, principle-centred leadership, self-leadership, servant leadership, and even spiritual leadership. Julian Barling, Amy Christie, and Colette Hoption (2010) of Queen's University in Kingston, Ontario examined the quantitatively oriented leadership research (research done using surveys or other numerically focused data collection methods) from 1980 to 2007 and found that two of the three most frequently studied leadership theories were charismatic leadership and transformational leadership. Many leadership researchers see charismatic leadership and transformational leadership as overlapping in a significant way, suggesting that transformational leadership is the dominant leadership theory studied. We'll examine this leadership style now in a little more detail.

Transformational Leadership

Studying political leaders in the United States, James Burns (1978, 20) developed the idea of the transformational leader as someone who interacts with employees in such a way as to "raise each other to higher levels of motivation and morality," with the key being shared values and goals. Bernard Bass (1985), studying military and business leaders, built on this work and collaborated with Bruce Avolio in the 1990s to identify four dimensions of a transformational leadership style. The first of these dimensions, idealized influence, concerns the behaviour of leaders and the ways in which they role-model appropriate action for the rest of the organization. The second, inspirational motivation, refers to the ways leaders motivate and challenge their employees, and provide meaning to their work. The third dimension, intellectual stimulation, speaks to the leader's ability to foster a work environment where employees are stimulated to develop new and creative ways to look at challenges and solve problems. Individualized consideration is the fourth and final aspect of transformational leadership. A leader demonstrating this dimension is one who acts as a coach and mentor, working with employees on an individual basis to help them develop to their full potential. The leader's focus is thus more on his or her employees' needs, rather than the leader's own self-interest.

Bass and fellow researcher Paul Steidlmeier (1999) have suggested that a transformational leadership style creates both more moral leaders and more moral organizations because of its reliance on such ethical principles as honesty and fairness, its strong focus on employees and their concerns, and its avoidance of manipulative and coercive leadership behaviours.

Ethical Leadership

Academic researchers have also developed a theory of ethical leadership. Linda Treviño, Laura Hartman, and Michael Brown (2000) first described this leadership approach in an article in the *California Management Review*, a business magazine published by the University of California at Berkeley. Working with other colleagues, they began conducting research studies to more clearly distinguish this form of leadership from other approaches. As a result of their work, they describe an ethical leader as a person who demonstrates "appropriate conduct through personal actions and interpersonal relationships, and the promotion of such conduct to followers through two-way communication, reinforcement, and decision making" (Brown, Treviño, and Harrison 2005, 120). They see ethical leadership as having two main components, one being the *moral person* and the other being the *moral manager*. The *moral person* is someone who acts with integrity, who shows concern for others, who is fair in his or her dealings with people, and who, as a result, can be trusted. The *moral manager* makes these personal characteristics and traits very visible in day-to-day behaviour by being an ethical role model, by talking about ethical standards, and also by acting on them in concrete ways that other members of the organization can see. For example, ethical leaders would reward ethical behaviour and, just as important, punish unethical behaviour.

Brown and Treviño (2006) acknowledge the similarities between ethical leadership and transformational leadership, noting the shared emphasis on integrity and role modelling, concern for employees, and fair and transparent decision making. They suggest that the biggest differences between the two are that, while transformational leaders focus their efforts on fostering a shared understanding of organizational vision and values, ethical leaders place more emphasis on communicating about ethics related concerns, such as the ethical standards of the organization, and then ensuring that those standards are followed. As they point out, these behaviours would be more consistent with a transactional leadership orientation.

TABLE 8.1   The Dimensions of Ethical Leadership

Moral person: (Leader's behaviour)	Moral manager: (Directs followers' behaviour)
Traits: *honesty, integrity, trust*	Role modelling: *visible ethical action*
Behaviours: *openness, concern for people, personal morality*	Rewards/discipline: *holds people accountable for ethical conduct*
Decision making: *values-based, fair*	Communicating: *conveys an "ethics/values" message*

Source: Treviño, Hartman, and Brown (2000). Reprinted by permission of the University of California Press.

Now let's consider what might make these leaders inclined to act in this way.

The Importance of Character in Leaders

As discussed in Chapter 2 on ethical theories, virtue ethics is a perspective that focuses specifically on moral character. When it comes to leaders, in particular good and ethical leaders, we expect to see certain traits and virtues. In his book linking personal integrity to corporate success, business ethics scholar Robert Solomon presents what he describes as a "catalog of business virtues" that ranges from *ability* to *zeal* or *enthusiasm* (1999, 69). Solomon emphasizes the importance of a leader's overall character and says that this sense of integrity, or wholeness, can stem from a number of key virtues, specifically mentioning the importance of "honesty, trustworthiness, and fairness" (1999, xiii). When we look at leaders in Canada or the United States who are recognized and celebrated for their leadership it's often for exhibiting these very traits (see sidebar "Leaders Who Stand Out in the Crowd").

SIDEBAR

Leaders Who Stand Out in the Crowd

If you were asked to identify a Canadian who is an ethical or transformational leader, could you? It might help to think of the significant accomplishments of some of our leaders, or moments when individuals demonstrated the strength of their moral character. For example, former prime minister Pierre Trudeau is often applauded for his success in creating the *Canadian Charter of Rights and Freedoms* in 1982. Scientist and CBC-TV personality David Suzuki is praised for raising global awareness of environmental concerns. Stephen Lewis, one-time Canadian ambassador to the United Nations, is celebrated for the work he has done to help draw attention to the HIV/AIDS epidemic in Africa. Sheila Fraser, Canada's auditor general until 2011, gained widespread recognition and trust for her efforts to hold high-profile politicians and civil servants accountable for the inappropriate use of taxpayers' money. Former General Romeo Dallaire is respected for his public acknowledgment in 2004 of his failure, and that of the United Nations, to prevent the inter-tribal violence that led to the deaths of hundreds of thousands of Rwandans.

However, similar examples in the business sector are somewhat harder to identify (see activities 2 and 3 at the end of this chapter). One business leader who has been characterized as transformational is Maple Leaf Foods CEO Michael McCain. In 2008, the company's sliced meat products were found to be contaminated with a dangerous bacterium called *Listeria monocytogenes*. The company quickly recalled dozens of products from grocery stores and stopped further meat production until the cause of the problem could be located and fixed. Unlike many CEOs whose companies are embroiled in a high-profile controversy, McCain immediately took a very active role in communicating directly with media about the crisis. He took the unprecedented step of publicly apologizing for the company's role in the illness and death that resulted from people eating Listeria-contaminated products, and outlined what the company was doing to address the issue. Media and public reaction to McCain's handling of the crisis, and in particular his apology, was very favourable and no doubt helped the company to recover more quickly from this tragic event.

Source: YouTube.

Findings from one of the largest leadership research initiatives suggest that Solomon's opinion on the importance of a leader being honest, trustworthy, and fair is universally shared. The GLOBE project, which stands for Global Leadership and Organizational Behavior Effectiveness, was started in 1994 by Robert House when he was with Pennsylvania's Wharton Business School. Over a ten-year period, House and 160 international research partners collected data from some 15,000 managers working for almost 780 organizations in 53 different countries. One of the areas explored in the GLOBE project was leader attributes. Deanne den Hartog and her four colleagues (1999) found that there were leadership traits that were seen as universally positive or negative by managers, while another group of traits was more culturally dependent. On the list of the universally positive leadership traits were honesty, trustworthiness, and justice/fairness. Among the negative leader attributes were ruthlessness and self-centeredness, while traits that seemed to vary from a culture standpoint included such things as sensitivity, ambition and individuality. This highlights how important it is for leaders to be aware of their leadership traits.

Now that we have some sense of the leadership traits and virtues that are important in many cultural contexts, let's turn our attention to the impact that leaders with positive virtues and traits can have.

Leadership and Ethical Climate and Culture

As noted in the introduction, one of the reasons we are so concerned about the character and leadership style of those in management roles is because of the significant influence they can have on the culture and climate of the organizations they lead. The concepts of climate and culture are likely familiar to you from courses on human resources, organizational behaviour, or business strategy. They are also very important in the area of ethics. Let's review quickly what we mean by these concepts and then discuss the specific links with ethics.

The terms *organizational climate* and *organizational culture* are sometimes confused, not surprising given that they both involve the study of organizational contexts. When we use the term *organizational culture* we are referring to the deeply rooted, and often unseen, values, beliefs, and assumptions about the way the organization operates that come to be shared by organizational members over time. We can often see these assumptions reflected in the language and stories of an organization, its rituals and traditions, as well as the ways organizational members work together. When we speak of *organizational climate*, we are talking about the impressions and perceptions employees have about such things as work procedures, policies, and practices. Because climate can be more easily altered by organizational leaders, it is considered to be more temporary than its culture counterpart (Denison 2003). Academics have been doing research in each of these related streams and explored linkages to the field of ethics.

An Ethical Work Climate and Its Outcomes

Bart Victor and John Cullen were the first to suggest that one aspect of an organization's overall climate is its ethical climate. By that, Victor and Cullen mean (1988, 101) "those aspects of work climate that determine what constitutes ethical behaviour at work" and they suggest that there are five possible ethical climate types (see sidebar for more details). The reason that ethical climate is important is that it can have a big influence on the work environment and, more particularly, on employees' ethical behaviour.

A significant amount of research has been done on ethical climate in the last 20 years. Cullen worked with Kelly Martin (2006) to review the published research on ethical climate and found that it was associated with higher levels of organizational commitment, job satisfaction, employee well-being, and lower employee turnover in organizations with ethical climate types such as *caring*, *law and code*, and *rules*. Just as important, the researchers also found lower levels of unethical workplace behaviours, such as stealing and sabotage.

SIDEBAR

Ethical Climate Types

Between 1987 and 1993, Bart Victor and John Cullen conducted research to develop their framework of ethical climate types. They drew on ethical theories associated with egoism, benevolence, and principles and then considered how these might be interpreted at the individual, organizational, and broader societal level. Here are the five climates that resulted from this research:

Instrumental: This climate type occurs in organizations where ethical decision making is approached from an egoistic or individual self-interest perspective.

Caring: Organizations with this climate type have a caring or benevolence orientation and take the well-being of employees and other stakeholders into consideration.

Independence: An independence climate exists in organizations where deeply held individual moral values are deemed the most appropriate reference point for ethical decision making.

Law and code: A climate of this type is found in organizations that support decision making based on principles that derive from external sources such as the Bible or other holy texts, the law of the land, or codes of conduct for various professions.

Rules: A climate of this type suggests a company that focuses on adherence to company rules and regulations when making ethical decisions.

Source: Adapted from Martin and Cullen (2006).

More recent research suggests other positive links between ethical climate and important aspects of organizational life, including promoting trust between employees and their managers, empowering employees to effect change, and reinforcing a safe and healthy workplace. This last effect is particularly important given that Canadian workers' compensation board data show that more than 1,000 people die each year on the job and close to 250,000 are injured, with related health care and insurance costs estimated to be over $5 billion (AWCBC 2012). Worker stress-related costs are estimated to be an additional $8 to $10 billion annually, or 20 percent of a company's payroll (Riga 2006).

An Ethical Work Culture and Its Outcomes

Just as with the previous discussion, when speaking of ethical culture we are referring to those aspects of organizational culture that are specific to ethics. Linda Treviño and colleagues see it as a combination of *formal* and *informal* systems that are capable of promoting either ethical or unethical behaviour (Treviño and Nelson 2004). They suggest that formal cultural systems include such things as leadership approach, reporting relationships in organizations, compensation systems, ethics policies (e.g., a code of ethics), and even training. Informal cultural systems consist of the behaviour of work colleagues and the norms for ethical conduct. In organizations where the formal and informal systems promote and reinforce an ethical culture, we expect to see more ethical behaviour and other positive individual and organizational outcomes.

Research suggests that these relationships do exist. As Brown and Treviño (2006) outline in their review of research in the area, organizations with leaders who promote ethical cultures with codes of conduct and reward systems see benefits in the form of positive attitudes and more ethical behaviour among employees. Muel Kaptein (2011) has found that a strong ethical culture is also associated with increased reporting of ethical issues, either through direct reporting to management or indirectly through a whistle-blowing channel such as a hotline. Similar to ethical climate research, employees working in organizations with ethical cultures also report being more satisfied in their jobs, more engaged with their work, and more committed to their organizations. In today's competitive work environment, this suggests that companies with ethical cultures could be at a distinct advantage.

For most of this chapter we have discussed the positive contributions that can be made by ethical leaders, but we also need to point out that there can be a dark, or unethical, side to leadership.

The Dark Side of Work Climate, Culture, and Leadership

Throughout history, many leaders have abused their power and privilege, and caused great harm. Adolf Hitler is often named as an example of this kind of leader. No doubt you can think of others.

In business, there have been several high-profile examples of unethical leadership and researchers have studied the individuals involved to try and help us learn some positive lessons from these negative situations. By studying destructive and toxic leadership, we hope to understand where problems can develop and use this knowledge to better promote and foster authentically ethical leadership in all organizations.

Although it has been over ten years since the collapse of the energy giant Enron, the case is somewhat like the Hitler example: a high-profile example of unethical leadership that has not lost its relevance over time. Many leaders are charismatic, people who are very skilled at using their communication abilities and influencing skills. In the Enron case, the world witnessed the destructive influence that such leaders can have. Depending on the skills of such leaders, we know that employees can tend to see such leaders in a positive light, even when their behaviour is ethically suspect.

Tourish and Vatcha (2005) describe the role of charismatic leadership in developing a corporate cult at Enron. They describe how charismatic leaders like Jeff Skilling and Kenneth Lay promoted a destructive and toxic culture that glorified executive privileges, Machiavellian tactics, and absolute conformity. As another example of the manipulative aspects of charismatic leadership, Enron trader Brian Cruver was known by his fellow employees as Darth Vader because of his ability to

Enron's Jeff Skilling ("The Prince") testifies before the Senate Commerce Committee in 2002.

Source: Stephen J. Boitano/Alamy Images.

seemingly control employees' minds. Jeff Skilling was referred to as "The Prince," following Machiavelli. Tourish and Vatcha (2005, 476) sum up the destructive culture that resulted at Enron:

> Once people over-align themselves with a company, and invest excessive faith in the wisdom of its leaders, they are liable to lose their original sense of identity, tolerate ethical lapses they would have previously deplored, find a new and possibly corrosive value system taking root, and leave themselves vulnerable to manipulation by the leaders of the organization.

Tourish and Vatcha also illustrate how, as in a cult, CEOs and other executives at Enron were privileged with extreme power and wealth. Despite the financial collapse of 2008, CEOs in large corporations today continue to have excessive salaries and compensation packages. In Canada, these levels have reached as high as 180 times the average employee's salary, while for some CEOs in the United States the multiple is as high as 1,000. This exorbitant compensation of CEOs is not limited to North America either. There appears to be a contagion effect in other parts of the world as well.

The Importance of Leadership in Fostering Ethical Climates and Cultures

So what specific roles do leaders play in fostering ethical climates and cultures? From research in the area, we know that their impact is significant and, in fact, some would argue they are the most important factor. Leaders who exhibit transformational or ethical leadership styles have been found to have significant positive effects on the ethical orientation of their organizations' climates and cultures.

Going back to the research review done by Julian Barling and his colleagues (2010), we see that transformational leaders can create work climates that foster trust and a sense of fair treatment. Such leaders have been shown to be more concerned about the health and welfare of employees, whether that is by promoting safety-oriented workplaces or ones that promote well-being, for example by removing workplace stressors or providing support for employees to deal with such stressors. Transformational leaders have also been shown to promote values that are in keeping with a deontological ethics perspective—that is, a focus on rights, duties, and obligations (Groves and Larocca 2011), and to have a positive influence on followers' moral identity (Zhu, Riggio, Avolio, and Sosik 2011). These attitudes and behaviours are necessary to promote ethical behaviour and a more socially minded orientation.

Given that ethical leadership is a newer concept, not as much research exists documenting its effects. We do know however that employees who perceive their leaders as ethical are more likely to report ethical concerns internally (Brown et al. 2005), and, significantly, are less likely to devote time to unproductive work-place behaviours (Avey, Palanski, and Walumbwa 2011). Employees of ethical leaders also report higher levels of job satisfaction and organizational commitment, and are willing to voluntarily put more effort into work (Ruiz, Ruiz, and Martìnez 2011). Brown and Treviño (2006) have found that ethical leaders are important role models for the development of future ethical leaders.

As a result of their extensive review of the ethical climate literature, Martin and Cullen (2006) recommend that leaders take a close look at their organizational climates and try to determine what kind of work environment they have. Companies can then consider what they might need to do to create more caring climates, and minimize possible perceptions of instrumental climates focused on individual self-interest or corporate profiteering.

Muel Kaptein's (2011) research highlights how important it is for organizational leaders to pay attention to the prevention of unethical behaviour, by examining its policies and procedures for encouraging the reporting of concerns. Marcia Miceli and colleagues (2008) stress that leaders need to ensure that employees are clear about what behaviours need to be reported and how they should go about doing so. Leaders then need to show strong support for such reporting by making it safe and easy for employees to raise concerns, and by acting quickly to investigate and deal with issues. Research done by Pablo Ruiz and his team (2011) also highlights continually reinforcing the importance of ethics initiatives, particularly by the communications activities of the most senior members of the organization.

Conclusion

In this chapter, we have focused on ethics and leadership and introduced you to two leadership theories with specific ties to ethics: transformational leadership and ethical leadership. We have discussed the critical role played by ethical and transformational leaders in shaping the ethical climate and culture of their organizations. We have reviewed the research on leader character traits and virtues, and discussed that leaders who are fair, honest, and trustworthy are valued by employees around the world. Such qualities can make leaders highly effective ethical role models, able to create work environments where employees feel trusted and are truly engaged and committed to helping meet their companies' economic, social, and environmental responsibilities. Again, research suggests that this may be increasingly important in tomorrow's corporations. For example, firms that are perceived as ethical may well have the upper hand in attracting the highly educated employees they will need to develop sustainable products and services for the world's increasingly socially conscious consumers and risk-averse investors. We hope this chapter has equipped you, as future leaders, to understand the key role that ethical leaders can play in tomorrow's sustainable organizations.

DISCUSSION QUESTIONS

1. Some of the first studies on transformational leadership style were carried out with leaders in the US military. How might this research setting introduce bias into the theory of transformational leadership? To what degree have such concerns been addressed?

2. How do the universally positive leaders traits identified in the GLOBE study match up with the descriptions of the behaviours of transformational leaders and ethical leaders? As a member of the "millennial" generation, are these positive leadership traits important to you? Are there other traits that you feel are necessary in an ethical leader?

3. Think about someone with whom you've had a relationship that you would consider to be an ethical leader. This person could be a boss at work, a teacher, a coach, or a parent or other close relative. What behaviours made them an ethical leader? Can you think of any specific actions they took to help promote ethical behaviour in others around them? What were those behaviours? How easy do you think it is to consistently exhibit those ethical behaviours? What would help you to do this?

SUGGESTED ACTIVITIES AND ONLINE RESOURCES

1. *Values in Action*
   What character strengths do you have? Find out by taking the Values in Action—Inventory of Strengths, by visiting this link and taking 15 minutes to complete the free online survey:
   https://www.viame.org/www/getyourviameprofile.aspx.

2. *Identifying Canadian Leaders*
   As mentioned in the chapter, people sometimes find it difficult to identify ethical or transformational business leaders. See whether you can come up with some ideas of your own by doing some web research to find Canadian CEOs who are consistently singled out for their behaviour on a variety of important ethical and social fronts. Look for leaders who are at the helm of companies being recognized as the best employers, the most generous on the community donations front, or those singled out for their CSR initiatives or deserving of business ethics awards, such as those in the program run by the Maritime Business Better Bureau:
   http://maritimeprovinces.bbb.org/bbb-ethics-awards/.

3. *An Online Apology*
   As discussed in the chapter, Maple Leaf CEO Michael McCain has been described as a transformational leader. Review the video the company posted on YouTube in August 2008, which was an apology to victims of

the Listeria bacterium outbreak that made many sick and ultimately resulted in the death of several people who ate Maple Leaf products.

Go to: http://www.youtube.com/watch?v=cSrazdNo55U.

Or go to youtube.com and search under "Maple Leaf Foods apology." You can also read the text of the apology below. After watching or reading the apology, reflect on the theories of transformational leadership and ethical leadership, and the traits/virtues of such leaders. To what degree do you think McCain's apology measures up to these ideals? (Adapted from Cannon 2009.)

Maple Leaf Foods Apology

My name is Michael McCain. As you may know, listeria was found in some of our products. Even though listeria is a bacteria commonly found in many foods and in the environment, we work diligently to eliminate it. When listeria was discovered in the product, we launched immediate recalls to get it off the shelf, then we shut the plant down. Tragically, our products have been linked to illness and loss of life. To the Canadians who are ill and the families who have lost loved ones, I offer my deepest sympathies. Words cannot begin to express our sadness for your pain.

Maple Leaf Foods is 23,000 people who live in a culture of food safety. We have an unwavering commitment to keeping your food safe, with standards well beyond regulatory requirements, but our best efforts failed and we are deeply sorry. This is the toughest situation we've faced in 100 years as a company. We know this has shaken your confidence in us. I commit to you that our actions are guided by putting your interests first.

REFERENCES

Association of Workers' Compensation Boards of Canada (AWCBC). 2012. Key statistical measure reports. *National work injury statistics program.* Vol. 2012.

Avey, J.B., M.E. Palanski, and F.O. Walumbwa. 2011. When leadership goes unnoticed: The moderating role of follower self-esteem on the relationship between ethical leadership and follower behavior. *Journal of Business Ethics* 98: 573–582.

Barling, J., A. Christie, and C. Hoption. 2010. Leadership. In *Handbook of Industrial and Organizational Psychology*, ed. S. Zedeck: 183–240. Washington, DC: APA.

Bass, B.M. 1985. *Leadership and performance beyond expectations.* New York: Free Press.

Bass, B.M., and P. Steidlmeier. 1999. Ethics, character, and authentic transformational leadership behavior. *The Leadership Quarterly* 10 (2): 181–217.

Brown, M.E., and L.K. Treviño. 2006. Ethical leadership: A review and future directions. *The Leadership Quarterly Yearly Review of Leadership* 17 (6): 595–616.

Brown, M.E., L.K. Treviño, and D.A. Harrison. 2005. Ethical leadership: A social learning perspective for construct development and testing. *Organizational Behavior and Human Decision Processes* 97: 117–134.

Burns, J.M. 1978. *Leadership*. New York: Harper & Row.

Cannon, M. 2009. The importance of apologizing for organizational transgressions: Lessons from the 2008 Maple Leaf meat recall. Halifax: Saint Mary's University.

Den Hartog, D.N., R.J. House, P.J. Hanges, S.A. Ruiz-Quintanilla, and P.W. Dorfman. 1999. Culture specific and cross-culturally generalizable implicit leadership theories: Are attributes of charismatic/transformational leadership universally endorsed? *The Leadership Quarterly* 10 (2): 219–256.

Denison, D. 2003. The handbook of organizational culture and climate. *Administrative Science Quarterly* 48 (1): 119.

Groves, K.S., and M.A. Larocca. 2011. An empirical study of leader ethical values, transformational and transactional leadership, and follower attitudes toward corporate social responsibility. *Journal of Business Ethics* 103: 511–528.

Kaptein, M. 2011. From inaction to external whistleblowing: The influence of the ethical culture of organizations on employee responses to observed wrongdoing. *Journal of Business Ethics* 98: 513–530.

Martin, K.D., and J.B. Cullen. 2006. *Continuities and extensions of ethical climate theory: A meta-analytic review*. Dordrecht, Netherlands: Springer Science & Business Media.

Miceli, M.P., J.P. Near, and T.M. Dworkin. 2008. A word to the wise: How managers and policy-makers can encourage employees to report wrongdoing. *Journal of Business Ethics* 86: 379–396.

Riga, A. 2006. Business awakes to cost of stress. *The [Montreal] Gazette*. February 27.

Ruiz, P., C. Ruiz, and R. Martìnez. 2011. Improving the "leader–follower" relationship: Top manager or supervisor? The ethical leadership trickle-down effect on follower job response. *Journal of Business Ethics* 99: 587–608.

Solomon, R.C. 1999. *A better way to think about business: How personal integrity leads to corporate success*. New York: Oxford University Press.

Tourish, D., and N. Vatcha. 2005. Charismatic leadership and corporate cultism at Enron: The elimination of dissent, the promotion of conformity and organizational collapse. *Leadership* 1 (4): 455–480.

Treviño, L.K., L.P. Hartman, and M. Brown. 2000. Moral person and moral manager: How executives develop a reputation for ethical leadership. *California Management Review* 42 (4): 128.

Treviño, L.K., and K.A. Nelson. 2004. *Managing business ethics: Straight talk about how to do it right*. 3rd ed. Hoboken, NJ: Wiley.

Victor, B., and J.B. Cullen. 1988. The organizational bases of ethical work climates. *Administrative Science Quarterly* 33 (1): 101–125.

Zhu, W., R.E. Riggio, B.J. Avolio, and J.J. Sosik. 2011. The effect of leadership on follower moral identity: Does transformational/transactional style make a difference? *Journal of Leadership & Organizational Studies* 18 (2): 150–163.

Making Ethical Decisions

Introduction

The purpose of this chapter is to explain how people make ethical decisions, to discuss the factors that help or hinder ethical decision making, and to help you learn how to improve your ethical decision-making skills.

Situations with ethical concerns or expectations are frequently encountered in the workplace. Knowing how to deal with them is critical in being able to assume your organizational and social responsibilities, and feel good about the work you do. The range and complexity of ethical issues, as well as expectations of responsible corporate conduct, have increased over the years. Knowing how to deal with these concerns is an important part of management today.

A common misconception about ethical decision making is that unethical decisions and behaviours in organizations are the result of "bad people." On the contrary, apart from extreme cases where some people clearly intended to do harm, decisions considered unethical are often a result of, to a certain extent, one or more of four factors: a lack of awareness of the ethical dimensions of the situation, ingrained habits that ignore the ethical implications of one's actions, rewards or punishments instilled by the organizational culture, or a lack of proper skills to analyze and resolve the situation using ethics. This chapter is meant to help you avoid these pitfalls.

We will begin by examining how decision making occurs in the workplace in situations with ethical concerns or expectations, what ethical awareness is about, and some of the factors that might hinder or help ethical awareness, reasoning, and behaviour. We will then consider different ways you can improve your ethical decision-making abilities.

How Decisions Occur in the Workplace

Understanding how decisions are actually made in situations with ethical concerns or expectations, and why people make the decisions they do, is the first step in improving ethical decision-making skills. Over the past several decades, considerable research has been conducted on these topics. Although it is not the purpose of this chapter to explain these findings in depth, we will provide an overview to point out some of the more important findings.

Many theoretical models have been developed over the years to try to explain how ethical behaviour occurs and the ethical decision-making process. Most of them describe a process where the decision-maker thoughtfully considers the situation and follows different steps before making a conscious choice (e.g., Treviño 1986; Hunt and Vitell 2006). However, as Trevino points out in her later writings, the models don't always reflect what people do when they make decisions. Human behaviour, she says, often "takes scripted form in that it is largely automatic, embedded in the routines of life, or triggered by particular contextual clues, and thus devoid of conscious deliberation" (Treviño and Weaver 2003, 161).

Routine and Non-Routine Decisions

Most decisions made every day by people in organizations can be characterized as "routine," and more or less spontaneous. In fact, as Klein (1989) concluded from interviews with 150 people making decisions, "relatively few decisions are made using analytical processes such as generating a variety of options and contrasting their strengths and weaknesses" (Klein 1989, 47). The busier people are, the more likely they are to rely on a faster, effortless, and routine decision-making process. With the frantic pace of today's workplace, it is thus to be expected that people often rely on such modes of thinking (Chugh 2004).

These routine decisions are "analyses frozen into habit" (Simon 1997, 139), created by past experiences. What seemed to work well once or twice is memorized as the way to do things. If a similar situation crops up, no further analysis is required; the habit is simply applied. Upon recognizing a familiar situation, a person rapidly responds to it, with minimal thought and little conscious awareness, applying the ingrained way of evaluating and managing the situation to achieve the desired results (Argyris and Schön 1974). This facilitates rapid decision making and also helps people maintain a certain degree of consistency in their decisions. Building on research in the field of neuroscience, Reynolds (2006) suggests a similar view of ethical decision making. The model he suggests consists of a first step of "non-conscious analysis," where information regarding the situation is compared with basic "prototypes." Prototypes are learned categorizations accompanied by norms about what "should be" and prescriptions about what to do to resolve a situation. For example, says Reynolds, if a supervisor offers you a promotion in exchange for sexual favours, the situation would be matched against a prototype of typical sexual harassment, where the norm is that a supervisor should not act that way. If your organization does not usually tolerate sexual harassment, the prototype would likely prescribe reporting the incident. In another example, if the situation is matched against a typical bribery prototype, in countries where bribery is viewed as unethical, the prototype would signal that the situation is not acceptable and prescribe that the bribe not be accepted. These prescriptions are brought to consciousness and may lead directly to action as prescribed. However, some other elements may make the decision-maker hesitate to act as prescribed—for example, consequences that one may find unacceptable or unbearable. In that case, everything will be brought to a second step: a conscious and more complex mode of reasoning in another part of the brain, to determine how to resolve the situation (Reynolds 2006, 739). This second step also occurs if the situation is novel or ambiguous and cannot be matched with an existing prototype. The conscious and more complex mode of reasoning will then be used to analyze the situation and decide on the best course of action.

The development of these patterned ways of responding, or prototypes, is strongly influenced by the organizational culture, which provides norms, expectations regarding appropriate behaviour, and pressures to conform. Although inevitable, this influence of the organizational culture can be problematic, especially if it supports habitual ways of responding that ignore ethical concerns. If no ethical concerns surfaced at the time the habitual response was constructed and memorized, or if they were silenced in some way, a person could go on for quite some time doing things the same way, with little awareness of the ethical nature of these recurring situations, and therefore with no opportunity to add ethics to the equation when solving the problem. Contextual factors such as organizational culture are thus of the utmost importance when trying to encourage ethical behaviour, as we will see.

The prototype model represents three challenges for ethics in organizations. First, organizations should make sure that their culture is strong enough so that initial prototypes, or habitual ways of responding, include solid ethical prototypes. With that in place, unless other factors lead them to act otherwise than prescribed by those prototypes, people will generally react as expected when faced with a situation involving ethical concerns or expectations. Second, organizations must ensure that employees are sensitive to ethics, through ethics training, dialogue, and ethical leadership. As a result, habitual ways of responding already in existence where ethical considerations were initially overlooked can be updated. Moreover, when a situation slightly different from the ones the prototypes have been designed for occurs, and the differences entail ethical considerations, people will be aware enough to use a more conscious type of thinking to resolve the situation. That, in turn, will lead to new prototypes that take ethical considerations into account. Third, organizations must be willing to question current practices to allow the prototypes behind them that might lack ethics to be reviewed.

As we have seen previously, in situations where the decision-maker does not have an available prototype or feels that he cannot use a prototype to deal with a given situation, a conscious and more complex mode of reasoning may be required. This will be the case in situations that are unusual, ambiguous, or more complex, or when the possible consequences are deemed troublesome (Miller, Hickson, and Wilson 1996; Legault 1999). For example, at a time when your department may be struggling under a considerable workload, one of your employees may request time off for serious personal reasons. According to company policy, personal time off is not granted when a department's productivity will suffer. However, you realize that the employee's well-being and his family's will also be adversely affected if he does not get the time off he is requesting. Such situations are what Toffler (1986), in her research on managerial decision making, termed "ethical dilemmas"—complex situations where managers don't know exactly what to do because of conflicting interests, norms, or values, or because of possible disturbing effects on the well-being of others.

To help the reader accomplish this mode of conscious ethical decision making, and do the best he can under the circumstances, we have developed an ethical decision-making framework that will be presented later in this chapter. But first we need to better understand what might undermine the decision-maker's best efforts. We will do that by examining the concept of ethical awareness and certain individual and contextual factors that may come into play, such as personal values and the organizational culture.

Ethical Awareness

The workplace is fraught with decisions and behaviours that often don't quite live up to ethical expectations. One important reason for this is lack of ethical awareness. Although most people easily recognize well-known ethical issues such as fraud, corruption, lack of product safety, and discrimination, many other ethical issues are not as clear and are unrecognized in daily interactions in the workplace. For example, situations in which honesty, fairness, respect, transparency, or other values are also at stake but where the actual consequences are less severe may not attract attention at the outset, or be seen as problematic or important enough to warrant attention.

People achieve ethical awareness in a given situation when they realize that their actions could affect the interests, welfare, or expectations of other people, even when a specific moral norm or principle does not come to mind (Rest 1986), and they recognize that they have a choice in the matter (Jones 1991). The awareness that a situation is ethically problematic can vary significantly from one person to another, as different studies have shown (Drumwright and Murphy 2004; Swenson-Lepper 2005; Simga-Mugan et al. 2005). Where some may see an ethical problem, others may see only a legal problem or a business problem without ethical content. Still others will not see a problem at all.

For example, if asked to cut corners on a project for a client, to maximize revenue for one's firm, some managers will simply do as they are told. Some may question the instructions on the basis that this might not be good for business—that is, the problem is seen only as a business problem. Others may view the situation as legally problematic, and worry about the possibility of the client suing them for not respecting the contract. Finally, some managers will view the situation as an ethical problem—while understanding the importance of revenue generation, they will question the appropriateness of the instructions that were given to them for reasons of honesty, respect for the client, possible consequences to the client or end users, or other ethical considerations.

People's ethical awareness in a given situation will vary, influenced in part by what values are important to them, their prior experiences, and their beliefs about their role in the organization. For example, a manager for whom fairness is important and who believes her role entails ensuring that employees are treated fairly will be more aware of the ethical implications when one of her employees asks for preferential treatment. A person who has suffered from unfairness in the past may also grasp the ethical undertones of such a request more easily. A manager who strongly values the well-being of end users may also be more aware than others when a situation presents ethical challenges related to product safety.

The characteristics of the situation itself may help trigger ethical awareness (Jones 1991). Situations of great moral intensity are more likely to be recognized as ethical in nature. This happens when important negative consequences are likely to occur or when the situation would be considered ethically problematic by our peers, our community, or the management of the organization (Jones 1991; Butterfield et al. 2000). It also happens when the negative consequences affect people close to us (Jones 1991). For example, we are more likely to be aware of the ethics in a situation when the consequences affect our employer or colleagues than when they might affect our customers or competitors (Blodgett et al. 2001). Moreover, if we evaluate a situation as undesirable or harmful, we may feel emotions such as anger or compassion, or anticipate feeling guilt or shame if the situation persists (Lazarus 1984). We recognize that the situation is inconsistent with accepted norms or with what we believe is appropriate, therefore triggering ethical awareness (Gaudine and Thorne 2001).

Ethical awareness is crucial to ensuring that ethical reasoning processes will be triggered (Butterfield et al. 2000; Jones 1991). If there is no such awareness, even when the situation calls for ethics, the decision will simply be taken according only to business criteria (Jones 1991). Using the above example, if business criteria alone are considered, the only reason the person would refuse to cut corners would be if he believes the firm may lose the client by doing so, thus affecting its bottom line. Once ethical awareness is experienced in a given situation, many factors, both individual and contextual, may influence how the decision process will unfold.

Factors That Influence Decision Making

People have an inherent capacity for making choices and regulating themselves. The capacity for self-regulation implies that people recognize that their liberty is constrained by the existence of others; they cannot simply do as they please. That realization allows them to then refrain from behaving in ways that violate their personal standards and affect their self-worth (Bandura 1986).

Normative ethical theories, such as those seen in Chapter 2, assume that acting morally is the result of a person's choices. Kantian ethics, for example, assumes that "rational" beings have the capacity to understand moral law and to knowingly and willingly act in accordance with it. Utilitarianism assumes that people can choose to consider certain consequences to others and act accordingly.

Notwithstanding the importance of these theories, however, a good deal of research on ethical decision making points out that multiple individual and organizational or situational factors can influence decisions. Even the best-intentioned people are subject to such influences. However, when these influences are well understood, people can take a more critical and self-aware stance, thus preserving as much agency and freedom in their decisions as possible.

Individual Characteristics

Most theoretical models that try to describe how ethical decision making occurs state that some individual differences influence ethical decision making (e.g., Treviño 1986; Hunt and Vitell 1986, 2006; Rest 1984). Although different factors have been studied over the years, three important ones stand out in understanding how people think and act in situations where ethics are involved: *personal values*, *level of moral development*, and *locus of control*. We will examine each one briefly.

Personal Values

Values are of particular interest in studying ethical decision making, because aiming to uphold values such as justice, respect, honesty, and equality is clearly linked to ethical concerns. Although definitions of values abound, the definition most used was provided by psychologist Milton Rokeach: "A value is an enduring (and relatively stable) belief that a specific mode of conduct or end-state of existence is personally or socially preferable to an opposite or converse mode of conduct or end-state of existence" (Rokeach 1973, 5).

Values play important roles in decision making. They serve to evaluate situations and others' behaviour: depending on their values, some people will see a problematic and worrisome situation, and others will not (Schwartz, Sagiv, and Boehnke 2000). Therefore, only some of the people observing a given situation will find that it warrants closer examination and action. Values also serve as guiding principles for making decisions and for justifying our decisions after the fact (Rokeach 1973). Values may also act as goals to be pursued—for example, some may aim to be compassionate managers, others to always act fairly. Individual variations in values may therefore lead to different choices among alternatives in a given situation (Guth and Taguiri 1965). They are important throughout the decision-making process.

Values are said to be a result of socialization and personal experience (Rokeach 1973; Schwartz 1994). A particular value may be very important to one person but unimportant to another. Research across different types of jobs, hierarchical levels, organizations, and cultures shows a significant diversity of values. For example, some managers' main values may centre more on ambition, success, competition, productivity, efficiency, and profit maximization, or "self-enhancement" values, whereas for others "self-transcendent" values such as trust, cooperation, compassion, tolerance, and employee and social welfare may be equally important (England 1967; Schwartz 1994). Self-transcendent values, focused on the welfare and interests of others, may therefore often be in conflict with self-enhancement values, which are focused on personal or organizational power or achievement (which includes success, influence, competitiveness, and efficiency) (Schwartz 1996). Such conflicts of values are often an inherent part of ethical dilemmas (Legault 1999; Toffler 1986). We mentioned earlier that there are cases where people feel that they cannot act as prescribed by their prototypes—such situations generally involve a conflict of values. For example, a newly appointed manager realizes that one of his employees is not very efficient, because his predecessor never allowed that employee to benefit from training to keep up to date. If the new manager simply applies a productivity and profit maximization prototype to the situation, the action prescribed would probably be to either terminate or relocate the employee. However, if the manager values fairness and employee well-being strongly, he might feel that the employee was not treated fairly by the previous manager and be upset by the consequences the employee would suffer if terminated or relocated. Feeling uneasy with what the prototype prescribes, the manager will set it aside and use a conscious and more complex mode of reasoning to re-solve the situation.

James Rest emphasizes the role of conflict of values in ethical decision making. He suggests that choosing between competing "moral" and "non-moral" values, deciding whether or not to fulfill what one's self-transcendent values would favour, is at the heart of ethical reasoning. While the individual is formulating an ethical course of action in a given situation, he may also be considering other courses of action, based on other values. In the context of business, "self-actualization values" such as efficiency, profitability, and personal or organizational success may come to mind; they often suggest courses of action quite different from those suggested by "self-transcendent" or "moral" values, when facing an ethical problem. "Often-times," says Rest, "other values are so important to a person that they pre-empt or compromise moral values" (Rest 1983, 564).

Level of Moral Development

Cognitive moral development theory suggests that there are different levels of reasoning that a person can apply to a given problem to determine what is right, or what "should" be done. Each level represents a different way of taking into ac-count one's personal interests and one's moral obligations toward others in a given situation. These cognitive levels of reasoning can be used to interpret situations and guide problem solving, and indicate what one should consider to determine what one should do (Kohlberg 1984; Rest 1983). Although not all theorists agree on just how central a role the level of cognitive moral development plays in ethical decision making, some models, such as Treviño's (1986), centre on it, and most theorists have integrated it over the years as a significant influence in their models.

Moral development theories suggest that people's way of reasoning in a situa-tion with moral components evolves over time. According to cognitive moral development theory (Kohlberg 1984; Rest 1986), children take into account only their own self-interest, external rewards, and punishments. As they mature, how-ever, they reach a second level of development where they refer to what is expected of them by others and seek to live up to what their peers or significant others expect them to do. At a slightly more mature stage of this second level, their basis of reference will rise to what they believe society or different stakeholders would deem acceptable. Theoretically, only a few individuals will use a third, more autono-mous, level of reasoning that is independent of others' expectations. At this level, their reasons for taking a certain decision are based on upholding basic individual rights or moral principles, such as justice, or on shareable ideals for organiza-tional cooperation, such as the common good. Even though someone may have developed the capacity to reason at higher levels, this does not mean that the person always reasons at that level: the actual level of reasoning used may vary quite a bit from one situation to another.

Most adults, when faced with a problem of an ethical nature, including managers (Weber 1990), will reason at the second level of cognitive moral development. This means that most people will be highly influenced by their organizational environment and the values and expectations it puts forward. Therefore, an environment where ethical conduct is expected and rewarded can encourage ethical decision making, just as the reverse situation can hinder it. Others may continue to reason at the initial level of moral development; therefore, their reasoning will lead to furthering their own self-interest, obtaining rewards, or avoiding punishment. A first step to making more ethical decisions is therefore being aware that, like most adults, we are probably reasoning at the second level, and therefore strongly influenced by our organizational environment.

Locus of Control

Locus of control refers to the extent to which one feels control over life events. Treviño and Nelson (2004) suggest that people with a high internal locus of control believe that their actions have a strong influence on what happens in their lives. They might then be more likely to take responsibility for the consequences of their actions, speak up when a situation does not meet their expectations, and be less inclined to be pressured by others to do something that they believe is unacceptable. Those whose locus of control is external will often blame fate, luck, or the influence of others for what happens to them. They will then be less likely to take responsibility for the consequences of their actions and be more susceptible to influences, such as peer pressure (Treviño and Nelson 2004). We can enhance our ability to make more ethical decisions when we are aware of our type of locus of control and try to develop a more internal one. Managers can also help foster higher internal locus of control in their employees by encouraging them to speak up and offer suggestions to improve ethics, acting on these suggestions, and then giving feedback about what has been done.

Contextual Factors

Codes of ethics, industry practices, organizational culture, and rewards have been the most studied factors affecting decision making in situations with ethical concerns or expectations (O'Fallon and Butterfield 2005). For the purpose of this chapter, we will focus on the two factors that seem the most influential to us: organizational culture and rewards.

Organizational Culture and Rewards

Organizational culture includes not only current practices and policies, but also beliefs, values, and assumptions that influence daily conduct (Schein 1985). Any type of social unit with a shared history will have evolved a culture, says Schein (2004, 11). An organization can include many subcultures in its different operational units and geographical locations.

Organizational culture can be useful because, by providing specific expectations of behaviour, it acts as a cohesive factor, reducing anxiety and uncertainty. That in turn helps colleagues work together (Schein 1985). It is an important concept for ethics because the culture conveys values and norms that influence decisions and behaviour, and clarifies expectations for behaviour (Sims 2002). It also shows quite clearly to what extent ethical concerns should guide behaviour, and which concerns are more important. Peer pressure and people's desire to belong to the group ensure that these informal norms are respected. Those who go against these norms will probably suffer certain consequences, such as being ostracized or considered unworthy of trust. For these reasons, organizational culture is recognized in most ethical decision-making models as a key factor of influence.

Managers' daily actions and ethical leadership show what is really valued in the organization and may set the ethical tone much more effectively than value statements and codes of conduct. Rewards, such as evaluations, bonuses, and promotions, but also informal perks, such as who gets a pat on the back or an invitation to have lunch with the boss, also show what is really valued in the organization and therefore may influence ethical behaviour (Treviño and Brown 2005). When such rewards are based mostly on performance and maximizing profits, and the way the objectives were achieved and their impacts are ignored, many unethical practices may occur (Kerr and Slocum 1987). This hard lesson was learned by Sears Roebuck in the early 1990s when it adopted more ambitious goals and incentives for its auto centre employees to try to counteract the downturn in revenues. Minimum quotas were given for different types of repairs, a bonus system was introduced for advisers' sales performance, and productivity incentives were introduced for mechanics. The end result was a significant increase in complaints and lawsuits for selling unnecessary parts and services (Sharp Paine 1994; Kidwell 2005).

As mentioned earlier, being aware of the factors that might tend to lower the level of our moral reasoning is an important step in making more ethical decisions. For example, when at work, ask yourself to what extent your behaviour is influenced by peer pressure and rewards. Are you really living up to your ethical ideals? If not, what can you do to change your way of doing things? We will now examine how you can enhance your ethical decision-making skills.

Enhancing Your Ethical Decision-Making Skills

We have noted that people have varying degrees of ethical awareness. The same can be said about their skills in analyzing ethical dilemmas and raising ethical issues in the workplace. In addition, many factors influence their ability to do the best they can in a given situation. The following section aims at providing certain tools to enhance your skills in all of these areas.

Enhancing Ethical Awareness

One of the most effective ways of enhancing ethical awareness, thus encouraging ethical behaviour in organizations, is increasing employees' sensitivity to different types of ethical issues (Sparks and Merenski 2000). Ethics training and team discussions about specific ethical issues can be helpful in this regard: if faced with a situation similar to one already discussed, a person is likely to recall the discussion and act with more ethical awareness.

It might also be helpful to make a habit of referring to a set of key questions designed to identify ethical considerations. Your organization may have already developed such a set of questions. If not, you might want to develop your own, based on those suggested here.

SIDEBAR

Key Questions for Enhancing Ethical Awareness

When considering an important decision or a situation that seems problematic, ask yourself the following questions to determine whether ethics are involved:

- Could the situation harm someone?
- Is it honest? Is it fair? Is it respectful?
- Does it violate someone's rights?
- Would it be embarrassing if information about the situation was known by others?
- Would I like to be treated this way?
- What if everybody else did this?
- Am I feeling pressured into doing something I feel uncomfortable about?

Improving Ethical Decision Making

Normative ethical theories, introduced in Chapter 2, suggest criteria that can be used to judge whether decisions made by others may be considered morally acceptable. They also tell us what we should consider in ethical decision making—for example, consequences to others, duties, rights, and justice.

We can add other theories to these considerations. We will not address them here in detail, but *ethics of care* (also called *feminist ethics*), for example, invites us to consider the importance of maintaining harmonious relationships and avoiding harm. *Postmodern ethics* suggests that listening to one's emotions and gut feelings about what one thinks is the best thing to do in the circumstances. *Discourse ethics* is a more process-oriented ethical theory. It suggests that the parties involved solve the problem together, aiming for a solution that is acceptable to all while respecting certain procedural rules in their exchanges, rather than try to impose a solution or manipulate others to do what one party believes is right.

None of these normative ethical theories alone is enough to provide us with a broad understanding of the different aspects that need to be examined when faced with an ethical dilemma, so that we can make the best possible decision under the circumstances. However, taken together, they can provide us with more considerations to take into account. That encourages a greater understanding of the different ethical components of the problem and allows for a more in-depth analysis, increasing our chances of making the best possible decision under the circumstances. The ethical decision-making framework suggested in this chapter was developed using such ethical theories. Moreover, because *values* are often more powerful references in actual decision making than the moral *principles* decreed by ethical theories, they have been added to the framework.

SIDEBAR

Ethical Decision-Making Framework

1. What are the facts?

- Don't assume: make sure there really is an ethical problem and, if so, that you have all the necessary facts to make your decision.

2. Alternatives

- What are the possible courses of action? Be creative and do not limit your options.
- *Analyze all of the alternatives with the following framework—don't jump to conclusions without proper analysis.*

3. Laws/policies/procedures

- What laws, policies, organizational rules, and professional or social norms are applicable to this type of situation, if any? Although there may be situations where following these is not appropriate for ethical reasons, they should be taken into consideration in your analysis.

4. Consequences (*Utilitarianism and stakeholder theory*)

- Who are the stakeholders in this situation?
- What could be the consequences of each alternative (short- and long-term, positive and negative), on each stakeholder?

5. Values

- What values are related to this situation (e.g., respect, transparency, loyalty, competency, honesty, impartiality, equity, efficiency, quality ...)?
- What values are in conflict in this situation (values for which upholding one would lead to a different solution than upholding the other)?
- Do any of the solutions considered go against any of these values?
- Which value(s) does it seem more important for you to uphold in this particular situation and why?

6. Relationships (*Ethics of care*)

- Can you avoid harming others?
- Which solution is more likely to preserve trustful and harmonious relationships with the different stakeholders?

7. Duties, rights, justice (*Ethics of duty, Ethics of rights*)

- Does each alternative respect fundamental human rights and human dignity?
- Does each alternative allow everyone to be treated fairly?
- Do some alternatives treat people as means to other ends, instead of treating them humanely and as ends in themselves?
- For each alternative, what would happen if everyone acted the same way as this option suggests? What if you were in the other person's shoes?

8. Moral impulse and emotions (*Postmodern ethics*)

- Do your emotions/gut feelings give you additional information about what to do or not to do?

9. Link with organization's mission and reputation

- What would be most consistent with your organization's mission while responding to the legitimate expectations of stakeholders? What would have the best impact on public trust toward your organization?

10. Possible influences and personal interests

- Do you feel pressured to act in a certain way, either because of your boss's or your peers' expectations, personal rewards or possible punishment, or because of deadlines or constraints?
- To what extent could your personal interests be affecting your perception of the situation?
- *Check if pressures or personal interests have altered your evaluation in previous steps and adjust accordingly.*

11. **Peaceful settlement/working together (*Discourse ethics*)**
    - Have you asked the people involved what they think about the situation?
    - Have you tried to understand the legitimacy of their position and take it into account?
    - Have you tried to work out possible solutions with the people involved?
    - *If you have answered NO to any of these questions, see whether you could adjust accordingly.*

12. **Decision**
    - Considering all of these factors, what would be the best decision under the circumstances, that would be considered reasonable to most people? Why?
    - *Justify your answer using the elements above, using either values, consequences, rules, etc.*
    - Is this decision the best you can make under the circumstances? Could you find a better solution if you were a bit more creative?
    - How can you minimize the negative impacts of this decision in the way you implement it? How can you take into account the important values and moral principles you've set aside to make your decision, in the way you implement it?

13. **Verify**
    - Could your decision be considered "unreasonable" by any of the stakeholders?
    - Would you be embarrassed or feel guilty or ashamed if your boss, your peers, or your family knew the decision you had taken?
    - How do you feel about your decision?
    - *If in doubt, maybe you should give it a bit more thought!*

© Diane Girard, 2005. Adapted in part from frameworks suggested by Legault (1999) and Treviño and Nelson (2004).

To learn how to use the framework, try to solve "Teamwork Required," the dilemma presented below, going through all the steps. The strength of the framework is its ability to allow you to analyze the situation more deeply through different ethical lenses. To fully benefit from this, make sure you don't jump over any of the steps, or stop midway because you think you've found the proper answer. Think of the framework as if you were constructing a particularly difficult puzzle: only when the last piece is in place do you know exactly what you are looking at, although the shapes will become clearer as you move forward.

Notice that in step #10 the framework encourages you to take into account the influence of different contextual pressures or personal interests on your decision making, and correct the situation accordingly. This allows you to be critical of your own reasoning (think back to the skills that were covered in Chapter 3, "Critical

Thinking for Business Ethics"). Notice also that the work doesn't stop with making the decision. To ensure that you've done the best you can under the circumstances, step #12 asks you to try to minimize the negative effects of your decision and take into account the other values or moral principles you mentioned in your analysis, but that weren't the determining factors of your decision, when you decide how you will implement your decision.

SIDEBAR

Ethical Dilemma: Teamwork Required

During the first class of your ethics course, the professor asked students to form groups of four or five people to work on a term paper. Thirty percent of their mark will depend on the group performance for this paper. You and three of your friends, who are used to working together, form a group. Some students were not in groups from the start because they joined the class late or didn't know anyone in the class. During the second class, the professor assigned these students to various groups that have fewer than five members. Alex has been told to join your group.

   Jacob, an influential team member and a high achiever, is displeased with this. Although Alex seems willing to do his fair share on the project, Jacob thinks Alex doesn't seem too bright and feels that he won't really contribute to the group. You and your three other teammates are used to working together efficiently and Jacob doesn't want to include an "outsider" who might not pull his weight. Because he knows that you do not have a choice in accepting Alex on the team, Jacob suggests making sure Alex's involvement in the project is minimal. He suggests, for example, giving Alex the less important tasks, and letting him know about group meetings at the last minute or scheduling them at times when he has classes.

   You feel very uncomfortable with Jacob's position, although you too are a high achiever, like the rest of the group. Jacob has a lot of influence on the group, and you don't know what to do. Using the ethical framework, how do you solve this dilemma? Justify your answer using elements of the framework.

Raising Ethical Issues Efficiently

An important part of learning how to solve ethical dilemmas, and therefore increasing your abilities in ethical decision making, is learning how to raise your ethical concerns with peers, employees, or your own manager, especially when you sense that you might not agree on what should be done. Here are a few suggestions to help you do this.

First, timing and attitude are everything. Make sure you choose the proper time and place to address this issue and do not be confrontational. For example, challenging your boss in front of your peers might not be the best way for him to be willing to address your concerns. State your concerns briefly and clearly in a way that person can relate to. For example, if you are talking to your senior manager, explaining how a situation might be detrimental to the reputation of the firm or harm clients' trust in the company, in addition to pointing out your ethical concerns, may be a more efficient way of making your point. Unless you are really sure of your facts, ask questions rather than assume that you know what is going on. Also, keep an open mind: the person you are talking to may have valid reasons for thinking or acting differently from what you believe should be done.

Conclusion

The purpose of this chapter was to discuss how people actually make decisions in situations with ethical dimensions, explain the factors that can help or hinder ethical decision making, and suggest ways to improve your ethical decision-making skills.

There are many approaches to ethical decision making and many theories about what influences it. Our goal was not to be exhaustive, but rather to provide students with a minimal understanding of what is involved in ethical decision making, and certain tools to help enable them to act, if they so choose, as responsible employees and managers in the workplace.

DISCUSSION QUESTIONS

1. Consider two situations you've experienced during recent years, as a student or in the workplace, where you were uncomfortable or troubled because certain values or moral principles you felt were important were difficult to uphold or because of possible consequences to other people. What did you do about the situation? How did the different individual and organizational factors explained in this chapter influence your decision (including if you decided to do nothing)?
2. Consider the scenario explained in the ethical dilemma "Teamwork Required" presented in this chapter. Analyze it using the ethical decision-making framework provided. What would you decide? Justify your answer using elements from the ethical decision-making framework.
3. In the ethical dilemma provided, how would you raise the issue with Jacob? What would you add to the suggestions as to how to raise ethical concerns with others?

SUGGESTED READINGS AND ONLINE RESOURCES

Treviño, L.K., and K.A. Nelson. 2010. *Managing business ethics: Straight talk about how to do it right*. 5th ed., Chapter 5: Deciding what's right: A psychological approach. Hoboken, NJ: John Wiley & Sons.

Anand, V., B.E. Ashforth, and M. Joshi. 2004. Business as usual: The acceptance and perpetuation of corruption in organizations. *Academy of Management Executive* 18 (2): 39–53.

REFERENCES

Argyris, C., and D.A. Schön. 1974. *Theory in practice: Increasing professional effectiveness*. San Francisco: Jossey-Bass.

Bandura, A. 1986. *Social foundations of thought and action: A social cognitive theory*. Englewood Cliffs, NJ: Prentice Hall.

Blodgett, J.G., L.-C. Lu, G.M. Rose, and S.J. Vitell. 2001. Ethical sensitivity to stakeholder interests: A cross-cultural comparison. *Academy of Marketing Science Journal* 29 (2): 190–202.

Butterfield, K.D., L.K. Treviño, and G.R. Weaver. 2000. Moral awareness in business organizations: Influences of issue-related and social context factors. *Human Relations* 53 (7): 981–1018.

Chugh, D. 2004. Societal and managerial implications of implicit social cognition: Why milliseconds matter. *Social Justice Research* 17 (2).

Drumwright, M.E., and P.E. Murphy. 2004. How advertising practitioners view ethics: Moral muteness, moral myopia, and moral imagination. *Journal of Advertising* 33 (2): 7–24.

England, G.W. 1967. Personal value systems of American managers. *Academy of Management Journal* 10 (1): 53–68.

Gaudine, A., and L. Thorne. 2001. Emotion and ethical decision-making in organizations. *Journal of Business Ethics* 31 (2): 175–187.

Guth, W.D., and R. Taguiri. 1965. Personal values and corporate strategy. *Harvard Business Review* 43 (5): 123–132.

Hunt, S.D., and S.J. Vitell. 1986. A general theory of marketing ethics. *Journal of Macromarketing* 6 (1): 5–16.

Hunt, S.D., and S.J. Vitell. 2006. The general theory of marketing ethics: A revision and three questions. *Journal of Macromarketing* 26 (2): 143–153.

Jones, T.M. 1991. Ethical decision making by individuals in organizations: An issue-contingent model. *The Academy of Management Review* 16 (2): 366–395.

Kerr, J., and J.W. Slocum Jr. 1987. Managing corporate culture through reward systems. *Academy of Management Executive* 1 (2): 99–108. Reprinted 2005. *Academy of Management Executive* 19 (4): 130–138.

Kidwell, R.E. 2005. Sears Automotive. In *Managing organizational deviance*, ed. R.E. Kidwell and C.L. Martin, 61–68. Thousand Oaks, CA: Sage Publications.

Klein, G.A. 1989. Recognition-primed decisions. In *Advances in man–machine systems research*, ed. W.B. Rouse, 47–92. Greenwich, CT: JAI Press.

Kohlberg, L. 1984. *The psychology of moral development: The nature and validity of moral stages*. San Francisco: Harper & Row.

Lazarus, R.S. 1984. On the primacy of cognition. *American Psychologist* 39 (2): 124–129.

Legault, G.A. 1999. *Professionnalisme et délibération éthique: Manuel d'aide à la décision responsable*. Sainte-Foy, QC: Presses de l'Université du Québec.

Miller, S.J., D.J. Hickson, and D.C. Wilson. 1996. Decision making in organizations. In *Handbook of organization studies*, ed. S.R. Clegg, C. Hardy, and W.R. Nord, 293–312. Thousand Oaks, CA: Sage Publications.

O'Fallon, M.J., and K.D. Butterfield. 2005. A review of the empirical ethical decision-making literature: 1996–2003. *Journal of Business Ethics* 59 (4): 375–413.

Rest, J.R. 1983. Morality. In *Cognitive development: Manual of child psychology*. 4th ed., ed. J. Flavell and E. Markman, vol. 3: 556–629. New York: John Wiley & Sons.

Rest, J.R. 1984. The major components of morality. In *Morality, moral behavior and moral development*, ed. W.M. Kurtines and J.L. Gewirtz, 24–38. New York: John Wiley & Sons.

Rest, J.R. 1986. *Moral development: Advances in research and theory*. New York: Praeger.

Reynolds, S.J. 2006. A neurocognitive model of the ethical decision-making process: Implications for study and practice. *Journal of Applied Psychology* 91 (4): 737–748.

Rokeach, M. 1973. *The nature of human values*. New York: The Free Press.

Schein, E.H. 1985. *Organizational culture and leadership: A dynamic view*. San Franciso: Jossey-Bass.

Schein, E.H. 2004. *Organizational culture and leadership*. 3rd ed. San Francisco: Jossey-Bass.

Schwartz, S.H. 1994. Are there universal aspects in the structure and contents of human values? *Journal of Social Issues* 50 (4): 19–45.

Schwartz, S.H. 1996. Value priorities and behavior: Applying a theory of integrated value systems. In *The psychology of values: The Ontario symposium. The Ontario symposium on personality and social psychology*, ed. C. Seligman, J.M. Olson, and M.P. Zanna, vol. 8: 1–24. Hillsdale, NJ: Lawrence Erlbaum Associates.

Schwartz, S.H., L. Sagiv, and K. Boehnke. 2000. Worries and values. *Journal of Personality and Social Psychology* 68 (2): 309–346.

Sharp Paine, L. 1994. Managing for organizational integrity. *Harvard Business Review* 72: 106–117.

Simga-Mugan, C., B.A. Daly, D. Onkal, and L. Kavut. 2005. The influence of nationality and gender on ethical sensitivity: An application of the issue-contingent model. *Journal of Business Ethics* 57 (2): 139–159.

Simon, H.A. 1997. *Administrative behavior*. 4th ed. New York: The Free Press.

Sims, R.R. 2002. *Managing organizational behavior*. Westport, CT: Quorum Books.

Sparks, J.R., and J.P. Merenski. 2000. Recognition-based measures of ethical sensitivity and reformulated cognitive moral development: An examination and evidence of nomological validity. *Teaching Business Ethics* 4 (4): 359–377.

Swenson-Lepper, T. 2005. Ethical sensitivity for organizational communication issues: Examining individual and organizational differences. *Journal of Business Ethics* 59 (3): 205–231.

Toffler, B.L. 1986. *Tough choices: Managers talk ethics.* 2nd ed. New York: John Wiley & Sons.

Treviño, L.K. 1986. Ethical decision making in organizations: A person-situation interactionist model. *The Academy of Management Review* 11 (3): 601–617.

Treviño, L.K., and M.E. Brown. 2005. The role of leaders in influencing unethical behaviour in the workplace. In *Managing organizational deviance*, ed. R.E. Kidwell and C.L. Martin, 69–87. Thousand Oaks, CA: Sage Publications.

Treviño, L.K., and K.A. Nelson. 2004. *Managing business ethics: Straight talk about how to do it right.* 3rd ed. Hoboken, NJ: John Wiley & Sons.

Treviño, L.K., and G.R. Weaver. 2003. *Managing ethics in business organizations: Social scientific perspectives.* Stanford, CA: Stanford University Press.

Weber, J. 1990. Managers' moral reasoning: Assessing their responses to three moral dilemmas. *Human Relations* 43 (7): 687.

Strategy and Ethical Decision Making

Introduction: What Is Strategy?

In answering the question "What is strategy?" noted Harvard University strategist Michael Porter (1996) explains that the essence of strategy is to be found in the choices and trade-offs a firm makes in its quest for a unique competitive position. As we will show in this chapter, these choices can range from a very narrow focus on the economic bottom line of a firm to an activist orientation that positions a company as pursuing a social goal quite distinct from profit maximization (although profits may still be critical to fund the noble pursuits identified in the mission statement of the firm). Managers strategize to make the firms they helm different from their rivals' firms. This differentiation can be rooted in ethics, particularly in thinking innovatively about the firm's value-creating activities. Ethics thus has the potential to be an integral facet of the strategic decision-making process.

However, as we will also demonstrate, while one approach to strategy may be motivated primarily by ethical activism, the goal of the majority of for-profit firms is to better garner economic rents. "Economic rents" refers to the payment received for a factor of production (i.e., a job or material used to produce a company's goods or services) over and above what is minimally required to keep that factor in its current use. For example, if I am prepared to do a particular job for no less than my current salary of $20 an hour, but I successfully convince my boss to give me a $5 raise, my rent seeking has resulted in an extra $5 per hour. In economic theory, a competitive firm is always trying to get more for doing what it is currently doing. A key question for strategy, then, is the extent to which rent seeking should be guided by ethical values.

Within this framework, strategic management and the pursuit of a sustainable competitive advantage is not a concern with *absolutes*, but rather a focus on the *relative*. That is, strategic success comes from how a for-profit firm positions itself in an industry relative to its competitors. What does it do differently to justify more profits? What does it do differently to convince potential customers to spend money on its product and not its competitors' products? Choices and positioning are no less important for survival for non-profit firms, because even they must compete for donor dollars and public attention. Choices are an essential piece of the strategy puzzle, because no firm can hope to be all things to all stakeholders.

Are Ethics Just Another Choice?

To strategists operating in this paradigm, ethics will be viewed as one of many variables that need to be assessed in the context of choices, trade-offs, and the pursuit of competitive success. The relative weight assigned to ethical concerns by individual strategists at particular firms will determine the ethical posture of that firm, and will be a function of broader strategic positioning choices. However, viewing ethical choices as a subset of strategic choice does not necessarily minimize the importance of ethics for practitioners of strategic management. Neither does it suggest that ethical considerations are less important than other strategic concerns.

Historically, the field of strategy has included a broad set of theoretical approaches and ethical perspectives. For example, Alfred D. Chandler's (1962) approach to strategy offers a complex holistic view of the realities facing management practitioners. While Chandler does not explicitly address the importance of ethics in his definition of strategy, his emphasis on the need to consider long-term goals and objectives can be seen as sympathetic to including the broader dimensions of ethics that managerial decision-makers face.

H.I. Ansoff (1965), another founding figure in the field, developed a theory of "enterprise strategy." This included a set of substrategies open to explicitly ethical thinking. Two examples of substrategies include a societal strategy and a legitimacy strategy. To Ansoff, firms had to be able to explain their role in society in a detailed way that goes beyond simple rent seeking. Early thought-leaders in the field of strategy encouraged practitioners to think about how their choices and trade-offs would affect society's view of their firm. These thinkers emphasized that firms needed to make strategic choices that would earn them social legitimacy and good standing in the communities in which they were competing, while warning firms not to take their status for granted. Writing in the early 1970s, Andrews (1971) noted that "coming to terms with the morality of choice may be the most strenuous undertaking in strategic decision making" (69).

The Influence of Economics

These classic thinkers demonstrate that viewing ethics as a part of strategic choice does not necessarily lead to its marginalization. Yet there is no question that through the 1980s and '90s the field of strategy suffered a sort of collective ethical amnesia. If you were to look at research taking place in the field at the time you would have found no mention of the social or ethical concerns that were so critical at the birth of the discipline.

While performance can be approached from different perspectives and viewed in different ways, the field of strategic management has come to define performance only through the lens of economic theory, narrowly understood. In other words, the goal of the publicly traded firm is simply to make money by doing whatever it takes to increase the value of its shares, within the limits of the law. This emphasis on financial bottom-line measures of success and the garnering of economic rents as the primary objective of the firm has turned managerial attention away from the social and legitimacy concerns that were central to the field in its early years.

Schendel and Hofer (1979) played a key role in defining strategy as an emerging field of management study in the 1970s. They adopted Ansoff's notion of enterprise strategy, but limited its focus to social-legitimacy concerns. A key virtue of this broad and inclusive approach to strategy was that it emphasized the role of business as one of society's important institutions and the critical role that businesses, in conjunction with government, must play in the everyday affairs of a healthy society. The 1980s, however, saw significant changes in strategy as a field of management study with the growth of dependence on economic theories to the exclusion of other disciplines such as ethics (Rumelt, Schendel, and Teece 1994).

Porter (1991) explains that the complexity, situation-specificity, and the changing nature of the firm and its environment seemed to have overwhelmed conventional approaches to theory building and hypothesis testing. Economic theories overcame these problems by creating a wide range of situation-specific mathematical models of limited complexity. That is, the models incorporated only a few variables and assumed away much of the complexity of real life, for example, always assuming that human behaviour is rational, selfish, and maximizing. These models specify only what is relevant and needs to be taken into account in specific situations. Strategists argue that they can explain "most" of the phenomena deemed worthy of study. For instance, economists would argue that most managers *are* selfish and rational, and that altruistic managers are statistical outliers not worthy of study.

Beginning in the 1980s, strategists embraced this approach and restricted their focus to the economic dimensions of management on the assumption that the purpose of business and the firm was profit maximization. This reliance on economics, economic models, and profit maximization resulted in ethics being marginalized within the discipline. In recent years, however, there have been clear signs of a reversal of this trend in the business world.

Ethics and Strategy: Four Models of the Strategic Firm

Today, that experience with a narrow economic focus on profit maximization is leading both theorists and practitioners to challenge the usefulness of this approach. Managers are increasingly discovering the need to formulate strategies that incorporate a much broader notion of value creation. Thinking about ethics more broadly has led in many instances to superior outcomes, including competitive positioning and enhanced share value. Weitzner and Darroch (2010) argue that this is no accident. Effective management requires that ethical reasoning and ethical principles and values play a central role in strategic management.

Classic Economic Model

A gradually broadening vision of the role of ethics in strategy has led to the emergence of four models of the firm: the classic economic model, the economic rationalist model, the good citizen model, and the activist strategist model. In the classic economic model that has come to dominate strategic thinking, strategic choice is limited to activities that serve the core corporate objective of improving the firm's bottom line (Weitzner and Darroch 2010).

There is power in this paradigm because it gives rise to strategies that provide solutions to a myriad of important problems facing a competitive firm, yet it also leaves practising managers with real and abiding problems, which economists label "externalities."[1] Externalities are the social costs that the firm, through its value-creating activities, creates but does not necessarily have to pay for. Think of pollution, for example. Factories create pollution, which harms the environment and causes local communities to suffer, yet most firms do not have to pay to eliminate all, if any, of the pollution that they have caused.

The classic economic response to the issue of externalities like pollution and climate change has been to rigidly define the boundaries between the responsibilities of civil society and those of the firm. Perhaps Milton Friedman (1970) captured this best when he famously exhorted that the social responsibility of business is to increase its profits. However, it should be noted that the corollary of Friedman's position is that social and ethical decisions are too complex to be left to businesses

---

1   For another recent critique of the profit maximization model of the firm, see Roger Martin's *Fixing the Game* (Boston: Harvard Business Review, 2011).

and that it is the role of civil society to establish the conditions under which businesses operate (Weitzner and Darroch 2010). This position has a certain pragmatic appeal because it lets capitalists focus on what they do best and leaves the challenge of regulating the social, economic, and environmental impacts of economic activity to the government so as to achieve ethically justifiable economic outcomes.

It is worth noting, however, that even this first model, with its narrow focus on share-value maximization, allows a role, though a very restricted one, for ethics. Friedman acknowledges that the pursuit of profits should be constrained by respect for the law and local ethical custom. With this model of the firm, it follows that there will be no room for strategies that involve fraud, deliberate deception, or illegal behaviour. Further, employees will be expected to respect fundamental moral values such as loyalty to the firm, honesty in their dealings with the firm, respect for and proper use of company property, and so on. These ethical constraints may or may not be explicitly articulated in ethical terms. However, they connect to strategy because of the negative impacts on firm performance should these issues, however they are labelled, be ignored.

Economic Rationalist Model

The second model explored is the economic rationalist model (Weitzner and Darroch 2010). In this model, the strategic decision-maker recognizes the importance of embracing multiple goals in assessing strategic choices, but assesses the trade-offs against a standard of enlightened self-interest. This model gives ethics a role beyond a narrowly interpreted ethics to address externalities such as social, economic, or environmental impacts, but only if reaching out in this way can be shown to "pay," or advance the bottom line. So, although this type of firm will still consider economic indicators of success as the optimal strategic choice when ethics and profit maximization conflict, this model nonetheless recognizes that addressing ethical concerns in an interesting way may be critical to the mission of the firm. A strategist working within the framework of this model will recognize the strategic importance of crafting a value proposition that incorporates an ethical vision to attract like-minded customers and employees. A firm's value proposition expresses the value that a firm

With public concern growing about e-waste, Hewlett-Packard saw an opportunity to use its huge logistical capacity to gain a competitive advantage through its "take-back" program, which keeps old equipment out of landfills.

Source: iStock.

promises to provide to its customers through its products and services. It also expresses what differentiates a particular firm from its competitors. It is tied to its mission statement and geared to motivate its employees as well.

What distinguishes this second model from the classic model is that managers recognize the importance of taking the time to think explicitly about ethics as a source of competitive advantage. Ethical stances can be priced, and as long as they lead to profitability they will be embraced. Information technology giant Hewlett-Packard actively campaigning to promote "take-back" of old equipment and recycling laws for the computer/home electronics industry is an example. Seen from a strategic perspective, not only is HP's strategy a good thing in and of itself, it also creates a competitive advantage for HP over its rivals, whose value and logistic chains are not as well constructed to deliver in this value dimension (Weitzner and Darroch 2010).

Corporate Citizen Model

The good citizen model is a third approach to strategy that embraces multiple goals and rationalities. It recognizes that it is not meaningful or practical to view the ethical elements of a business decision as distinct from the strategic elements. It acknowledges, as the economic rationalist model does, the costs and benefits of acting on or ignoring ethics. But this paradigm rejects enlightened self-interest as the sole ethical criterion for determining the role of ethics in strategic management.

This third approach to strategy refuses to limit ethical choices to the pursuit of profit maximization. Strategists governed by this model see themselves as both an agent of the firm and a responsible member of society, with moral and fiduciary obligations. The good citizen model poses strategic challenges not faced by the first two models because it offers no easy prescriptions, formulas, or templates to guide strategic choices. On the other hand, its strength lies in the way in which it is able to encompass the world of the visionary and those committed to disruptive change (Weitzner and Darroch 2010). Think of Ballard Power Systems. Its business is creating clean-energy hydrogen-powered fuel cells. Its goal is to make money by having its product dominate the energy market. Of course, if it is successful, it will have reshaped many industries by moving them away from classic "dirty" energy sources toward a more environmentally responsible model.

Strategist as Activist Model

The final model is that of the activist strategist who sees the limits in a bottom-line-focused economic rationality and therefore reaches out to embrace multiple rationalities, rejecting the notion that the corporate objective should be profit maximization (Weitzner and Darroch 2010). Managing a firm with an activist stance may be profitable and may require profitability—"may" because some firms are allowed by their owners to operate at a loss, with, say, tax write-off incentives. The owner's ideological stance can create a situation where profitability is not critical. The strategic logic of business entities adopting this model will not be driven by profit maximization, but some other ethically significant goal, like sustainability.

Managers of firms that adopt this model will require that the entire organization recognize the existence of competing rationalities and goals. This approach will usually be tied to a niche or differentiated strategy where the firm's values can be readily identified by prospective market segments. Take the example of TOMS' shoes—buy one pair of shoes and a second pair will be given to a child in need. One could equate this position with ethical positions driven by metaphysical, religious, or ideological concerns. For this model, while profit maximization is not the goal, the potential for significant profits cannot be ruled out. Organizations governed by this strategy model may and do find willing shareholders, as the field of ethical, socially responsible investment (SRI) and responsible investment (RI) demonstrates. On the other hand, refusing to pursue profit maximization as the core strategic objective may mean that firms and other business entities that embrace this model will need to seek investors that share their commitment to this model.[2]

Choosing Values

The boundaries defining the role of ethics in strategic thinking vary with each of these four models. What the existence of four alternative approaches to strategy implies, however, is that developing an effective, well-thought-out strategy requires decision-makers to determine what ethical values will guide the operations of the business and the strategic model that will govern their strategic thinking. This will involve, for example, determining the goals and objectives of the firm or organization, and developing an understanding of its social, economic, and environmental responsibilities.

In short, in a 21st-century marketplace, effective strategic thinking requires that business entities must select the values that will guide their choices and be able to articulate what kind of business they are and want to be. This will be particularly true of businesses for which the goal of strategic thinking is the achievement of a sustainable competitive advantage—an advantage, in other words, not gained at the cost of environmental or social problems.

Ethics and Corporate Social Responsibility (CSR)

A key question for strategists is how best to achieve ethical credibility in a competitive landscape. Porter and Kramer (2006) propose that this requires defining

---

2   The growing field of social enterprise is an example of a strategic approach to business that embraces this model.

strategic value creation so it contains an explicitly ethical dimension. They contrast this approach to business with some popular notions of corporate social responsibility that see these ethical activities as "add-ons" that are not integral to the core value-creating activities of a competitive firm. By presenting the salient ethical issues under the mandate of the "social," as opposed to the "strategic," CSR pressures companies to think about some very critical issues in generic ways, rather than firm-specific and value-specific ways. In Porter and Kramer's view, a firm's response to ethical issues will be weakest when stimulated by public responses to issues that were not on its strategic radar—for example, Nike and the sweatshop controversy in the 1990s. In fact, in their view, managers lacking a strategic understanding of the ethical issues faced by a firm are likely to postpone the costs of resolving the issues, which can lead to far greater costs later when the firm is judged to have violated an important ethical rule or principle (Porter and Kramer 2006).

Problems with CSR

Porter and Kramer (2006) reject many of the classic arguments in favour of CSR on the grounds that while they may be philosophically sound, from a practical perspective they are strategically weak. For example, theorists have argued that societies give firms a licence to operate in their midst based on an unspoken expectation that the firm's economic activities will generate societal benefits as well as private benefits for shareholders. This may be a justifiable expectation, but if in practice managers view CSR only as a way to silence noisy social critics and activists, then ethics just devolves into a series of short-term defensive moves of little strategic benefit.

Even worse, in certain stigmatized industries, CSR is pursued as a form of insurance in the hope that a firm's reputation for social consciousness will temper public criticism in the event of an ethical crisis. For example, think of multinational oil company BP, and the massive 2010 oil spill in the Gulf of Mexico, just off the coast of Louisiana. In light of this disaster, both BP and other companies in the oil and gas industry went out of their way to highlight their past CSR-type activities to suggest that they were not as bad to society as current news stories might have suggested. These approaches to CSR fall well short of the holistic approaches to incorporating ethics into the strategy-making process described earlier.

Shared Value

The solution lies in the principle of shared value, which involves creating economic value in a way that *also* creates value for society by addressing its needs and challenges (Porter and Kramer 2011). Businesses must reconnect company success with social progress. Porter and Kramer (2011) identify three key ways to do this:

- reconceiving products and markets in ways more aligned with the classic notion of enterprise strategy, where social concerns are as important as profit seeking;
- redefining productivity in the value chain (i.e., the activities a company engages in to create value) to move away from the narrow focus on only economic variables; and
- enabling local cluster development (encouraging the local development of supporting industries) to support healthy societies. For example, Hollywood is the centre of movie making, so businesses that support movies, such as set design, acting schools, and equipment-makers, thrive in the Los Angeles area.

Porter and Kramer (2011) emphasize that this approach to shared value is not about personal values or "sharing" the value already created by a firm's economic activity, an approach that focuses on the redistribution of economic benefits. Rather, it is about expanding the total pool of economic and social value.

What makes the shared-value approach "strategic" according to Porter and Kramer? To begin with, in contrast to the notion of "doing good" in CSR, the language is not solely ethical. Instead, the emphasis is on the firm generating goods and services that create value, as seen from both a societal and a profit-oriented perspective. This will require the firm to think strategically about all aspects of its value chain, balancing its assessments of costs and benefits. Instead of a focus on citizenship, philanthropy, sustainability, and so on, the focus is on joint company and community value creation. And it resolves Friedman's critique (1970) in that the motivation is no longer the discretionary interests of managers nor is it a response to external pressure. Instead, the value creation is understood to be integral to competition.

A Fifth Model

Porter and Kramer's focus on value creation as the goal of strategic management can be seen as a fifth or hybrid model of strategic choice, which incorporates three key elements of all four models described earlier. It rejects the profit maximization models whose focus is narrowly economic. Instead, it accepts profitability as a core element in the value-creation matrix, and is therefore central to strategic management. It also rejects the idea of corporate citizenship where corporate social responsibility is defined not as a core strategic input but as a management responsibility distinct from and in addition to producing goods and/or services profitably. Instead, it sees the corporation as a social institution embedded in the communities in which it does business. Finally, the hybrid model sees societal value creation as integral to strategic management, not a niche business activity or an alternative to business as usual.

According to this hybrid view, business is a societal institution with clear societal responsibilities where success is unavoidably determined by ethical criteria that incorporate social, environmental, and economic values.

Case Study: The Shopping Mall Challenge

Imagine that you have recently been appointed manager of a shopping mall. Your job is to manage 16 acres of commercial space, a mall, in the heart of a decaying area of your city. Local merchants were up in arms because the crime rate was rising and the number of people visiting the mall was dropping. As a result, the mall had acquired a bad reputation in the minds of local shoppers, who had no shortage of shopping options. The quality of merchandise was declining because, increasingly, local retailers were writing off the area, paying less attention to appearances and upkeep, and stocking their shelves with cheap goods. A troubling picture was emerging.

The demographics of the area had begun to change several years before. The neighbourhood, at the centre of a large urban area, had started seeing an influx of refugees, low-income housing, apartments, increasing numbers of homeless people, and a growing mix of cultures and races. With those changes had come drug dealers, youth gangs, poverty, racial conflict, and violent crime, including a headline-grabbing brawl that had left two local high school students beaten and stabbed and four other students arrested on weapons charges.

These changes had left their mark on the mall, which many regarded as "the centre of it all." The mall had always been the local hangout for students at the six surrounding schools. But, gradually, the loitering students were almost outnumbering shoppers. Increasingly, irritated mall retailers were pointing at "hoodlums" as the source of their problems. But the students had little else to do. The mall was a place to socialize, fill the lunch hour, and put in time after school. Many students were from single-parent families or came from homes where both parents worked to make ends meet. So heading home after school was not an attractive alternative. On the other hand, drugs were becoming a problem and the mall was becoming a place for drug dealing. Clashes with mall security were becoming more common and merchants were beginning to ask for security guard escorts when they dropped off their deposits at the bank in the mall after stores closed.

But the picture was not all bleak. The schools were working hard to find solutions. There was still a good mix of income groups, education levels, and housing in the neighbourhood. A number of community organizations had formed to address local problems. A recent study by the Canadian Centre for Justice Statistics had found that social and economic factors correlated with reported crime in the 26 largest municipalities across the country. In other words, the communities most at risk were those whose members were the most disadvantaged.

An item in *The Globe and Mail* also attracted your attention. The blurb described a crime-prevention conference in the United States using "target hardening and hardware." You attended and learned about upgraded security systems, surveillance cameras, eviction techniques, legal services, highly trained security personnel, and related options. This was clearly an attractive alternative. It was what the merchants in the mall seemed to want. The prevailing attitude revolved around getting the teenagers off mall property and restoring "law and order."

You now have to make some tough decisions. The direction the local merchants wanted to take was clear. But were they right?

DISCUSSION QUESTIONS

1. As mall manager in the case described above, you are unable to put off decisions much longer. What should you do in this situation? Discuss or write down your possible options, and then list the ethical pros and cons for each.

2. Several local citizens' groups and a school principal are asking for appointments. And a delegation of mall merchants has arranged a meeting for the next afternoon. It appears that for these stakeholders, a drug bust at closing time the night before was the final straw. How will you deal with these groups? What actions or strategies will you suggest, and how will you justify them?

3. What are the trade-offs between strategic and ethical concerns?

SUGGESTED READINGS AND ONLINE RESOURCES

Cragg, W., M. Schwartz, and D. Weitzner, eds. 2009. *Corporate social responsibility.* Surrey: Ashgate Publishing.

Freeman, R.E., J.S. Harrison, A.C. Wicks, B.L. Parmar, and S. de Colle. 2010. *Stakeholder theory: The state of the art.* Cambridge: Cambridge University Press.

Porter, M.E., and M.R. Kramer. 2011. Creating shared value. *Harvard Business Review* (January–February): 62–77.

REFERENCES

Andrews, K.R. 1971. *The concept of corporate strategy.* Homewood, IL: Dow Jones-Irwin.

Ansoff, H.I. 1965. *Corporate strategy.* New York: McGraw-Hill.

Chandler, A.D. 1962. *Strategy and structure.* Cambridge, MA: MIT Press.

Friedman, M. 1970. The social responsibility of business is to increase its profits. *New York Times Magazine*, September 13.

Porter, M.E. 1991. Towards a dynamic theory of strategy. *Strategic Management Journal* 12: 95–117.

Porter, M.E. 1996. What is strategy? *Harvard Business Review* (November–December): 61–78.

Porter, M.E., and M.R. Kramer. 2006. Strategy and society: The link between competitive advantage and corporate social responsibility. *Harvard Business Review* 84: 78–92.

Porter, M.E., and M.R. Kramer. 2011. Creating shared value. *Harvard Business Review* (January–February): 62–77.

Rumelt, R.E., D.E. Schendel, and D.J. Teece, eds. 1994. *Fundamental issues in strategy.* Boston: Harvard Business School Press.

Schendel, D., and C. Hofer, eds. 1979. *Strategic management: A new view of business policy and planning.* Boston: Little, Brown.

Weitzner, D., and J. Darroch. 2010. The limits of strategic rationality: Ethics, enterprise risk management and governance. *Journal of Business Ethics* 92: 361–372.

PART THREE
Applying Ethical Principles: Cases and Analysis

Socially Responsible Small Business and Entrepreneurship

Case Study: The Fidditch Lumber Company

Kaitlyn Saunders had been working at Fidditch Lumber Company for two years. She had graduated with a joint degree in environmental management and business administration from the local university. Her family had been woodlot owners for three generations and she had found the job at Fidditch intriguing, so she was thrilled to be offered the position of general manager. Fidditch had been the first lumber company in the region to provide co-generated electricity derived from sawmill waste to the local power company. This was a company that she could feel good about working for and she enjoyed being able to apply her university knowledge and skills.

However, Kaitlyn was now facing her first real ethical dilemma and was not quite sure what to do about it. She sat at her desk on Tuesday afternoon staring at the latest text that had come in from Louis Marchand, Fidditch's largest supplier and the source of Kaitlyn's dilemma.

Fidditch Lumber Company: An Overview

Jade and Buddy Fidditch were cousins who had founded and still jointly owned Fidditch Lumber Company. The company produced pine lumber and wood products, which were sold wholesale and retail through the Fidditch Lumber Store and delivered to retail customers in Eastern Canada and Maine. The three primary product lines were domestic pine decking, wood shavings, and firewood. The decking accounted for 75 percent of Fidditch's revenues. The primary buyers for the wood shavings were two garden centres in town. The primary buyer of the firewood was the national park 10 kilometres down the road and two campgrounds on the lake just north of town. Although the company sold some firewood to local customers, most of the people in town switched to natural gas when the gas company ran a line into town five years ago.

Fidditch Lumber was now 20 years old and had 10 employees in addition to Jade and Buddy. Neither Jade nor Buddy had ever attended university or college. Jade was the president and oversaw the logistics side of things. Buddy headed up the sales and marketing and public relations side of the business. Both dealt with strategic planning. As the general manager of operations and the retail store, Kaitlin covered all of the accounting and personnel management. The employees included four mill workers, three drivers who did shift work, and two store employees. Jade and Buddy also took a couple of shifts a day in the company store. They liked the opportunity to stay in touch with their customers and enjoyed the social aspect of sales.

Kaitlyn Saunders and Fidditch

Kaitlyn distinctly remembered the day that Buddy had interviewed her.

She had asked him, "What are the values of Fidditch Lumber?"

He had paused and stammered, "We all know what our values are—what this company stands for. Jade and I are entrepreneurs and that is how we have been successful in this business for 20 years."

A few months later, at a general meeting, Kaitlyn had suggested, "Could we plan a meeting to discuss our company values and our CSR strategy?"

Buddy had looked puzzled and whispered to Jade, "What is CSR?"

"I'm worried about us making decisions that might have an impact on our community that could come back to haunt us," said Kaitlyn.

Buddy looked indignant. "We give more than our fair share back to the community. We have supported the Red Fox hockey team for the past 10 years. We just gave $2,000 to the elementary school library."

Kaitlyn tried to stay calm and said, "All I'm suggesting is that we sit down and discuss our values and a social responsibility strategy for Fidditch. Don't you think if we had a mutual understanding of the purpose of Fidditch and outlined who our stakeholders are and what our responsibilities are toward them, it would help us make strategic decisions?"

"We don't have time for that soft stuff. Go group-hug some of your college buddies. I have work to do." And with that Buddy had stormed out of the room.

Jade had given Kaitlyn an understanding look and said, "Don't take it personally. The US recession is hitting us hard. You know what our accounts payable is looking like these days. Buddy is just a bit stressed."

The Ethical Dilemma

Louis Marchand was Fidditch's largest supplier. Louis owned 17 woodlots scattered throughout the province. Kaitlyn had been working closely with Louis over the past two years. She had recently discovered that Louis was using an extremely hazardous pesticide on his woodlots. An article in the local newspaper had reported that several children living near Louis's woodlots were developing bloody noses and hives all over their bodies. Louis had called Kaitlyn on Friday to say that he had a supply to deliver. Later that day at the manager's weekly Friday meeting, Kaitlyn had raised the pesticide issue. Buddy had quickly shut her down. He had said that he wanted to introduce a new product line to grow the company and that they needed the wood from Louis to do that.

"We have never told our suppliers how to manage their woodlots and we're not going to start now," Buddy had said angrily.

"Our larger competitors are advertising with the FSC label," Kaitlyn had replied, trying to stay calm, although she could feel her frustration mounting.

"FSC?" asked Jade.

"The Forest Stewardship Council," explained Kaitlyn. "They independently certify woodlots. With that labelling, we could let customers know that our lumber is coming from forests using responsible forestry practices. There are other standards we could consider as well."

"How expensive is it?" asked Jade.

"I can look into it," said Kaitlyn as she saw Buddy rolling his eyes.

"Okay," said Jade. "We can pick this up at next week's meeting."

Now here it was Tuesday and Louis's texts were getting more and more demanding. Kaitlyn heard her phone ping.

"Not another one," she thought to herself. But the text was from Jade.

"I want to find out more about CSR. Where can we get some help?"

Socially Responsible Small Business and Entrepreneurship

When we think about business ethics and corporate social responsibility (CSR) we often focus on the big players. Large multinational corporations (MNCs) are frequently the focus of television and newspaper stories, sometimes for responsible business practices, but mostly for irresponsible or unethical business practices.

Most of the research and textbooks on business ethics and CSR also focus on large corporations and executive-level decision making. Karakowsky, Carroll, and Buchholtz (2005, 6) have suggested some of the reasons why they believe large companies are given more attention by business researchers and educators. First, big businesses are more visible than small and medium-sized businesses (SMEs), and large MNCs are constantly under pressure to be more transparent and accountable. Second, large corporations' products and advertising are more widely known. Consequently, big businesses are in the spotlight more frequently. In addition, people in our society often associate size with power, and the powerful are often given closer scrutiny. Large transnational corporations have been called the dominant institutions in our world (Korten 1995). Thus, there are significant ethical issues connected with the impact of these large corporations on society and the natural environment. Large companies are also more likely to advertise their socially responsible behaviours. For example, companies such as Canadian Tire, Scotiabank, and Tim Hortons often promote their charitable activities or sustainable business practices.

However, we believe that a narrow focus on large corporations and executive-level decision making is limiting. In most developed countries around the world, SMEs account for approximately 98 percent of all business and employ 50 percent of the workforce. It is, therefore, important to discuss the ethical issues and social impacts that are unique to different-sized firms. In addition, small and medium-sized businesses should not necessarily benchmark CSR activities and ethical business practices against large MNCs. Even though the scale of the economic, societal, and/or ecological impact for a SME might not be as great as the impact for a transnational corporation, it is still important for students to understand the unique ethical issues and dilemmas of smaller organizations and the effect that SMEs have on society. It is also critical for students to recognize the interconnectedness of ethical issues in different business contexts and to practise ethical decision-making skills in different contexts. For example, small businesses are influenced by different organizational, sectoral, and economic factors than large businesses.

Entrepreneurship and innovation are increasingly seen by governments and businesses as critical to a competitive global economy. Canada is said to be one of the most entrepreneurial countries in the world and many Canadian post-secondary institutions incorporate small business and entrepreneurship into their curricula and programs. Entrepreneurship is now accepted as a core concentration or major area of study at both graduate and undergraduate levels in many business schools around the world. In addition, other faculties, such as engineering, natural sciences, and other applied social sciences have incorporated entrepreneurship as a course in their curricula. However, most business education, business education textbooks, and academic business research continue to focus on large corporations and executive-level decision making, including the study of business ethics and CSR. At the same time, many business schools have broadened entrepreneurship education to include ethical and social entrepreneurship. This allows students to understand the vital role of entrepreneurship education in creating economic values that are guided by ethically and socially responsible business practices. There are many examples of entrepreneurial activities that have led to noble societal goals, such as green agriculture and fair trade initiatives.

In this chapter, we provide some convincing reasons for combining small-business management and entrepreneurship in our discussion of business ethics and CSR.

SMEs in Canada

Despite the focus on "big" business and "big business" ethics in business schools, the majority of Canadian business school graduates, like Kaitlin, will end up working for SMEs like Fidditch Lumber Co., not large MNCs. Industry Canada reports that approximately 98 percent of Canadian businesses have fewer than 100 employees (Industry Canada 2011). As of 2009, Statistics Canada reported that approximately 48 percent of the total private sector labour force worked for small businesses (fewer than 100 employees) and that these small businesses contributed to 23 percent of GDP in Canada (Industry Canada 2009). Moreover, in Canada, approximately 80 percent of the SME population consists of fewer than 10 employees. Table 11.1 illustrates the number of employees in Canadian businesses by percentage of total for each province.

Over 100,000 new businesses are created in Canada each year (Industry Canada 2010). Canadian SMEs contribute to society through job creation, the provision

Table 11.1   Number of Employees in Canadian Businesses (by percentage of total for each province)

	1–4	5–9	10–19	20–49	50–99	Small < 100	Medium 100–499	Large 500+
				percent				
NL	55.8	22.7	11.1	6.7	2.0	98.2	1.5	0.3
PE...........	52.0	22.4	13.1	8.4	2.4	98.3	1.4	0.2
NS	55.0	20.5	12.0	7.8	2.5	97.8	1.9	0.3
NB	54.8	20.7	13.1	7.9	2.4	98.1	1.6	0.3
QC...........	51.1	22.2	13.1	8.8	2.8	97.9	1.8	0.3
ON...........	55.2	19.5	12.1	7.9	2.9	97.5	2.2	0.3
MB...........	50.2	21.6	13.7	8.9	3.2	97.5	2.1	0.3
SK...........	55.0	21.0	12.4	7.7	2.3	98.4	1.4	0.2
AL	59.2	18.0	11.2	7.1	2.5	98.0	1.7	0.2
BC	56.6	20.0	12.1	7.3	2.4	98.3	1.5	0.2
YT	49.2	23.3	13.5	9.6	1.9	97.6	2.2	0.2
NWT........	34.7	23.8	20.1	13.8	4.5	96.7	3.1	0.2
NU..........	24.1	25.0	22.9	18.6	6.5	97.1	2.7	0.3
Canada	54.8	20.2	12.3	7.9	2.7	97.9	1.9	0.3

Source: Excerpt from Statistics Canada, *Business Register*, June 2009.

of products and services, taxes, and innovation and entrepreneurship. SMEs, therefore, have a huge impact on the Canadian economy, communities, and the natural environment.

Ethics and Small Business

SME owners and employees, as well as all entrepreneurs, deal with ethical issues and ethical decision making in their business practices. Justin Longenecker, an expert in small business and entrepreneurship, and his colleagues at Baylor University have been studying small business, entrepreneurship, and ethics for over three decades. Longenecker and some of his colleagues (2006) found that both large publicly traded corporations and smaller companies have changed their standards of ethics and that business leaders in all sizes of organizations are making more ethical decisions. Although SMEs face different pressures than large companies, SMEs also face pressure from customers and suppliers, and they are often faced with the same regulations as large companies. At Fidditch, Kaitlyn is feeling pressure from a major supplier.

However, Longenecker and his colleagues also reported that small businesses face different ethical issues from large corporations. Small-business owners and entrepreneurs experience uniquely complex ethical challenges about issues of ownership (Kuratko, Goldsby, and Hornsby 2004); fairness, personnel, customer, and distribution issues (Hannafey 2003); ethical dilemmas when introducing new technologies, products, and services (Etzioni 1988; Hannafey 2003); and ethical issues, in particular conflicts of interest, involved in all stages of an innovative start-up (Fassin 2005).

Additional conflict of interest issues arise if the SME is family-owned and several family members are owners and/or employees. These issues are often connected with human resource functions, such as hiring, firing, and succession planning. Family-owned businesses often get a bad reputation for things such as preferential treatment, governance problems, and feuding. The case hints at a potential clash between the management philosophies of the cousin co-owners, Jade and Buddy. Jade appears to be showing more of an interest in CSR and sustainability, whereas Buddy appears to be more focused on the innovation and bottom-line aspects of growing the business.

However, a recent study found that family-owned firms actually respond more to institutional pressures than large publicly traded corporations (Berrone, Cruz, Gomez-Mejia, and Larraza-Kintana 2010). This research found that family-owned businesses want to have a positive image within their local communities. For example, they are more likely to be more environmentally friendly than large, public corporations whose sustainability efforts are often more symbolic than substantive.

Other researchers have discussed how small businesses face particular barriers (e.g., limited time, resources, and capabilities) related to ethical responsibilities (e.g., Karakowsky et al. 2005; Lepoutre and Heene 2006). In the Fidditch case, neither Jade nor Buddy has post-secondary education or training in CSR and sustainability. In addition, Buddy appears to be facing time and financial pressures that are blinding him to some of the ethical and strategic issues facing Fidditch.

Graafland, van de Ven, and Stoffele's (2003) study of business firms in the Netherlands found that, in contrast to large firms, which prefer an integrity strategy to promote ethical behaviour, small businesses prefer a dialogue strategy. For example, they found that small businesses often assign one board member to informally deal with ethical questions. Small businesses are also less likely to have formal codes of conduct or codes of ethics. Although many SMEs have no formal ethics training or institutionalized ethics programs, this does not mean that they are not ethically responsible. Having a formal ethics program in place does not necessarily translate into ethical business practice. For example, Enron had a lengthy code of ethics and claimed to be doing triple bottom-line accounting, which measures social, environmental, and financial performance, at the time of its ethical downfall.

The process of applying for a business ethics award, such as the Better Business Bureau (BBB) Business Ethics Award, can provide SMEs with an opportunity to benchmark against other ethical leaders in business. Many regional BBBs present annual business ethics awards, which include categories for SMEs. Award-winning SME owners and entrepreneurs have often combined entrepreneurship with ethical leadership and social responsibility.

CSR and Small Business

The idea of CSR also differs between small and large firms. Many small businesses are focused on growing their companies and they face many competing priorities, as the case illustrates. Related to our discussion in the previous section, often SMEs do not have the financial resources and CSR knowledge of larger companies. North American small businesses have been hit especially hard after the market meltdown that followed the 2008 collapse of the financial services industry in many parts of the world. SMEs are often overwhelmed with tax burdens and cannot seek offshore tax havens the way that many large MNCs can. Therefore, many small businesses will claim that they cannot "do CSR" because they are barely surviving. However, SMEs also tend to have a narrow view of CSR and associate it only with donating time and money to their local community. (This is Buddy's perspective in the case study.)

When you probe into the vision, goals, and day-to-day activities of SMEs, though, many of these companies are taking good care of their employees, providing a quality product or service, trying to reduce their ecological footprint, and giving back in some way to their community. To many SME owners and managers, that is just the way you do good business.

Another important area where we see SMEs taking a different CSR approach is in the area of stakeholder management. Fuller and Tian (2006, 295) suggest that SMEs' "legitimacy with immediate stakeholders, employees, customers, suppliers, and their 'local' community is at stake in a far more direct and personal way than it is with major corporations." Small businesses often have a closer relationship than MNCs do with their stakeholders, especially employees, customers, the local community, their business partners, and the natural environment. In the case, Kaitlyn is feeling pressure from Louis Marchand, a primary supplier with whom she has worked closely during her time at Fidditch.

However, SME's close relationships with employees, customers, suppliers, and the community often bring them a greater sense of social responsibility. Adam Smith, the founding father of modern-day economics, promoted the idea that business acting in its own self-interest will result in the greatest benefit for the community. Yet, in 1776, Adam Smith's idea of community was pretty local, not the global marketplace of the 21st century. The transportation and technology of the 18th century certainly did not allow businesses to have customers and suppliers on the other side of the world the way that large MNCs do today. Businesses in Adam Smith's community would have actually seen the impact of their decisions on their stakeholders and they knew that they had to conduct their businesses in a socially responsible way. So, in this sense, a small business that focuses on a local and/or regional market might be more inclined to act in an enlightened self-interest manner that benefits the local and regional communities.

It has been reported that many SMEs approach CSR in an implicit, informal, unstructured manner. In fact, the language of "CSR" is as unfamiliar to many small-business owners and managers (Russo and Tencati 2009) as it was to Buddy and Jade. Many SMEs do not use terms such as stakeholders, stewardship, or sustainability. Think about it: the acronym CSR stands for *corporate* social responsibility. For SMEs, what is most important is responsible business practice or considering the "right thing to do" (Fassin 2008).

Just as the values of a large company are often developed and instilled by its CEO, we find that the values of a SME are strongly influenced by the personal values of the business owner(s) or manager(s). Often the business owners have a strong belief in giving back to the community. Whereas in large MNCs the efforts that drive CSR often come from mid-level human resources and public relations staff, in SMEs the internal champion of CSR is most often the owner–manager. In a study of 24 SMEs across the United Kingdom, every company identified the owner–manager or senior partner as the guiding force behind CSR in their company

(Jenkins 2006, 251). Because the owner–manager is closer to employees in a SME, they can more readily serve as CSR champion and engage all employees in CSR initiatives. In the Fidditch Lumber Co. case, Kaitlyn appears to be the internal champion of CSR, but is butting up against one of the owner's beliefs and values.

However, SMEs don't necessarily champion CSR within their organizations in the same way that larger companies do. Russo and Tencati (2009) studied 3,626 Italian firms of different sizes. They concluded that Italian SMEs are increasingly familiar with the concept of CSR, yet are unwilling to formalize CSR strategies into specific and explicit management systems. Table 11.2 summarizes some of the differences that these researchers found between small and large Italian companies and their approach to CSR.

Canadian Business for Social Responsibility (CBSR), a non-profit organization representing Canadian member companies, is part of a global network committed to CSR. It sponsored a 2003 study to better understand the unique business realities, challenges, and opportunities of SMEs in practising CSR. One of the findings of this study is that many SMEs are looking for guidance and support for their CSR activities (Princic, Floyd, and Bonham 2003). Table 11.3, a condensation of that report, considers the biggest challenges that Canadian SMEs are faced with when developing and implementing CSR activities. Note how the first two points are particularly applicable to the Fidditch Lumber Co. case.

Related to the fourth point in Table 11.3, many environmental management programs, mechanisms, and standards, such as the ISO 14000 series and Account-Ability, are costly to implement, especially for SMEs. There seems to be a growing understanding of this fact and organizations are trying to develop standards that are geared more to smaller organizations. The Global Reporting Initiative (GRI) has recognized this gap and its website offers various materials for SMEs. The

Table 11.2 Small Versus Large Italian Company Approaches to CSR

Small business	Large business
Strong relationship with local community guides CSR	Business benefits guide CSR
Low degree of formalization of CSR strategies	Capacity to extend CSR along supply chain
Specific responsible behaviours toward specific stakeholders	Focus on financial initiatives regarding stakeholders
Environmental focus on reducing consumption and pollution	Comprehensive environmental strategies
Informal responsible strategies toward employees and other stakeholders	Specific formal procedures; ethical codes; social reporting

Table 11.3   Core CSR Challenges for SMEs—Costs, Resources, and Time

1. The cost of implementing CSR is high, particularly in the primary resource and manufacturing sectors, where the cost of industry regulations and technical overhead is seen as quite high.

2. Sourcing environmentally friendly products is problematic because of limited availability. SMEs rarely have the purchasing power to influence their local suppliers to provide environmentally and socially responsible products.

3. While purchasing trends show a shift in demand to more socially and environmentally responsible products and services, most consumers are not yet making their purchasing decisions according to these criteria. Educating consumers about the impacts of their purchasing decisions is difficult, and makes it less appealing for SMEs to shift their products/services to more socially and environmentally responsible ones.

4. Internal communications and training for employees on CSR practices is challenging for SMEs because of resource constraints and the lack of affordable, external support (Princic et al. 2003, 4).

Caux Round Table, with its project for Moral Capitalism, has released the *CSR Handbook for Small and Medium Enterprises*, which can be accessed online (see end of chapter for website information). These are two examples of places where Fidditch Lumber Co. can go to get help with CSR.

At the same time, Heledd Jenkins of Cardiff University used data from 24 exemplary SMEs in the United Kingdom to show how smaller firms can use CSR opportunities to their competitive advantage. For example, she found that SMEs' flexibility, creativity, and innovativeness can help them to quickly take advantage of emerging products and services as well as to develop innovative approaches to CSR (Jenkins 2006).

Ethics and Entrepreneurship

Although a great deal of complexity and vagueness surrounds the definition of entrepreneurship, the concept most often refers to the behaviours and traits most commonly used to identify and exploit opportunities that involve risk-taking, innovativeness, proactiveness, and continuous improvement in business operations (Covin and Slevin 1991). Entrepreneurs realize their entrepreneurial ideas by starting up and managing new ventures, which, though small at the beginning, often grow, expand, and become more sophisticated. Think of Canadian companies such as Boston Pizza, Research in Motion (RIM), and auto-parts manufacturer Magna International.

Hannafey (2003) suggested that extremely competitive market pressures can distort an entrepreneur's ethical focus. He concluded that although most entrepreneurs have a good grasp of the moral climate inside their organizations, the particular demands of the entrepreneur's environment may lead to unique ethical dilemmas and questionable ethical practices. For example, entrepreneurs often work long hours and make decisions in isolation. In their research, Longenecker, McKinney, and Moore (1988) found that egoism and individualism traits among entrepreneurs sometimes lead to unethical business practices. As the popular television program *Dragons' Den* often shows, entrepreneurs can sometimes be opportunistic and cutthroat.

Unfortunately, there is no shortage of past and present cases of irresponsible entrepreneurship. The 1990s era of the dotcom entrepreneur (Global Crossing,

---

SIDEBAR

Egoism

Egoism refers to an ethical theory that holds that self-interest is the foundation of morality. Individualism refers to the habit or principle of being independent and self-reliant.

WorldCom, Satyam Computer Services, and Nortel, for example) illustrated quite well how entrepreneurial expansion is sometimes connected to accounting fraud and insider trading. There are also cases of intellectual property theft of patents, copyrights, trademarks, trade names, trade secrets, and their accumulated know-how.

Some of the entrepreneurship literature reveals that discussions of relevant stakeholders typically focus on investment bankers, securities analysts, institutional investors, venture capitalists, certification gatekeepers such as ISO, and those who review products (Lounsbury and Glynn 2001). Some entrepreneurs are short-sighted and fail to see the complexity of stakeholder relationships and how they affect their entrepreneurial activities. At the same time, we said earlier in the chapter that small businesses often have close relationships with their immediate stakeholders. Stakeholder analysis, as described in Chapter 6, could be helpful in identifying both opportunities and threats for entrepreneurs.

We suggest that a *genuine entrepreneur* is ethically, socially, and environmentally responsible, and a keen contributor to sustainable economic and community development. The genuine entrepreneur focuses on the purpose of business and the purpose of entrepreneurship, what Longenecker described as the close connection between entrepreneurial spirit and integrity. What does it mean to be a good entrepreneur? How does the entrepreneurship define success? Is it about making money? Is it about using entrepreneurial talent to contribute to the common good? What is the purpose of business? How does it connect to life purpose? We ask these questions because it makes sense to bring critical and reflective questions related to social justice, the meaning of work, and human dignity into discussions of responsible entrepreneurship.

The European Commission Directorate-General for Enterprise produced a report entitled, *A Collection of Good Practice Cases Among Small and Medium-Sized Enterprises Across Europe* (2003). The cases included in this report aim to illustrate responsible entrepreneurship among 25 SMEs in Europe. The European Commission feels that *responsible entrepreneurship*, rather than corporate social responsibility, is a better term to use for SMEs. The term *responsible entrepreneurship* was originally coined by the United Nations in the context of its work on sustainable development.

> Responsible entrepreneurship associates the individual entrepreneurial drive and attitude necessary for creating and running a small business with a wider sense of societal responsibilities that often forms part of the personal values of the SME owner/manager.

This collection of cases would also serve as a good source of information for the folks at Fidditch Lumber Co.

Communicating Responsible Entrepreneurship

Although large companies are more likely to communicate about ethical, social, and environmental goals and outcomes, this does not imply that large companies are more socially responsible or ethical than SMEs. As touched on earlier in the chapter, SMEs often carry out CSR activities without ever formally integrating them into their management processes, without ever communicating them to external stakeholders and, in some cases, without ever recognizing them as CSR-type initiatives.

A Danish study of 1,071 SMEs found that SMEs do not typically communicate to external stakeholders about their CSR activities. Rather, SMEs tend to focus their CSR communications on their internal stakeholders (Nielsen and Thomsen 2009). CSR initiatives are highlighted on some small businesses' company literature and websites and many SMEs communicate CSR initiatives internally to employees through newsletters, staff meetings, and speeches by the owner or senior management team. Large companies can communicate lofty CSR goals because their impacts are seen as farther reaching, but some SME CSR communications might be scrutinized more closely because SMEs are more visible in their local and regional communities.

Conclusion

Strengthening the link between business ethics, small business, and entrepreneurship is critical to the development of ethical and socially responsible entrepreneurs and businesses. All business owners and entrepreneurs experience ethical dilemmas and ethical decision making, no matter what the size or nature of the enterprise. In short, "big" business should not dominate the discussion of business ethics and CSR.

CASE STUDY DISCUSSION QUESTIONS

1. What special challenges is Kaitlyn facing in implementing CSR in a small business?
2. If Kaitlyn and Jade work to develop a CSR strategy for Fidditch, who or what should they consider as relevant stakeholders? What kinds of responsibilities does Fidditch have to its stakeholders?
3. How might Jade and Kaitlyn gain Buddy's support? How can they help him develop a broader understanding of CSR, as described in Chapter 6?
4. Where could Fidditch Lumber Co. go to get help on CSR initiatives for small business?

GENERAL DISCUSSION QUESTIONS

1. How might the responsibilities of a small business differ from the responsibilities of a large corporation? How might ethical responsibilities related to environmental management and ecologically sustainable business practices differ among different-sized organizations?
2. Is bigger business better business?
3. What does it mean to be a good entrepreneur?
4. How do informal social controls such as family-owned businesses' desire to fit in the local community relate to Adam Smith's idea of self-interest and collective interest?
5. In one of your Entrepreneurship classes, you are asked to create a new venture. One of the students in your group comes up with the idea of developing a University Girlie Calendar, using scantily dressed, provocative pictures of some of the more popular girls on campus. How does this entrepreneurial idea fit in with the idea of genuine entrepreneurship discussed in the chapter?

ACTIVITIES

1. Research the website of a small business in your local community. Look for evidence of socially responsible activity. See whether the terms CSR, ethics, stakeholders, or sustainability are used. What factors would you use to decide whether or not this is a business that exemplifies responsible entrepreneurship as defined by the United Nations on page 164 of your text?

2. As mentioned in the chapter, many regional BBBs present annual business ethics awards, which include categories for SMEs. Go to your regional BBB website, if there is one in your region, and look up a recent winner. Consider nominating a small business in your community that exhibits responsible entrepreneurship.

SUGGESTED READINGS AND ONLINE RESOURCES

Better Business Bureau (BBB). Business Ethics Award. http://maritimeprovinces.bbb.org/bbb-ethics-awards.

Caux Round Table. 2008. *CSR handbook for small and medium enterprises.* http://www.cauxroundtable.org/index.cfm?&menuid=104&parentid=16.

European Commission, Directorate-General for Enterprise. 2003. *A collection of good practice cases among small and medium-sized enterprises across Europe.* http://ec.europa.eu/enterprise/policies/sustainable-business/files/responsible_entrepreneurship/doc/resp_entrep_en.pdf.

Global Reporting Initiative (GRI). https://www.globalreporting.org/reporting/reporting-support/support-for-SMEs/Pages/default.aspx.

REFERENCES

Berrone, P., C. Cruz, L.R. Gomez-Mejia, and M. Larraza-Kintana. 2010. Socioemotional wealth and corporate response to institutional pressures: Do family-controlled firms pollute less? *Administrative Science Quarterly* 55 (1): 82–113.

Covin, J.G., and D.P. Slevin. 1991. A conceptual model of entrepreneurship as a firm behaviour. *Entrepreneurship: Theory and Practice* 16 (1): 7–25.

Etzioni, A. 1988. *The moral dimension: Toward a new economics.* New York: Basic Books.

European Commission, Directorate-General for Enterprise. 2003. *A collection of good practice cases among small and medium-sized enterprises across Europe.* http://ec.europa.eu/enterprise/policies/sustainable-business/files/responsible_entrepreneurship/doc/resp_entrep_en.pdf.

Fassin, Y. 2005. The reasons behind non-ethical behaviour in business and entrepreneurship. *Journal of Business Ethics* 60: 265–279.

Fassin, Y. 2008. SMEs and the fallacy of formalizing CSR. *Business Ethics* 17 (4): 364–378.

Fuller, T., and Y. Tian. 2006. Social and symbolic capital and responsible entrepreneurship: An empirical investigation of SME narratives. *Journal of Business Ethics* 67: 287–304.

Graafland, J., B. van de Ven, and N. Stoffele. 2003. Strategies and instruments for organizing CSR by small and large businesses in the Netherlands. *Journal of Business Ethics* 47 (1): 45–60.

Hannafey, F.T. 2003. Entrepreneurship and ethics: A literature review. *Journal of Business Ethics* 46: 99–110.

Industry Canada. 2009. Key small business statistics—July 2009. http://www.ic.gc.ca/eic/site/sbrp-rppe.nsf/eng/h_rd02395.html.

Industry Canada. 2010. Key small business statistics—July 2010. http://www.ic.gc.ca/eic/site/sbrp-rppe.nsf/eng/h_rd02488.html.

Industry Canada. 2011. Key small business statistics—July 2011. http://www.ic.gc.ca/eic/site/sbrp-rppe.nsf/eng/h_rd02596.html.

Jenkins, H. 2006. Small business champions for corporate social responsibility. *Journal of Business Ethics* 67: 241–256.

Karakowsky, L., A.B. Carroll, and A.K. Buchholtz. 2005. *Business and society: Ethics and stakeholder management.* Toronto: Nelson.

Korten, D. 1995. *When corporations rule the world.* West Hartford, CT/San Francisco: Berrett-Koehler/Kumarian.

Kuratko, D.F., M.G. Goldsby, and J.S. Hornsby. 2004. The ethical perspectives of entrepreneurs: An examination of stakeholder salience. *Journal of Applied Management and Entrepreneurship* 9 (4): 19–43.

Lepoutre, J., and A. Heene. 2006. Investigating the impact of firm size on small business social responsibility: A critical review. *Journal of Business Ethics* 67: 257–273.

Longenecker, J.G., J.A. McKinney, and C.W. Moore. 1988. Egoism and independence: Entrepreneurial ethics. *Organizational Dynamics* 16: 64–72.

Longenecker, J.G., C.W. Moore, J.W. Petty, L.E. Palich, and J.A. McKinney. 2006. Ethical attitudes in small businesses and large corporations: Theory and empirical findings from a tracking study spanning three decades. *Journal of Small Business Management* 44 (2): 167–184.

Lounsbury, M., and M.A. Glynn. 2001. Cultural entrepreneurship: Stories, legitimacy, and the acquisition of resources. *Strategic Management Journal* 22 (6/7): 545–564.

Nielsen, A.E., and C. Thomsen. 2009. Investigating CSR communications in SMEs: A case study among Danish middle managers. *Business Ethics* 18 (1): 83–93.

Princic, L., M. Floyd, and J. Bonham. 2003. Engaging small business in corporate social responsibility: A Canadian small business perspective on CSR. *Canadian Business for Social Responsibility.* http://info.worldbank.org/etools/docs/library/114189/Engaging%20SME%20in%20CSR%202003.pdf.

Russo, A., and A. Tencati. 2009. Formal vs. informal CSR strategies: Evidence from Italian micro, small, medium-sized, and large firms. *Journal of Business Ethics* 85: 339–353.

International Business and Globalization

Case Study: Gildan Activewear

Even as Montreal-based T-shirt manufacturer Gildan Activewear was receiving the 2003 award for "excellence in corporate, social and ethical responsibility" from Canada's minister of international cooperation for its business ventures in Honduras, Gildan executives must have been worried. Trouble was brewing in Honduras at its El Progreso factory. Gildan was attracting the wrong sort of attention, having been accused in the media and by Canadian and foreign non-governmental organizations (NGOs) of engaging in a pattern of labour rights violations at one of its Honduran factories. The situation was quickly deteriorating.

Gildan is typical of modern apparel and fashion companies in that most of its products are sourced from factories in economically developing countries, where there is little regulation of labour and business and what regulations exist are often poorly enforced. Gildan owned the El Progreso factory in Honduras, whereas in many instances the corporations behind the famous brands we all recognize prefer to contract out their manufacturing to third-party businesses, which assume most of the risk and costs of compliance with local laws and norms where factories are located.

Back in 2001, the labour conditions in factories supplying Gildan had caught the attention of a Canadian workers' rights NGO called the Maquila Solidarity Network (MSN). MSN teamed up with other NGOs from Honduras, Mexico, El Salvador, and Haiti to exchange information about working conditions in Gildan factories, and accused Gildan of violating local employment and health and safety laws. Gildan denied the allegations. Then, in 2002, the Canadian Broadcasting Corporation (CBC) aired a documentary entitled *Sewing Discontent*, in which it alleged that workers in the El Progreso factory were being subjected to forced pregnancy tests, had excessively high production quotas, were exposed to dangerous levels of fabric dust, and were routinely dismissed if they attempted to organize trade unions.

Gildan again denied the allegations. It gave the CBC affidavits from workers who claimed that they had been pressured to lie to the CBC reporter. When 38 employees were later dismissed from the Honduran factory, the workers, a local union, and the NGO coalition alleged that they had been fired for exercising their legal right to organize a union. Gildan officials met with MSN in Montreal in late 2002 and denied that the workers had been dismissed for union activity. In early 2003, the Quebec Federation of Labour (QFL), Oxfam Canada, and Amnesty International called on Gildan to initiate an independent investigation into the dismissals. Around the same time, the Solidarity Fund of the QFL, a major Gildan shareholder, conducted its own investigation into the dismissals in Honduras and concluded that Gildan had violated the workers' legal right to unionize. When Gildan refused to rehire the workers, the Solidarity Fund sold its Gildan shares, and its representative on Gildan's board of directors resigned in protest. In 2004, the coalition of NGOs released its report of working conditions in Gildan's Honduran factory under the title *A Canadian Success Story? Gildan Activewear: T-Shirts, Free Trade, and Worker Rights*. Gildan quickly threatened the report's authors with a defamation lawsuit, but the NGOs were undeterred and continued their public criticism of Gildan's labour practices.

Labour relations issues at a factory thousands of kilometres away had reached the attention of Canadian organizations and media, and there was little sign that the negative attention was dissipating. There was now a real risk that these issues would begin to affect Gildan's reputation and bottom line. Gildan needed to demonstrate to its customers, investors, and the marketplace that it took labour standards issues and its responsibility as a global citizen seriously. It took a step in that direction when, in the fall of 2003, it joined an American-based initiative, the Fair Labor Association (FLA).

The FLA had emerged in the late 1990s at the urging of President Clinton and his administration. Clinton was under public and political pressure to respond to the surge in media reports about American corporations engaging in or condoning unethical and unlawful practices in foreign countries. In particular, there was heightened sensitivity in the United States in the immediate post–North American Free Trade Agreement (NAFTA) era to the "export of American jobs" to low-wage developing countries. NAFTA, and other global and regional trade agreements, make it cheaper and easier for businesses to source from foreign countries, but these trade agreements do not require compliance with any basic minimum labour standards. President Clinton had promised that he would address the use of foreign "sweatshop" labour by American corporations. He encouraged the apparel industry, unions, and NGOs to come together to develop a way to self-regulate supply-chain labour practices.

The result, the FLA, has no legal powers, but a corporation that voluntarily joins the FLA is expected to abide by the FLA's rules and procedures. For example, members are required to adopt a code of conduct and require their suppliers to comply with it. The code includes a list of nine core labour standards, including a requirement to respect "freedom of association" and the right of employees to access collective bargaining, a prohibition on child labour, and rules applying to wages, hours of work, discrimination, and health and safety. By joining the FLA, Gildan pledged to adopt that code and to take steps to ensure compliance at all of its supplier factories, whether it owned the factories or not. Membership in the FLA also subjected corporations to occasional audits of supplier factories by FLA staff, and a complaint mechanism. This permits the FLA to investigate allegations that there has been a violation of the code by a corporate member or one of its suppliers.

It did not take long for Gildan to become the target of an FLA complaint. The Toronto-based MSN, along with the Canadian Labour Congress (the umbrella organization for most Canadian unions) and a Honduran workers' rights NGO together filed a complaint, alleging that the dismissals were in violation of the FLA code because they occurred in retaliation for the employees' attempts to organize a union. To make matters worse for Gildan, a second complaint was filed against it for the events in Honduras—this one through an organization called the Worker Rights Consortium (WRC). The WRC was formed in the late 1990s by the activist student organization United Students Against Sweatshops, which wanted to ensure that university-branded apparel was made under decent working conditions. Universities and colleges were pressured by students to join the WRC, and those that did were required to adopt a supplier code of conduct and to monitor their suppliers' compliance with it. Because Gildan was a large supplier of T-shirts to the universities that had joined the FLA, it was bound by the WRC's rules, including its complaints procedures. When the NGOs that had filed the FLA complaint also filed a WRC complaint, Gildan was suddenly faced with an obligation to consent to two independent investigations of the mass dismissals of employees in Honduras.

Both organizations (the FLA and WRC) conducted their own investigations, and released reports in 2004, finding multiple violations of local labour laws and the codes of conduct. Soon after, Gildan announced that it was closing the Honduran factory, claiming it was for business reasons completely unrelated to the labour issues and complaints. The factory closed in September 2004 and all remaining employees were dismissed. This decision provoked a number of responses. An investment fund called Real Assets Investment Management divested its shares from Gildan, issuing a press release that asserted that Gildan's actions in Honduras threatened the "long-term sustainability" of the company. The WRC called on all participating universities to cancel their orders with Gildan for its non-compliance with the WRC rules and the FLA passed a motion to terminate Gildan's membership unless the company implemented an acceptable corrective plan.

The Rewards and Challenges of Economic Globalization

Economic globalization is the subject of much debate. Its origins, causes, values, and impacts are all contested. Economic globalization describes the processes of integrating businesses beyond national borders through global sourcing, global networks and managers, and global markets (see sidebar for a discussion of factors that have contributed to economic globalization). For some, globalization is the inevitable result of economic and social evolution, a powerful force for good that will raise living standards around the globe. For others, it represents a set of policies designed primarily to benefit global corporations and the wealthy at the expense of the global masses, a system that, both in theory and in practice, will increase global economic and social inequality and fuel political instability. These are complex debates that have no easy or clear answers.

In Canada's case, the trend toward the globalization of business is very clear. In 1987, the value of goods imported into Canada was approximately $93 billion. By 2007, the amount was $390 billion. Between 1987 and 2007, the amount of goods exported ballooned from approximately $98 billion to $418 billion. Overall, the percentage of Canada's GDP (gross domestic product) derived from global trade (imports and exports combined) rose from 43 to 62 percent between 1987 and 2007 (Hunter and Bryant 2008, 3).

Canadian businesses can save substantially on their costs by manufacturing their products in economically developing countries (EDCs). As noted in the case study above, one source of savings is the dramatically lower wage and benefit levels in countries in South Asia, Africa, and Central and South America compared with levels in Canada. Other business expenses, including taxes, are often lower as well, and the degree of regulatory oversight by government, and the costs associated with it, is usually much lower in EDCs than in more economically advanced nations like Canada.

The lower level of government oversight of business activities in EDCs is sometimes a result of a lack of government capacity—local officials may lack the financial resources or technical expertise necessary to effectively regulate business activities. However, often it is by design. Many EDC governments have created export processing zones (EPZs), or "free-trade areas," to entice foreign corporations to invest there. EPZs are geographically defined spaces within a country where foreign

SIDEBAR

Contributing Factors in Modern Economic Globalization

"Economic globalization" describes a process of greater economic integration across national borders, facilitated by several key developments: (1) "free-trade" laws; (2) new information technologies; and (3) improved transportation systems.

- *Free-trade laws* reduced or eliminated tariffs on imported goods, making it more economically viable for corporations to source their products from economically developing nations, where production costs are lower. Free-trade laws also imposed restrictions on the right of national governments to give legal or financial advantages to domestic companies over foreign companies ("most-favoured-nation" clauses). For example, a Canadian policy designed to give a Canadian-based company a market advantage over foreign competitors could violate a free-trade agreement signed by the Canadian government.

- *New information technologies*, including the Internet, email, and video-conferencing, have made global business integration and control more feasible and cost-effective than in the past.

- *New or improved transportation systems*, including faster ships that can carry more cargo and systems that enable businesses to better track their goods, thus reducing the time and cost of global sourcing.

Source: NOAA photo library/ Creative Commons.

corporations are promised special treatment. This can include: low or zero corporate and property taxes, government subsidies, security services, free or cheap electricity and water, and a promise by government officials to waive or reduce labour, environmental, and other forms of regulation that would otherwise apply to local businesses operating outside the EPZ.

During the past quarter-century, the promise of lower operational costs has persuaded many Canadian corporations to outsource their production requirements from Canada and the United States to EDCs. Even companies that had carefully cultivated the business image of a responsible, homegrown producer found it difficult to resist the pull of economic globalization. For example, when Roots closed a Toronto factory in the mid-1990s and shipped those jobs overseas to an EDC, the company issued a statement explaining that it could no longer compete by producing in Canada (see sidebar). Even after the additional expense of shipping goods from EDCs in the southern hemisphere to North America, North American companies in labour-intensive industries, including fashion, sporting goods, footwear, and toys, have reaped huge savings in production costs from global outsourcing.

The Ethics of Conducting Business in Foreign Countries

While the economic benefits to Canadian businesses of global sourcing are obvious, those benefits come fraught with business risks and ethical dilemmas. Cultures, ethics, religions, laws, and business practices vary widely across nations. A business practice that is considered unethical and is unlawful in Canada might be perfectly acceptable, lawful, and even expected in other countries. Consider three examples: (1) the practice of bribing government officials to acquire a business

---

SIDEBAR

"How We Do Business": Letter from Roots Canada (excerpt)

Roots

Toronto, Summer 2009

Dear Roots Customer,

For the longest while, we made most Roots products in Canada but in recent years we have shifted some of our manufacturing abroad as a result of technical, economic and capacity challenges.

In early 2004, with great reluctance and much disappointment, we closed one of our own manufacturing facilities in Toronto where we made much of the Roots apparel line. For seven years, we tried to compete with offshore manufacturing companies. Unfortunately, it proved a largely unprofitable and unrealistic exercise.

The sad reality today is that there are fewer available suppliers in Canada, and certain products can no longer be made in Canada. It's a shame that free trade, globalization and the saturation of the Canadian market by major US and European companies manufacturing overseas have made this situation worse. The result: the technical capacity simply no longer exists in Canada to make certain categories of merchandise.

Source: Roots Canada (2009). www.roots.com. Reprinted by permission.

advantage; (2) the use of child labour; and (3) the emission of toxic substances into the environment.

- Bribery is a criminal offence and considered unethical in Canada, but it is a normal and expected way of conducting business in many EDCs.
- Canadian laws require children to attend school full-time, and most Canadians would be appalled if five- or six-year-old children were pulled from school to work in factories. However, in many poor Asian countries, child labour is a normal part of family life, necessary to ward off extreme poverty or even starvation.
- Canadian environmental laws restrict the right of businesses to release harmful chemicals and substances into the environment, and require businesses to track and publish the amounts of the toxins they release. In many EDCs, it is lawful to release the same harmful chemicals into the environment.

Is it "unethical" for a Canadian corporation to bribe officials, use child labour, or release toxins into the environment in an EDC, where those practices are both lawful and common? At the core of this debate is whether Canadian companies should be expected to adhere to "Canadian" ethics and legal standards in their activities in other countries, where laws and notions of ethics differ. When Canadian businesses operate abroad, should they export Canadian ethics, or should they adopt the ethical code of the host states in which they choose to operate?

On the one hand, we might subscribe to the notion of *ethical relativism*, the idea that there are no absolute, universal ethics that apply in every setting and, instead, what is ethical depends on the cultural and social norms that dominate in particular places at specific times. Applying this approach, a Canadian company that uses child labour to sew soccer balls in rural Pakistan is not acting "unethically" if child labour is considered a normal and acceptable practice there, even when the same practice is considered unethical in Canada.

Since Pakistani governments, communities, and parents should be deciding what is best for Pakistan and for Pakistani children, it would be inappropriate and paternalistic for Canadian corporations to impose Canadian values and ethics on their Pakistani operations and suppliers (Basu 2001). Canadian corporations should therefore respect the laws and ethics of the countries in which they are operating, without importing "Canadian" ethics.

A child sewing a soccer ball at a factory in Asia. When a company from the developed world produces goods in developing countries, should it export its ethics, or adopt the ethical codes of its host country?

On the other hand, we might reject ethical relativism, in whole or in part, and assert instead that there are *universal business ethics* that apply across geographic space and time. Slavery is an example. If a foreign country offered modern-day businesses the use of slaves to produce their goods, a Canadian corporation that took advantage of the offer to increase their profits would no doubt attract a considerable public backlash in Canada. The argument directed at the corporation would be that slavery is universally condemnable and unethical, and that no government, individual, or business is free to use slaves for personal or economic benefit. The argument that slavery is "lawful" in the foreign country would not likely satisfy the corporation's critics.

The difficulty with the argument for universal business ethics is that someone needs to decide what types of behaviour make the list. Who makes that decision and on what basis? Governments, political and religious leaders, poets, and philosophers, among others, have long wrestled with these questions.

An important attempt to define a set of universal ethical principles is the Universal Declaration of Human Rights (UDHR), introduced by the United Nations in 1948 in the wake of the horrific events of the Second World War. The UDHR presumes that there is a bundle of rights or entitlements to which all humans are entitled, regardless of where they happen to live. It includes the fundamental freedoms of right of expression and belief, for example, and some economic rights as well, such as the right to equal pay for equal work regardless of sex, the right to "just and favourable conditions of work and to protection against unemployment," and the "right to form and join unions." The UDHR is directed at governments, providing politicians with a roadmap of what rights and responsibilities they are expected to ensure for their citizens.

As the volume of global business and the influence of multinational corporations grew during the latter part of 20th century, a variety of instruments were adopted by international organizations to target the conduct of global corporations. One example is the *Guidelines for Multinational Enterprises*, issued by the Organisation for Economic Co-operation and Development (OECD), originally introduced in 1976 and substantially revised in 2000 (Murray 2001). The Canadian government has endorsed these guidelines and encourages all Canadian corporations to abide by them when they engage in business outside Canada (Canada 2011).

The guidelines stress that businesses have the responsibility to avoid certain types of conduct—including bribing public officials and using child labour—wherever they operate. These obligations exist even if local laws or norms do not prohibit the practices, as noted in this passage from the OECD guidelines:

> A State's failure either to enforce relevant domestic laws, or to implement international human rights obligations or the fact that it may act contrary to such laws

or international obligations does not diminish the expectation that enterprises respect human rights (OECD 2011, 30).

The OECD guidelines presume a set of universal business ethics to which all organizations should adhere. A range of other global codes of conduct targeting global business practices do the same, including, for example, the United Nations Global Compact (see Appendix 1 at the end of this chapter). These codes reject the central claim of ethical relativism, that there are no absolute, universal ethics that apply in every setting. However, these business codes are voluntary. They act as a guide to ethically responsible business behaviour, but there are no formal legal sanctions for non-compliance.

This lack of legal redress produces a common dilemma for business leaders responsible for global activities. Some activities that are listed as unethical in non-enforceable instruments like the OECD guidelines are also lawful, or at least commonly practised even if technically unlawful, in countries where Canadian businesses operate. If you were operating a Canadian business abroad, and you could earn your company substantial profits by violating an ethical "rule" listed in the guidelines but permitted in the host country, would you do that? Is your primary obligation to maximize profits on behalf of shareholders, or to comply with the OECD's list of non-enforceable universal principles of business ethics?

Codes of Conduct and Other Private Initiatives

In the case study that opened this chapter, Gildan *owned* the factory in Honduras that became a flashpoint. Because Gildan was the direct employer of the workers affected, what happened in the Honduran factory was clearly Gildan's responsibility. It is more common for multinational corporations to contract out their production needs to third-party suppliers in EDCs. That way, corporations save costs and avoid many of the challenges and risks associated with running a business in a foreign country. However, this model of global outsourcing creates its own ethical issues. When a Canadian corporation, like the Hudson's Bay Company (HBC), contracts with Factory X in China to produce clothing for an HBC brand, is HBC ethically responsible for the actions of Factory X?

In the past, most executives would likely have answered "no" to that question. For example, in 1991, a Nike executive was asked whether Nike was responsible for labour practices in its supplier factories in Indonesia. He answered: "It's not within our scope to investigate. I don't know that I need to know" (Esbenshade 2004, 119). That was a common perspective at the time. The position then was that it was the responsibility of the owners of the supplier factories to ensure that local laws were being complied with, and the responsibility of the local government officials to make and enforce whatever laws they deemed appropriate. It was not the responsibility of a corporation placing orders from those foreign factories to police legal compliance there, or to impose moral or ethical standards on foreign businesses or governments.

This hands-off position was challenged in the 1990s by a wave of labour, human rights, and environmental activists, who argued that multinational corporations were responsible for the conduct of their suppliers. The activists investigated and publicized the actions of the foreign-factory owners, identified which corporations they supplied, and then waged negative and damaging publicity campaigns against them. In 1996, an American labour rights activist publicized the story of young girls working in very poor labour conditions in a Honduran factory to make clothes for a Kathie Lee Gifford line of apparel sold at Walmart stores. This was one of many stories in the media during the 1990s describing how North American and European corporations were profiting from business practices of their foreign suppliers that many northern consumers found objectionable.

As a result of that activism, many corporations found it increasingly difficult to deny all responsibility for the conduct of their suppliers. Beginning with denim clothing company Levi Strauss in 1992, many began introducing *supplier codes of conduct*. Through these codes, corporations acknowledged that they had some responsibility to police their suppliers and to hold them to a set of standard rules (see Appendix 2: "Roots Workplace Code of Conduct" at the end of this chapter). Various other initiatives and codes also emerged, including the Fair Labor Association and the Worker Rights Consortium, mentioned in the Gildan case study, that addressed labour practices, others that addressed environmental practices, and still others that focused on specific industries (such as forestry) or professions (such as accounting).

By adopting a code of conduct, a corporation signals to its stakeholders and the public its support for a set of universal standards that it believes apply worldwide. This can, and often does, create a set of difficult challenges for corporations. First, it may be difficult for a corporation to decide which standards to include in its code. If the standards are set too low, the code may be dismissed as a public relations gimmick. If the standards are set too high, the corporation risks negative publicity every time a supplier is discovered violating the code.

Second, some standards could disqualify an entire country. For example, in China, workers are not legally entitled to join any trade union other than the official state-sanctioned union. Therefore, a corporation that includes in its supplier code a requirement that workers be free to join unions of their own choosing may be disqualifying itself when sourcing from any Chinese factories.

Third, corporations must decide how much money to invest in monitoring compliance with their codes, and how to respond when violations of a code are identified. Companies like Nike and Gap, which have experienced some of the highest levels of scrutiny, have invested millions of dollars to implement and monitor their codes; whereas other corporations do little more than post a code on their website, investing little or no money to monitor compliance levels. When a supplier violates the code, is the appropriate response to cancel all orders from that supplier, or to pressure the supplier to bring its behaviour into compliance with the code? The wrong response could open the corporation to harmful negative publicity.

Fourth, adopting a code of conduct usually attracts a variety of private watchdogs that are interested in what steps are being taken to ensure compliance. Nongovernmental organizations, academics, media, unions, consumer groups, and investors may all be interested in knowing how well the code is being implemented. Corporations need to decide how to deal with those actors. Is the best course of action to open a dialogue with these private watchdogs, or to adopt a more secretive strategy designed to keep information about code compliance in-house?

Case Study Discussion and Conclusions

There are no easy answers to these questions. While there may be great economic benefits associated with a global production strategy, operating a global business is also complicated, risky, and fraught with ethical challenges. Think back to the case study that opened this chapter. Do you think Gildan should have responded differently to the situation it faced?

Gildan responded to the allegations made against it by the NGOs in a defensive manner that is quite common. The first inclination of many business leaders faced with accusations of unlawful and unethical behaviour in a foreign country is to deny the allegations, and to threaten or ignore the accusers. It is interesting to note that some of the companies that faced the most intense scrutiny for their global activities, such as Nike and Gap, acknowledged over time that a more fruitful response was to enter into a dialogue with their accusers, to agree to look into the allegations, and to discuss possible resolutions if the allegations were confirmed. For example, a Nike executive said this about Nike's initial approach to allegations made against its global activities:

> Nike made a real mistake. I think we reacted negatively to the criticism. We said, wait a minute, we've got the best corporate values in the world, so why aren't you yelling at the other folks. That was a stupid thing to do and didn't get us anywhere. If anything it raised the volume louder. (Murphy and Mathew 2001, 7)

Similarly, Gildan found that the more it denied that there were any problems at its Honduran factory, the more the volume of criticism escalated. Gildan executives were probably surprised by the persistence of the NGOs, and by the range of other actors that soon joined in the chorus of criticism as time went on.

Eventually, Gildan decided to join the Fair Labor Association. Corporations join organizations like the FLA in an attempt to demonstrate that they take their ethical responsibility to monitor their supply-chain labour practices seriously. However, there are also risks in taking this step, as Gildan learned. Once a corporation adopts a code of conduct and accepts responsibility for policing it, it can expect to be held accountable to the code, even though the code itself is "voluntary." The finding of the FLA and the Worker Rights Consortium, that Gildan had violated its code (and local labour laws), was a public relations blow for Gildan. It undermined the credibility of Gildan's claims that the NGOs were selling falsehoods and that the sudden closure of the Honduran factory was completely unrelated to the workers' complaints.

Following the threat by the FLA to suspend its membership, Gildan entered into discussions with the FLA and the NGOs. In early 2005, Gildan submitted a corrective-action plan to those groups. The plan included offering preferential hiring rights to all of the dismissed employees at a new factory Gildan was opening in Honduras, an offer to provide free commuting costs or to pay moving expenses for the former employees to enable them to get to the new factory, and a promise not to discriminate against employees who support unions. Gildan also agreed to provide a Honduran workers' rights NGO with ongoing updates about the implementation of the plan. Gildan agreed to aggressively advertise the new jobs in ways most likely to reach the former employees, including using a loudspeaker mounted on a car in communities where those workers lived. Roughly 77 percent of former employees that applied for work at the new factory were eventually rehired by Gildan. As a result of this remedial plan, Gildan was permitted to remain a member of the FLA.

In 2007, when Gildan decided to close two factories in Northern Mexico, it took a different approach than it had in Honduras. It contacted MSN and a leading Mexican workers' rights NGO to seek their input into how to properly manage the process and avoid the sort of negative criticism it had endured in Honduras. Gildan discussed the closures, which affected some 1,300 workers, with the NGOs and local government officials. As a result, Gildan agreed to provide extended health benefits and notice pay that exceeded local legal requirements, and to pay local state officials $200,000, to be used as a fund to retrain and help dismissed employees find alternative work. The Mexican NGO that had participated in the discussions announced that Gildan's approach to the factory closures in Mexico set a positive precedent for how foreign multinationals should behave in economically developing countries.

DISCUSSION QUESTIONS

1. Do you think Gildan responded properly when first confronted by the NGOs with allegations of labour law violations at its Honduran factory?
2. Why do you think Gildan decided to join the Fair Labor Association and thereby subject itself to the FLA's complaint mechanism?
3. Is it appropriate for NGOs to be engaged in campaigns designed to influence and perhaps harm the reputation of corporations?
4. What should Gildan do next?

SUGGESTED READINGS AND ONLINE RESOURCES

Asgary, N., and M. Mitschow. 2002. Toward a model for international business ethics. *Journal of Business Ethics* 36: 239.

Canada. Foreign Affairs and International Trade. 2011. *Canada's national contact point for the OECD guidelines for multinational enterprises.* http://www.international.gc.ca/trade-agreements-accords-commerciaux/ncp-pcn/index.aspx?lang=eng&menu_id=1&menu=R&view=d.

Cetindamar, D. 2007. Corporate social responsibility practices and environmentally responsible behavior: The case of the United Nations Global Compact. *Journal of Business Ethics* 76: 163.

Frieden, Jeffrey. 2006. *Global capitalism: Its fall and rise in the twentieth century.* New York: W. W. Norton & Company.

Hunter, Trevor, and Murray Bryant. 2008. *The globalization of Canadian corporate leadership: 1987–2007.* Ivey School of Business, University of Western Ontario. http://www.ivey.uwo.ca/centres/engaging/research/Globalization_of_Canadian_Corporate_Leadership.pdf.

Organisation for Economic Co-operation and Development (OECD). 2011. *OECD Guidelines for multinational enterprises: Recommendations for responsible business conduct in a global context.* http://www.oecd.org/dataoecd/43/29/48004323.pdf.

Rivoli, P. 2009. *The travels of a T-shirt in the global economy.* New York: John Wiley & Sons.

Stiglitz, J. 2002. *Globalization and its discontents.* New York: W. W. Norton & Company.

United Nations. Global Compact. http://www.unglobalcompact.org.

REFERENCES

Basu, K. 2001. The view from the tropics. In *Can we put an end to sweatshops?*, ed. A. Fung, D. O'Rourke, and C. Sabel, 43. Boston: Beacon Press.

Canada. Foreign Affairs and International Trade. 2011. *Canada's national contact point for the OECD guidelines for multinational enterprises.* http://www.international.gc.ca/trade-agreements-accords-commerciaux/ncp-pcn/index.aspx?lang=eng&menu_id=1&menu=R&view=d.

Esbenshade, J. 2004. *Monitoring sweatshops.* Philadelphia: Temple University Press.

Hunter, T., and M. Bryant. 2008. *The globalization of Canadian corporate leadership: 1987–2007*. Ivey School of Business, University of Western Ontario. http://www.ivey.uwo.ca/centres/engaging/research/Globalization_of_Canadian_Corporate_Leadership.pdf.

Murphy, D., and D. Mathew. 2001. *Nike and global labour practices*. Unpublished manuscript. January. New Academy of Business Innovation for Socially Responsible Business.

Murray, J. 2001. A new phase in the regulation of multinational enterprises: The role of the OECD. *Industrial Law Journal* 30: 255.

Organisation for Economic Co-operation and Development (OECD). 2011. *OECD Guidelines for multinational enterprises: Recommendations for responsible business conduct in a global context*. http://www.oecd.org/dataoecd/43/29/48004323.pdf.

Roots Canada. 2009. *How we do business: An open letter about our standards and approach to social responsibility*. http://about.roots.com/on/demandware.store/Sites-RootsCorporate-Site/default/Link-Page?cid=MSTR_HOW_WE_DO_BUSINESS.

APPENDIX 1: The United Nations' Global Compact's Ten Principles

The UN Global Compact's ten principles in the areas of human rights, labour, the environment and anti-corruption enjoy universal consensus and are derived from:

- The Universal Declaration of Human Rights
- The International Labour Organization's Declaration on Fundamental Principles and Rights at Work
- The Rio Declaration on Environment and Development
- The United Nations Convention Against Corruption

The UN Global Compact asks companies to embrace, support and enact, within their sphere of influence, a set of core values in the areas of human rights, labour standards, the environment and anti-corruption:

Human Rights

- Principle 1: Businesses should support and respect the protection of internationally proclaimed human rights; and
- Principle 2: make sure that they are not complicit in human rights abuses.

Labour

- Principle 3: Businesses should uphold the freedom of association and the effective recognition of the right to collective bargaining;
- Principle 4: the elimination of all forms of forced and compulsory labour
- Principle 5: the effective abolition of child labour; and
- Principle 6: the elimination of discrimination in respect of employment and occupation.

Environment

- Principle 7: Businesses should support a precautionary approach to environmental challenges;
- Principle 8: undertake initiatives to promote greater environmental responsibility; and
- Principle 9: encourage the development and diffusion of environmentally friendly technologies.

Anti-Corruption

- Principle 10: Businesses should work against corruption in all its forms, including extortion and bribery.

Source: United Nations. Global Compact. http://www.unglobalcompact.org/AboutTheGC/TheTenPrinciples/index.html.

APPENDIX 2: Roots Workplace Code of Conduct

Roots Canada Ltd. ("Roots") aims to do business with suppliers that respect the culture in which they operate, the local law, and the workers who manufacture Roots products.

Roots has developed this Workplace Code of Conduct ("Code"), which sets forth the basic minimum requirements that all suppliers must meet in order to do business with Roots.

In addition to the specific provisions in this Code, Roots expects its suppliers to act reasonably in all respects and to do their best to ensure that no abusive, exploitative or illegal conditions exist at their workplaces.

I. SUPPLIER AGREEMENT

Country Law: Roots suppliers must operate in full compliance with the laws of their respective countries and with all other applicable laws, rules and regulations, including those relating to labour, worker health and safety, and the environment. In cases where the Roots standard is more stringent, the Roots standard will apply.

Subcontracting: Roots will only work with subcontractors who comply with this Code and who have signed a copy of this Code. Supplier must agree to disclose to Roots the name and address of every subcontractor used in the production of Roots garments and products.

Recordkeeping: Suppliers and subcontractors must agree to permit Roots and their representatives to inspect all facilities and documents to ensure compliance with local laws and international standards. All documents provided must be accurate and must be presented in a manner that allows for a complete inspection by auditors.

Communication of Standards: Roots expects our suppliers to support and co-operate in the distribution of this code. This includes posting the Code of Conduct document in the local language, as well as English, in an area where all workers may regularly view these principles.

II. EMPLOYMENT STANDARDS

Wages and Benefits: Suppliers must pay all employees who manufacture Roots garments, products, or components at least the minimum wages and benefits mandated by local law, including an annual paid holiday as required by law or which meet the local industry standard. Wages must be paid directly to the worker in full in legal tender. Only legal deductions are permitted, and workers must be notified of these deductions.

Payment of wages must be made at or near the workplace. In addition to their compensation for regular hours of work, employees shall be compensated for overtime hours at such premium rate as is legally required in the country of manufacture or, in those countries where such laws do not exist, at a rate at least equal to their regular hourly compensation rate.

Work Hours and Overtime: Except in extraordinary business circumstances, employees shall (i) not be required to work more than the lesser of (a) 48 hours per week and 12 hours overtime or (b) the limits on regular and overtime hours allowed by the law of the country of manufacture or, where the laws of such country do not limit the hours of work, the regular work week in such country plus 12 hours overtime and (ii) be entitled to at least one day off in every seven day period. Each employee must be notified at the time of hiring that compulsory overtime may sometimes be necessary.

Child Labor: Suppliers to Roots shall employ workers who meet the applicable minimum legal age requirement of their country or are at least 15 years of age.

Forced Labor: No forced labor, in any form, may be used by any Roots supplier, whether prison labor, indentured labor, bonded labor or otherwise.

Discrimination and Harassment: No employee of Roots suppliers shall be subject to workplace discrimination, harassment or abuse. Discrimination must not occur on the basis of race, color, sex, religion, political opinion, nationality, social origin, maternity or marital status.

Health and Safety: The workplace must be safe and healthy, and suppliers must comply in all respects with all applicable laws regarding the provision of a safe, hygienic, and healthy working environment. Suppliers must take steps to prevent workplace injuries and illnesses, and must train employees to use safe workplace practices.

Freedom of Association: Employers shall recognize and respect the right of employees to freedom of association and collective bargaining.

Environment: Vendors must comply with all local laws protecting the environment.

Roots will favor suppliers and contractors who take steps to ensure that their operations have the least impact possible on the environment.

Monitoring and Verification: Roots, by our representatives, may audit the facilities of any supplier and the facilities of any subcontractor. All suppliers and subcontractors shall fully cooperate and provide access to all facilities and documents to ensure compliance with this Code. Roots reserves the right to perform unannounced audits when deemed appropriate.

Source: Roots Canada. https://canada.roots.com/on/demandware.store/Sites-RootsCorporate-Site/default/Link-Page?cid=MSTR_WORKPLACE_CODE. Reprinted by permission.

The Individual in the Workplace

Case Study: The Student Counsellor

A new office was created for a newly appointed student counsellor at a university. A modest window was included in the door with the expectation that student passers-by would not interrupt with a knock if they saw that another student was being counselled. Soon after, a senior colleague of the counsellor offered to spray the window so that it would appear to be frosted and provide much more privacy for the occupant. He accepted the offer. Sometime later, the manager in charge of the unit noticed the frosted glass and sent an email asking that the glass be replaced with a clear pane, arguing that the prospect of passers-by looking through the clear window was intended to deter allegations of or attempts at sexual harassment on the part of the counsellor. The counsellor responded by noting that he preferred the frosted glass because, as a Muslim, he prayed several times a day, and the frosting afforded him some privacy during his prayers. Whose rights should take precedence in this case—the employee's or the employer's? Why? Is there additional information that you would like to have before deciding? Are there other ways of resolving this matter?

Introduction

In the modern business ethics reality, Canadian corporations—and those in most English-speaking countries—are increasingly accountable for their actions (and inactions) to a broad range of stakeholders. Moreover, because the support of stakeholders is now generally regarded as essential for a corporation to reach its strategic objectives, measures to gain and keep this support are now expected to be integrated into governance procedures, policies, strategies, and actions. Directors are expected by investors and regulators to oversee these aspects within their governance responsibilities and to ensure that executives and managers do likewise. Consequently, the time is long past that a corporation can take actions without concern for the rights of its employees. Leaving the observance of employee rights to happenstance can risk lawsuits, low morale and productivity, loss of excellent employees and prospects, and damage to the reputation of the corporation, its directors, and executives. As a result, there is an emerging emphasis on the development of a culture of integrity that will provide guidance and encouragement for executives, managers, and employees on a broad range of ethical behaviour, including the treatment of employees (Brooks and Selley 2008).

Employees have become very attuned to their employer's behavioural intentions by observing how their executives and managers behave, the application of penalty and reward systems, and the promotions and respect accorded to other employees or themselves. In addition, many experts and researchers support the view that employees infer how ethical their employer's non-employee activities are based on how ethically they perceive themselves to have been treated (Brooks and Dunn 2012, 508). As a result, it should be recognized that how an employer treats its employees carries significant ethical signalling functions for both internal and external stakeholders.[1]

These developments should not be taken to indicate that employers should acquiesce to whatever demands are made by employees and ignore the reasonable and legitimate interests of shareholders. Instead, the treatment of employees (which might include requests, directions, discipline, risks imposed, and so on) should be, and be *seen* to be, a reasonable balance of employee and employer (i.e., investor) interests. Difficulties usually arise when the interests of one significantly outweigh those of the other.

However, because law and regulation frequently do not provide good or comprehensive guidance in determining the appropriate balance between employees and employers' interests, judgment is required to develop a balance that takes social expectations or norms into account. It is those expectations that often grow in response to scandals or perceived corporate misbehaviour, which in turn drive changes in laws and regulations. Corporate policy-makers are well-advised to maintain a constant awareness of both actual and probable trends, and to provide up-to-date guidance for employees.

---

1 Internal stakeholders include executives, managers, employees, company agents, and some current investors. External stakeholders include prospective executives, managers, employees, and some current and all prospective investors; and customers, lenders, partners, and local government.

In such a dynamic environment, it would be folly to presume without checking that employee treatment patterns established long ago would still be the norm, and that they are still desirable or appropriate. Employee treatment patterns and decision criteria need to be revisited frequently to ensure they continue to be relevant and effective. Nonetheless, for some time, several developments and trends that facilitate good decisions about employee treatment have been strengthening, such as:

- the development and maintenance of an ethical culture or culture of integrity in an organization to provide ongoing guidance for decisions; and
- increasing respect for:
  - the exercise of employee conscience;
  - physical and mental health;
  - civility, privacy, and dignity;
  - fair and equitable treatment; and
  - diversity.

Moreover, there is a growing understanding that the values inherent in a culture of integrity and in the development of a sound reputation provide good reference touchstones for decisions related to appropriate employee treatment.

These themes will be developed below to provide a framework for decisions affecting the general treatment of employees, as well as several specific topics, including:

- procedural justice: needed or not?;
- whistleblowing: frill or necessity?;
- respect for privacy and dignity;
- autocratic or democratic management styles;
- civility in the workplace;
- healthy and safe work environment; and
- harassment—sexual and otherwise.

The Shifting Balance of Rights Between Employee and Employer

"An employer has the right to a fair day's work for a fair day's pay." This sentence has long been used to summarize the balance of power relationship between employer and employee, and the expectations for each. However, the definition of fairness, which has been changing continuously, has been a challenge for both sides to understand. The trend has been to enhance employee interests, rather than the short-term interests of employers. For example, during the Industrial

Revolution in the 18th and 19th centuries, and into the 1940s, the workweek was six days long, and ten-hour days were not unusual, except on Saturdays. Slowly, the workweek has shortened to five days, and the expectation for daily hours of work has dropped to seven or eight hours, so that a 35–40 hour workweek is the expectation for most.

While respect for employee rights has been growing, raising the concern of some that profits will be eroded in the process, it is evident that the longer-term interest of investors has been well served by employees who are healthier and more able to perform at a high-quality level. In addition, well-trained and motivated employees are less likely to leave and the resulting work environment is more likely to attract new employees. These positive changes for employees are most valuable in modern occupations that require more skill and training than the physical jobs that dominated in earlier decades. Consequently, although the balance of rights has shifted toward more respect for employee interests, the overall interests of employers have been better served as well.

Employee Rights Themes in North America

Fairness: Reasonable Expectations for Employers and Employees

Fairness expectations, earlier taken to refer to fair treatment regarding pay and working conditions, have been expanded to include employment opportunity, gender, race, and age. For example, it is no longer considered appropriate and may be illegal to limit or discriminate against women or men by:

- restricting employment opportunities to men, without very specific justification;
- paying women less than men for equal work; or
- restricting promotion opportunities.

Similarly, it is not appropriate and, depending on the jurisdiction, may be illegal to discriminate against or give preference to persons on the basis of their race or religion, or their age, provided that they can continue to perform their duties at a satisfactory level. Nor can there be any harassment or hazing of individuals on the basis of gender, race, or age differentials—or on any basis for that matter.

Supportive Governance Policies, Their Application, and Leadership Expectations

Expectations of fairness have also expanded beyond the evident actions or decisions involved to include corporate governance and the processes that shape those decisions. Company policies, approved by the board of directors, that provide guidance for decisions that are fair, and for recourse if they are not, are expected to be in place and observed. For example, employees must be given sufficient information and time to make an "informed choice" on difficult decisions. Procedural justice needs to be evident, and reasoning relatively transparent, or the decisions made may be regarded as tainted or biased. Whistleblower mechanisms that incorporate fair treatment (i.e., protection from retaliation) are becoming the norm, and are mandated in some industries and jurisdictions, or with regard to sensitive areas such as reporting pollution. Although at first glance it seems unfair, it is now recognized that disabled persons need to be given extra consideration for access and workspace requirements to make their overall treatment fair in comparison to healthy normal individuals.

It is now well understood that just having appropriate policies governing employee relations is not enough to ensure their application. They also need to be appropriately monitored and enforced. More important, there is the growing realization that corporate leaders must strive to create and sustain a culture of integrity within their corporation. It is also now understood that senior leaders, including the CEO, must be vocal in visibly advocating and supporting such a culture or it will not be viewed as worthy of employee support. Without that culture, an atmosphere of trust cannot prevail in the workplace and many of the trends described here cannot come to fruition. Without trust in the workplace, innovation, loyalty, and shared commitment to corporate goals will be stultified at best. CEOs are now screened as to their "tone at the top," a phrase that describes their commitment to ethical principles that support a culture of integrity.

Increasing Concern for Physical and Psychological Aspects of Employment

In addition to higher expectations of fairness for actions, decision making, governance, and leadership processes, there is now greater respect for many physical and mental aspects of employment. For example, for decades there has been a trend toward improving the safety of working conditions, and the risks to health that employees were expected to take 50 or even 20 years ago are now relatively low.

But the more significant recent trend is the increasing sensitivity to the psychological concerns of employees, such as the concerns for:

- privacy and dignity, such as during substance-abuse testing;
- harassment, both sexual and otherwise;
- the ability to exercise their conscience (for example, to ignore or report decisions to pollute);
- quality of life balance, including family-friendly workplaces, smoking bans, etc.; and
- civility of expression and conduct.

These concerns spring from the public's view that the workplace should have values and policies that are acceptable to society at large, and that should mirror issues that society deems appropriate. In this context, as will be seen below, it is only with less frequency, and only with good cause, that the rights of employers are allowed to impinge upon the rights of employees.

Specific Employee Rights, Interests, and Concerns

Discrimination

Discrimination results from the prejudicial or negative treatment of an individual or group, or the preferential treatment of an individual or group over another. In either instance, an individual or group is disadvantaged relative to others, and is therefore treated unfairly.

This kind of treatment was once normal, but society has gradually become less tolerant of discrimination, and laws now exist to prevent it. Types of discrimination that have become illegal over time include: slavery; lower pay for women doing work equal to men; fewer opportunities for promotion for women than men; lower pay or job opportunities for black or coloured people, or based on

Society's changing attitudes toward discrimination have allowed women to pursue new career paths, and resulted in an African-American (Barack Obama) becoming president of the United States—something that would have been unthinkable a generation ago.

Source: iStock.

race or creed or age or sexual preference, unless there are carefully determined justifications involved.

It used to be that women were prevented from becoming police or firefighters, but within the past ten years, tests of strength, stamina, dexterity, and so on have been developed to provide reasonable thresholds for women to demonstrate that they can exceed to be hired. From the time of the slave trade until quite recently, black people or people of colour were considered by some to be too limited in intelligence or inferior and therefore not hired for certain jobs; but that is no longer the case and is ridiculous in hindsight. Non-discriminatory tests should be developed and universally applied to ensure that those who are not hired will not seek legal recourse against a company for what they see as unfair hiring practices. In addition, cases of discrimination can be identified in public blogs to the detriment of corporate reputation, even if no lawsuits are launched. Tests now applied to choose among applicants are subject to scrutiny, and employers need to adopt practices that manage their risks proactively.

Another instance of changed attitudes is discriminating against women who are pregnant. It is now considered unethical, and is illegal, to deprive pregnant women of pay increases or job opportunities because they are pregnant, or to discriminate against women who might become pregnant. Questioning women about their intentions to become pregnant is considered an invasion of privacy and could be taken as evidence of intent, at least, to discriminate. In Canada, pregnant women are allowed paid maternity leave to give birth, and have the right to return to their jobs when that leave is finished. Maternity leave comprises two weeks of unpaid leave and 15 weeks of paid (employment insurance) leave. In addition, the birth mother may also take up to 35 weeks of parental leave (which can be shared with the father), thus totalling a maximum 52-week leave for the birth mother. Adoption leave, which is referred to as "parental leave," allows each partner to share up to 35 weeks. Some employers also give men the right to paternity leave to help out when a new baby—by birth or adoption—arrives.

Dismissal

In earlier times, people could be fired or dismissed on a whim, or because they were pregnant, or a person of colour, or for whatever reason, which may or may not have been advanced. That time is long past, and fair treatment is now expected. Dismissal must now be for a real cause related to the employee's inability to perform their duties satisfactorily, or for causing a disruption in the workplace. To avoid lawsuits for improper dismissal, care must be taken to document these causes objectively and to ensure that the reasoning is sound, fair to the employee, and not biased.

When an employee is dismissed appropriately for cause, there may be contractual severance payments, but generally no other departure payments are expected.

Sometimes an employer will want to terminate an employee where no cause can be found. In that case, the employer can terminate the employee, but is required by law to give notice of termination to the employee and to provide a payment equivalent to the salary during the notice period. The employee may be required to work during the notice period.

Sometimes an employer cannot identify a legitimate cause for dismissal and decides to "encourage" a person to leave by mistreating them and/or by impinging on their ability to do their job. That person may then be considered to be "constructively dismissed" by those actions, and can sue for significant damages on the basis of constructive dismissal that can amount to up to one month's salary per year of employment, depending on the type of job, length of service, age of employee, and amount of salary.[2] It should be noted that the conditions necessary for constructive dismissal can be created knowingly or unknowingly, so employers often educate managers to minimize the risk involved, by making sure that she or he will not unknowingly cause a constructive dismissal of an employee by imposing restrictions or cutting off the capacity of the worker to do their job.

In summary, dismissal must be done fairly *for cause*, or with a legal notice period and pay, or else the employer will likely have to pay legal penalties to the employee.

Harassment—Sexual and Otherwise

Individuals now have the right not to be harassed in the workplace—sexually or otherwise. This right developed its current strength gradually and emerged in its current form in the mid-1990s.

Harassment occurs when someone directs improper behaviour at you that you find offensive, and that the other person knew, or should have known, was offensive. Several aspects of this definition are noteworthy, including that it is the aggrieved person who initially determines what is offensive, a perspective that is frequently upheld in later proceedings. What the giver of the harassment believes is or is not offensive usually does not matter unless the claim is deemed by human rights adjudicators to be in error. Many managers or other employees left unchecked by their superiors have found to their surprise that what they considered to be acceptable personal, or racial, or sexual references, or jokes, or behaviours (even if inadvertent) were considered offensive. Managers should also be aware that in disputes over potential harassment, the person with the power (the manager)

---

2   For junior-level employees, the rule of thumb is usually one week per year of service. For more senior employees, one month per year of service is more the norm. There is usually a statutory minimum of notice for employees of any level, which would start at one week of salary for one year of service.

is usually presumed to have been in control of the encounter and therefore responsible for the harassment charged. Many managers have found that a zero-tolerance policy avoided painful incidents and unfortunate surprises.

The most appropriate and practical approach is to educate all employees about unacceptable behaviour, and to institute policies that ensure zero tolerance. It is the responsibility of the company and ultimately the board of directors to ensure that there are effective policies and guidance in place, and that effective rapid action is taken on all reported instances of harassment to avoid legal action and loss of reputation. In fact, each company is expected to ensure that its workplace is free from harassment even if harassment occurs when employees are not in the company's buildings. For example, a salesperson calling on customers at their premises needs to be protected since the customer's offices are considered part of the salesperson's company's workplace. Reported harassment problems need to be acted upon by contacting the customer's executives as soon as possible.

Employees should also be educated to be always on guard against situations that could lead to spurious charges of sexual harassment in situations such as the case that opened the chapter. A fellow employee, or a student who is unhappy with his or her perceived treatment by a manager, counsellor, or teacher, can charge sexual or other harassment to get revenge. Unfortunately, although the individual charged may be innocent, the impact on the reputation of the person charged can take significant effort and time to reverse. Sometimes the individual charged never fully recovers.

Civility

Employees now expect to be treated *civilly*—that is, in accord with existing social norms—by their employer, and enlightened companies are doing so, although the expectation is not yet a right enforceable by law except for a few specific aspects, such as harassment or invasion of privacy. Employees who are not treated with civility, however, are frequently demotivated and likely to seek employment elsewhere. Prospective employees are unlikely to join a company if they find out that they will not be

- treated with dignity, courtesy, respect, politeness, and consideration;
- spoken to in tones that are appropriate for the circumstances;
- able to express contrary views;
- in an environment where conflicts are managed respectfully rather than confrontationally.[3]

---

3   See University of Toronto, "Human Resources Guideline on Civil Conduct," available at: http://www .hrandequity.utoronto.ca/Asset952.aspx?method=1.

Uncivil behaviour is a relatively new umbrella concept that includes such specific behaviour as:

- shouting;
- profanity, abusive, aggressive, or violent language directed at an individual or individuals;
- using props suggestive of violence;
- slamming doors;
- throwing objects;
- humiliating, degrading, demeaning, belittling, insulting, frightening, or intimidating another person;
- distributing comments about an individual, whether verbally or in writing, including online, that are unjustified and are likely to have a negative impact on the individual if he or she were to see them; and
- telling inappropriate jokes.[4]

Because of the growing sensitivity of employees, and of public displeasure at uncivil acts, leading-edge companies are creating codes[5] to guide behaviour and guard against problem activities and actors. Employees (particularly executives) showing a pattern of misbehaviour may be referred for professional counselling if they are thought worthy and likely to be responsive.

Privacy and Dignity

Privacy in the workplace context refers to the ability or right of an employee to keep information about themselves private, or within their control, and not to share it with their employer or the public. Privacy is related somewhat to *dignity*, which refers to an individual's right to receive respect and appropriate or ethical treatment, in that a breach of privacy may often lead to a loss of personal dignity or respect.

Generally, in North America, there is an understanding that an employee's personal or private information should not be accessed by a corporation unless the employer's interest is reasonable, legitimate, and morally acceptable. For example, an employer cannot ask for or access an individual's health data before or during employment unless it can be shown that the information is important to the role to be played within the organization or with society on behalf of the employer. It would not be appropriate for an employer to ask for stress test data as a condition for an office job, or for past illness data to avoid hiring those with high risks from

---

4   Ibid.

5   Ibid.

> ### MINI-CASE
>
> ## Misbehaving Boss Fired for Bullying Gets $25,000
>
> Sharon Rodrigues, the manager of a Dairy Queen restaurant in British Columbia, was fired on June 25, 2009 for "rudeness, swearing, bullying, insubordination, anger and tardiness." However, in a strange twist, she sued for wrongful dismissal and won $25,000. How could such an outcome occur?
>
> Sharon had been employed at the restaurant for 16 years by a total of four owners before receiving any formal indication that her work had been problematic. She was given a letter on June 24, 2009 outlining the allegations, and was put on probation with a review in four weeks. Nevertheless, she was fired abruptly one day later without any severance or other payments.
>
> The judge found that, while her behaviour was unacceptable, it did not represent a sufficient cause for immediate dismissal. Instead it was evidence of poor performance of her managerial role, which called for a warning and remediation. As described in a newspaper report of the incident, "[b]ecause the company had not challenged her conduct before the probation letter and did not give her a reasonable opportunity to improve herself after the letter was delivered, the judge concluded that [the employer] terminated Rodrigues without cause … . Taking into consideration her age (46), limited education, the availability of similar work, the nature of the employment and the years of service, [the judge] found that the appropriate notice period for the wrongful dismissal was 16 months." Her employer had made three offers to settle, which Rodrigues rejected. But because these offers were less than the judge awarded, her employer had to pay part of her legal and court costs as well as her salary for the 16-month notice period.
>
> What are the lessons to be learned from this case?
>
> Source: Adapted and with quotations from Sheryl Smolkin, "Misbehaving boss fired for bullying gets $25,000," *The Toronto Star*, October 10, 2011, B7. Accessed October 17, 2011. http://www .moneyville.ca/blog/post/1060394---bullying-boss-fired-for-insubordination-gets-25-000.

a pension perspective. On the other hand, psychological or substance abuse testing before and during employment may be acceptable where the position involves working in high-stress environments or provides ready access to drugs or alcohol, or where machinery is being operated that could risk the lives of the individual or others. Similarly, an employer cannot begin surveillance (by camera or in person) of employees unless there is a compelling reason, such as trying to stop instances of drug use or sale, intimidation, or physical abuse. Monitoring for efficiency is not usually considered a compelling reason. It is wise, however, to consult a lawyer before instituting tests or surveillance in order to be apprised of the local legality of the actions planned. Penalties for invasion of privacy can be severe.

It is also important for employers, even where an invasion of privacy is authorized, to inform employees, where practicable, about the testing or surveillance plan and obtain their consent. Sometimes employers have informed employees about a test immediately before it takes place, and have not allowed any time for reflection before requiring submission, or have given an ultimatum such as "take the test or leave our employ." Unless the employees know of the plan in advance and consent to it after being given a reasonable period of time to reflect on a set of reasonable choices, the employer's action may be judged as lacking *informed consent*, and legal penalties may be applied. On the other hand, an employer may introduce a program of random testing if appropriate notice is provided, the nature of the work legally warrants the tests, and remedial action is judged reasonable.

Moreover, in the case of a substance abuse testing program, employers should be prepared to preserve the dignity of employees who test positive by repeating the test to make sure the result is not a *false positive*, and by keeping the first result confidential until it is confirmed. The loss of reputation that an employer may incur can be significant, as well as the charges of defamation of character.

Employees also need to be careful not to take advantage of employer rights. For example, they should not presume that they have the right to use company assets for personal matters without authorization or reference to company policy. Employees should also not presume that it is appropriate to use their work computers for their own private work, or for browsing illicit websites and downloading materials from them. Employees are increasingly finding that employers are within their rights to inspect and review company computers, including personal emails. Similarly, employees should be wary of using company phones for personal calls because their presumption of privacy for such use is not well founded.

Employers that violate an employee's rights to privacy and dignity pay a steep price financially and reputationally, and also because the *trust relationship* between employer and employee may be damaged beyond repair. Trust is critical for sustained high performance, and for employee cooperation, retention, participation in innovation programs, and tolerance when issues arise that negatively affect their expectations. The reverse is also true—employers who show continued respect for their employees' rights to privacy and dignity can achieve competitively high levels of trust and loyalty. Although employers will always be tempted to exercise their perceived power over employees, they need to be constantly aware that they are very vulnerable to overstepping and invading the privacy or undermining the dignity of their employees, thus triggering consequences that may not be evident for some time.

Health and Safety Risks

Employees have the right to expect that they will not be harmed in their workplace, and that they will be told of any abnormal risks, whether they are apparent or not. This represents a considerable change from the 1940s and 1950s in North America, when employees could be ordered to undertake risky activities or to work in environments in which air quality was poor, or even hazardous, and conditions were so unsafe that employees had to be lucky to finish without harm. Working conditions have been subject to increasing regulation for decades and workplaces are much changed from the days when employees were just glad to have a job and were thus willing to assume dangerous risks to their health and safety.

Harmful conditions continue to exist outside of North America, although the efforts of activists have raised public awareness, caused customer boycotts, and developed international performance standards and audit protocols in such areas as sweat-shop labour, child labour, and unsafe mines or factories. But problem areas still exist, such as the production of "blood diamonds" in unsafe mines in oppressive regimes. Another hotly debated issue remains the continuing sale of the cancer-causing mineral asbestos from Canada—where it is tightly restricted—to factories in India, where regulations and employee awareness are minimal. Companies should be aware that their reputations may be damaged by continued activities or relationships with employers that do not adhere to North American standards and expectations.

Quality of Life and Work–Life Balance

The growing concern for improved quality of life has affected not only employees' expectations for their health and safety, but also the time they want to spend away from work with family and friends, or on personal pursuits. In growing numbers, employees are resisting spending time on work that is well beyond what is expected as a normal workweek in their chosen occupation. If they are asked to work overtime, they are likely to expect overtime payment rather than working the extra time out of a sense of duty, because they are putting an ever-higher valuation on their leisure time. Even so, employees are now more likely to refuse extra-hour work even if paid at a premium, if the total number of hours exceeds a reasonable level that impinges on their needed leisure and/or family time. The reasonable level involved varies depending on the region and job or profession involved. Employees, even in professions such as accounting or law, have a higher regard for their quality of life—and the work–life balance that involves—than ever before, and corporations that are not mindful of these changed expectations will probably lose employees who have other attractive options, as well as losing the cooperation of those who remain.

Ability to Exercise One's Conscience

One of the emerging trends in employee expectations is the desire for employees to exercise their conscience—to not dump hazardous waste irresponsibly, to speak up against the unethical treatment of employees or customers or other stakeholders, or to refuse to bribe or commit other illegal or unethical acts. In many jurisdictions, individual employees can themselves be charged for illegal acts such as dumping hazardous waste, and can no longer successfully use the "loyal agent" or "Nuremberg" defence, in which an employee claims that "my boss told me to" or "I was just following orders."

It is also evident to employees who are deterred from exercising their conscience that their employer either doesn't care about their views, or perhaps has some illicit reason for endorsing the practice in question. In either case, doubt may be raised in the minds of employees about the *ethicality of their employer*. Sometimes, however, it is their *boss's* lack of ethics they are seeing, not the company's, but they are unlikely to identify the difference unless there is a protected ethics inquiry service for them to consult. Such an inquiry service would also be useful in identifying problems and heading off those instances where the exercise of employee conscience would cause significant problems for the company and for society.

Whistleblowing: Frill or Necessity?

"Blowing the whistle"—reporting questionable acts to someone within the organization, to the press, or to outside authorities—is a specific case of exercising one's conscience that has recently gained prominence. Enlightened directors and management have been encouraging whistleblowing for more than ten years because they have realized that they cannot be everywhere and hear all problems, so they need the cooperation of employees to report when questionable acts are being planned or are in progress. This encouragement, along with the creation of whistleblower mechanisms (including protection programs), has become an important aspect of sound, modern, risk-management programs.

In addition, after the Enron, Arthur Andersen, and WorldCom governance and reporting breakdowns—which gave rise to the "credibility crisis" and spawned remedial legislation in the form of the *Sarbanes-Oxley Act of 2002* (SOX) in the United States—corporations wishing to raise funds in the United States (including the largest 250 firms in Canada) must now install the whistleblowing mechanisms necessary to keep their boards of directors apprised of unethical acts related to financial matters. Consequently, for most large companies, whistleblowing mechanisms are not frills—they are now a necessity.

Even so, most people have been raised not to "tell" on anyone. As they grew up, they were taught that tattletales were despicable and deserved to be called "rats" or "snitches." Moreover, prior to the advent of protected whistleblower programs, most whistleblowers found that they were stigmatized by their bosses and colleagues, and often denied promotion and fired. This means that a company must do what it can to reverse the general cultural bias against telling on colleagues and encourage inquiries for clarification. Experience suggests that roughly 50 percent of the calls to hotlines, set up as a focal point to whistleblowing mechanisms making it easier for employees to blow the whistle, are from callers wanting clarification on the ethicality of acts, so it follows that without such a reporting/inquiry point, many questions will go unanswered and problematic acts will take place.

Even with a focal point for reporting, organizations must commit to a fair, speedy investigation (that is, to a fair process and treatment); otherwise, reporting calls will be minimal. This need for fair, due process means that the nature of the hotline or reporting centre needs to ensure that it signals values that will engender trust and attract reports. Companies sometimes find that lawyer-staffed hotlines are considered by some employees to be neither as fair, nor their actions as transparent, as their employees would prefer.

Autocratic or Democratic Management Styles

For decades, a debate has been under way about whether an *autocratic* (or "top-down" command) or *democratic* (participative or input-encouraged) management style should be adopted. Although each may be needed in different settings, it is noteworthy that the democratic style of management is a better fit with most of the trends and specific issues discussed above.

Conclusion

The rights and expectations of workers have increasingly been gaining respect from both the public and employers, and employment laws have provided minimum levels of treatment. In general, employee treatment is fairer, safer, healthier, and more ethical. Where the employer used to be almost omnipotent, the legal and reputational repercussions of poor or unfair employee treatment are now likely to be severe and lingering. However, the positive aspects of fair, ethical treatment of employees are now much better understood. In the longer term, the interests of employees and employers in fair and reasonable treatment are increasingly seen as synergistic, not corrosive. To assure their status as good corporate citizens and attractive places to work, employers should scrupulously respect not only existing employee rights, but also employee and societal expectations likely to affect their future.

DISCUSSION QUESTIONS

1. Several trends in employee treatment are identified in this chapter. What are they, and are there dangers if these trends continue?
2. Whistleblower protection programs can be very useful, but how can abuse be prevented, such as false anonymous reporting to stigmatize a colleague who is competing for a promotion?
3. Should the standards of reasonable behaviour be more lax for a woman who harasses a man than for a man who harasses a woman?

SUGGESTED READINGS AND ONLINE RESOURCES

Canadian Employment Law Today. http://www.employmentlawtoday.com.

Human Resources and Skills Development Canada. http://www.hrsdc.gc.ca/eng/labour/index.shtml. See tabs on employment standards, equality, etc.

Kerns, C.D. 2003. Creating and sustaining an ethical workplace culture. *Graziado Business Review* 3: 3. http://gbr.pepperdine.edu/2010/08/Creating-and-Sustaining-an-Ethical-Workplace-Culture/.

REFERENCES

Brooks, L.J., and D. Selley. 2008. *Ethics and governance: Developing and maintaining an ethical corporate culture*. 3rd ed. Toronto: Canadian Centre for Ethics & Corporate Policy.

Brooks, L.J., and P. Dunn. 2012. *Business and professional ethics for directors, executives and accountants*. 6th ed. Mason, OH: South-Western, Cengage Learning.

Financial Reporting and Ethics

Case Study: ABCCo

The following is based on a true story. The names have been changed to protect the guilty.

Hugh's stomach lurched as the doorbell rang. He knew who it was; he had just seen the breaking news on TV: "Top executives of ABCCo arrested in massive accounting fraud." Hugh thought he had avoided this day by leaving the company two years ago.

The story began when Hugh met Jeb at a university in the western United States, where they were both studying business—Jeb in management, Hugh in accounting. Hugh pegged Jeb as someone who would succeed. Jeb was very competitive; he did not accept losing. But he was also smart and naturally gregarious. Hugh marvelled at Jeb's ability to sell just about anything to anyone. Though Hugh shared Jeb's competitive nature, he was not as outgoing. Hugh was a bit quieter and more conservative.

Hugh and Jeb went their separate ways at graduation. But their paths crossed again many years later when Hugh took a job with a large health-care company. Jeb had been working there for a year. They got together frequently to commiserate about their jobs in middle management. Both were dissatisfied and felt that they could run a similar organization more successfully with a better business model. After a few years of learning the business and planning their own, they took that leap of faith—they founded ABCCo, their own health-care business. With his leadership and sales skills, Jeb took the position of CEO, whereas Hugh was a natural fit as the CFO, having obtained his certified public accountant's licence (the equivalent of a chartered accountant in Canada) while working for a Big Four accounting firm. Hugh thought they were a great executive team with complementary skills.

Things went quite well for ABCCo. In its first five years of operation, ABCCo's income grew by an average of 22 percent each year (starting with a growth spurt of 36 percent from its first to second year, followed by growth rates of 22, 17, and 13 percent in each successive year). Though this growth rate was admirable, both men knew they could grow the company at a faster pace if only they could access more financing. After six years as a private company, they took the company public, offering it on the NASDAQ stock exchange. The troubling thing for Hugh was that, during the initial public offering (IPO) discussions, Jeb promised the underwriters, key investors, and financial analysts that the company would grow by 25 percent *every year* for the foreseeable future. Hugh felt uncomfortable with this promise. He believed that they could meet a 25 percent growth rate on average, but he didn't see how they could meet it every single year. Despite his misgivings, he said nothing because he trusted Jeb's foresight and confidence. Besides, Hugh was riding high—the company he co-founded was in the big time!

The problems started immediately after the company went public. Each quarter, Hugh would take the preliminary financial statements to Jeb to review together. Jeb wasn't a professional accountant like Hugh, but he knew accounting well enough. Instead of reviewing the activity in the financial statements, Jeb would calculate how much the company "should" grow, based on the 25 percent promised growth rate, and discuss ways they could change the numbers to meet that target. During the first year, they were behind by a small amount and it was easy to re-calculate estimates like bad debt, warranty, or pension expenses (acceptable within accounting rules) to reach their target. For example, they changed their earlier estimate of uncollectible credit sales from 3 to 2 percent. This change, within ac-ceptable accounting rules, would decrease expenses, thus increasing income for the period. As he made these changes, Hugh didn't argue with Jeb. But with each quarter's reports, the company got farther and farther behind Jeb's expectations and it became more difficult to meet Jeb's quarterly earnings targets by just tweak-ing estimates. And the estimates were becoming a bit too aggressive. Soon they wouldn't pass muster with the auditors.

During the company's second year as a publicly traded organization, Hugh found it nearly impossible to make the numbers "work." He and Jeb began to argue vehemently. Hugh realized that Jeb wasn't going to accept anything less than meeting the 25 percent growth rate he had promised the world. Hugh began to falsify transactions to increase current income. Because he knew how the auditors performed their annual audit procedures, he knew how to create false sales trans-actions and hide them so they wouldn't be detected. Hugh was torn about doing this. On the one hand, he was so proud of the successful company he had built that he felt he was helping the company and its employees. On the other hand, he knew he was committing fraud. He found it hard to sleep at night. He started drinking.

In the third year of the company's public trading, Hugh made the gut-wrenching decision to leave his beloved company. It was very difficult, but he decided to take early retirement and he found part-time work to keep himself occupied. He lost his love for his work, but at least he could sleep at night … or so he thought.

The end of the story: After his arrest, Hugh agreed to testify against Jeb in exchange for a lighter sentence. The trial was long and gruelling, after which Hugh spent several months in prison. He now spends his time on the speaking circuit, sharing his experience in the hopes that others will learn from it.

What Is the Issue?

Top executives of publicly traded organizations often feel intense pressure to meet earnings targets, whether they set those targets themselves or financial analysts set the targets. If an organization fails to meet earnings targets, its stock price usually drops, the executives may be perceived by the market as incompetent, and they might miss out on bonuses. Given this pressure, the issue is *whether or how financial statements can be "true and fair" representations of the organization's financial performance rather than a "managed" view of its performance.*

Before discussing this case, it is helpful to review some background about financial reporting.

The Role of Financial Reporting

Corporations—and virtually all organizations, for that matter—must "account" for their activities. This is especially true when stakeholders are not nearby and can't easily access information about the organization, as is the case with publicly held organizations. All stakeholders, which include current investors and creditors, as well as potential business partners, employees, or the government, have a right to information about the organization's current financial status and how well it is performing. The organization itself obviously wants all stakeholders to have this information; without it, the organization would not gain access to financing. Financial statements are the key mechanism for meeting stakeholders' need for information.

Organizations that are publicly held, or traded on a stock exchange such as the Toronto Stock Exchange (TSX), must issue financial statements quarterly and annually. A complete set of financial statements usually consists of the following separate statements:

1. *Balance sheet*: reports the current financial status of the organization, through assets (what the organization owns), liabilities (what the organization owes others), and equity (the shareholders' claims to the organization);
2. *Income statement*: reports how well the organization performed during the period; revenues minus expenses results in the income for the period;
3. *Statement of cash flows*: reports what the organization did with cash coming in and going out; and

4. *Statement of Changes in Shareholder Equity:* reports changes in the capital or owner's investments in the organization.

Together, these statements provide useful information to virtually all stakeholders. For example, a banker who extended a loan to the organization might be interested in the statement of cash flows, to determine how the organization is using its cash and whether it is in a position to easily pay off the loan. An investor might be especially interested in the income statement because income often has a direct impact on the organization's stock price. A long-term investor might also be interested in studying the balance sheet to understand the organization's current and potential future financial status. Other stakeholders might be interested in simply knowing that the organization remains a viable business.

Ensuring High-Quality Financial Reporting

Financial statements can be of poor quality—in other words, inaccurate or misleading—due to error or fraud. Though the definitions of error and fraud are clear, distinguishing one from the other is not so easy. An error is an unintentional misstatement. If an error is found, the financial statements must be reissued with the correct information. As long as the corrections are made in a timely manner, no laws are violated. Fraud is an *intentional misrepresentation in the financial statements, whether by commission or omission.* Financial statements that contain intentionally false information represent fraud by commission. Financial statements that do not contain the information they should represent fraud by omission. If a fraud is found, not only must the financial statements be reissued with the correct information, but the organization and its executives may be prosecuted in criminal, or civil court.

Because the definitions of error and fraud seem clear, how do ethics apply to financial reporting? Some argue that unethical behaviour lies somewhere in between error and fraud. That is, they think of the quality of financial statements as being along a continuum from honest and error-free (highest quality), through various levels of severity of unethical reporting, to blatant fraudulent reporting (lowest quality). Because accounting rules allow for discretion, the more opportunistic executives are with that discretion, the more unethical the resulting reporting. In this light, fraud represents an extreme case of unethical behaviour. Others view the distinction more simply, and in only one of two ways: error or fraud. If an error is caught and fixed, there is no violation. If intentional misrepresentations are found, but the financial statements are within the law or accounting rules, that is acceptable. In this view, ethicality is irrelevant—there is no grey area (Knechel et al. 2007).

How can stakeholders be assured that the organization's financial statements do not contain any significant errors or fraud? For one thing, most organizations have a board of directors and a subcommittee of the board (an *audit committee*) that is responsible for overseeing the process of producing accurate financial statements. Second, publicly held organizations are required to issue audited financial statements. Every year, auditors are hired to determine whether the financial statements are free of material misstatements, and whether the misstatements are a result of error or fraud. Third, an organization's financial statements can be subject to scrutiny by regulatory agencies such as the Ontario Securities Commission or the US Securities and Exchange Commission. Even before financial statements get to these levels of oversight, however, the road to high-quality financial reporting begins within the organization itself (Knechel et al. 2007).

SIDEBAR

What Is an Audit?

An audit ascertains the reliability or validity of information. The most common is the financial statement audit. Every year, the organization hires an independent *external auditor* (a public accounting firm) to render an opinion on the financial statements. If the auditor does not find significant errors or fraud, the *audit opinion* states that the financial statements present, in all material respects, a true and fair picture of the organization's condition and activity for the year, in accordance with international financial reporting standards.

Additionally, many organizations hire *internal auditors* as permanent employees. Internal auditors typically report to the highest levels within the organization and perform a wide variety of audit functions. They usually assist the external auditor in the audit of the financial statements, while also performing audits of selected departments for efficiency, effectiveness, fraud, or compliance.

Fraud Triangle

The fraud triangle can be a useful tool for understanding the likelihood that financial statements may contain fraud or significant errors. According to the fraud triangle, three conditions affect the likelihood of fraud: (1) opportunity, (2) motivation, and (3) attitude/rationalization. If all three conditions are present, it is very likely that fraud exists within the financial statements (IAASB 2009; Murphy and Dacin 2011).[1]

---

1   Though the fraud triangle is used to assess the risk of fraud only, not error, I include a discussion of the risk of error as well. Implementing good internal controls is the best way to reduce the risk of errors. Thus, I discuss internal controls, within the opportunity section, as a way to reduce both fraud and errors.

Figure 14.1   The Fraud Triangle

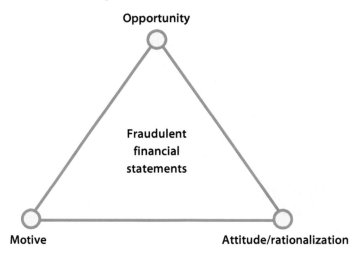

Opportunity

Opportunity exists when a person perceives that she or he has the ability to perpetrate a fraud *and* get away with it. For example, a manager of a division may perceive that she could create false sales transactions and enter them into the accounting system with no one knowing. Or the top finance/accounting executive could order a subordinate to make accounting "adjustments" without being questioned. Opportunity is usually thwarted by instituting strong internal controls. Those same internal controls also prevent errors from reaching the financial statements.

Components of Internal Control

To implement strong internal controls, it is important to use a framework that is congruent with other key management goals and objectives. The Committee of Sponsoring Organizations (COSO)[2] developed an internal control framework now used by many organizations around the world (COSO 1992). This framework describes five interrelated components that work together to form a comprehensive system of internal controls:

---

2   The Committee of Sponsoring Organizations of the Treadway Commission (COSO) was established in 1985 with the goal of providing thought leadership in three interrelated areas: (1) enterprise risk management, (2) internal control, and (3) fraud deterrence. Its internal control framework is used by organizations worldwide (COSO 1992).

1. the control environment
2. risk assessment
3. control activities
4. information and communication
5. monitoring

These five components must work together for effective internal control. Each is discussed briefly here.

Good internal controls must begin with a strong control environment. The control environment is defined as the "tone at the top" and consists of top management's integrity, ethical values, philosophy, and operating style. This tone sets expectations for employees. If management doesn't take internal controls seriously, employees won't either. The control environment also includes the way management assigns authority and responsibility to employees and the way it develops employees. Thus, the control environment not only helps set expectations for all employees, it provides the discipline and structure within which all employees perform their jobs. Many people argue that the control environment is the most important element of internal control because, without it, the remaining four elements will not be sufficient to prevent fraud.

Every organization faces risks from both inside and outside the organization. Risk assessment is the identification of risks that may cause the organization to fail to achieve an objective. To enable the company to achieve the objective of issuing high-quality financial statements, management assesses where the greatest risks are and implements controls best suited for reducing those risks. For example, if an organization's inventory consists of expensive and easily stolen items, then management would likely deem the warehouse a source of increased risk of theft. If the inventory is subject to a great deal of valuation fluctuation, management should emphasize controls over the process of adjusting inventory values within the accounting department. Risks vary a great deal from organization to organization. Management must prioritize risks because it would be too costly to implement strong internal controls over absolutely everything. Risks should be reassessed and reprioritized often in today's fast-paced business environment.

Once risks are identified, management must put control activities in place. These include physical safeguards, required approvals or authorization, segregation of duties, reconciliations, and reviews of operation performance. Following the same examples above, there are many control activities that management would likely implement to safeguard expensive inventory. Management might require password entry into the warehouse; only employees needing access to the warehouse would be issued a password, and a monitoring system would log every entry and exit. Cameras might be installed. Inventory counts would be scheduled at regular intervals, and possibly on a surprise basis. For the risk of valuation fluctuations, management may implement segregation of duties and/or an approval system. For example, one person within the accounting group might perform the valuation calculations, while another reviews and approves it, and a third person actually makes the adjusting entry. The choices of control activities are almost endless, but they must be reasonable, cost effective, and work well within the organization's structure. In essence, management performs a cost–benefit analysis of control activities for the associated risk. Areas of greater risk will have more control activities, and perhaps more elaborate control activities associated with them. Areas of high risk may even have redundant or backup controls in place so that if an error or fraud is not caught by one control, then it may be caught by the second or third control.

For the internal controls to work properly, communication of information must be ongoing both up and down the chain of command. Information must be identified, gathered, and communicated in a useable form and a timely manner. This idea applies not only within the organization, but outside it as well. For example, some organizations automatically link their inventory ordering system with a vendor's sales system, so they can order inventory immediately and seamlessly without formal communication (often referred to as just-in-time [JIT] inventory ordering using electronic data interchange [EDI] communications). The vendors with whom the organization partners must understand some of the organization's control activities to work smoothly together.

Finally, the system of internal controls would not work properly without continuous monitoring. Monitoring includes assessing the quality of the system's performance over time. The strongest internal control systems are updated and improved regularly to fix actual and potential problems, and to adjust to changes in the environment. Monitoring can be performed within each department, by a compliance department, or by internal auditors.

These five components of internal control are essential to a well-run organization that produces high-quality financial statements. However, it is important to note that internal controls are rarely foolproof. They do not provide 100 percent assurance that the financial statements are accurate; they provide only reasonable assurance. Also, to effectively reduce perceived opportunity and the potential for error, internal controls should not be so onerous that employees find a way around them. And top executives always have the ability to override or ignore controls. After all, who else is left to approve a directive from the CEO?

Motive

A motive is a reason to commit fraud, usually in the form of an incentive or pressure (IAASB 2009). Incentives are often financial. The term "greed" has been used a great deal to describe perpetrators' motives for committing financial statement fraud. Greed is a powerful incentive. For example, executives may receive a bonus or additional stock options if they issue financial statements that meet earnings targets. But incentives can also be social. That is, executives may feel that their reputation as good leaders is heightened when they report solid performance in the financial statements.

Pressure can come from external or internal sources. For example, shareholders of an organization may put pressure on the executives to increase the organization's stock price. Executives know that if earnings, as reported in the financial statements, do not meet the market's expectations, the organization's stock price will fall. Internal pressure is the opposite of the social incentive discussed in the previous paragraph. Executives may feel that their reputation as good leaders will be harmed if they issue financial statements that fail to meet expectations (Graham et al. 2005). Whether the pressure comes from external or internal sources, it tends to "flow downhill." That is, executives who feel this pressure will place the same degree of pressure on their subordinates, who will place pressure on their subordinates, and so on.

In the previous section, two examples of perceived opportunity were described. Here, I provide examples of a related motive for each:

- A manager of a division may perceive that she could create false sales transactions and enter them into the accounting system without anyone knowing. She may have an incentive to do so if her bonus is tied to the division's sales reports. She may feel pressure to do so to meet a certain sales target or else lose her job.
- The top finance/accounting executive could tell a subordinate to make accounting "adjustments" without being questioned. He may use this perceived opportunity to present a picture of the organization that is more positive than it actually is. He may be motivated to make himself appear to be a successful executive and leader.

Attitude/Rationalization

Because they exist within the mind, both an attitude and a rationalization are difficult to observe (Hogan et al. 2005). However, behaviour and speech can be indicators (Murphy and Dacin 2011). With regard to *attitude*, certain individuals may be "predisposed" to commit fraud. For example, psychopaths would not hesitate to commit fraud if the opportunity and motive are present. How do we identify such individuals? One way is to ask potential employees to complete a series of psychology tests. If that is not feasible, prior behaviour may be an indicator. Someone who has been in trouble with regulators or law enforcement is more likely to have an attitude favourable to committing fraud or to taking rules too lightly. Luckily, most people consider themselves to be ethical, and thus do not have an attitude that favours committing fraud. However, rationalization appears to be a different story.

Rationalization is something we do when we contemplate or commit an un-ethical act. We rationalize the unethical act to avoid or reduce the bad feelings that accompany it (Murphy and Dacin 2011). For example, let's say we receive a significant amount of change back in error from a department store, and we decide to keep it. We might argue that the store is a large organization that won't miss the extra money. We might argue that the store charges high prices and owes us money. We might argue that we are university students who need money for school—a worthy cause. All these arguments, whether true or not, are rationalizations. They allow us to act unethically but still feel fine about it. There are six categories of rationalization:

1. Shifting the blame: "Everyone does it."
2. Pleading ignorance: "I don't see that I'm hurting anyone."
3. Moral justification: "I'm protecting the company ... the employees ... my family ..."
4. Advantageous comparison: "This is nothing compared to ..."
5. Letting the victim take the fall: "They had it coming."
6. Euphemistic labelling: "I am trying to level the playing field."

Hearing someone use a rationalization might be a psychological red flag for fraud. Hearing yourself using a rationalization should make you think twice before acting.

In cases where executives knowingly issued fraudulent financial statements, the first three rationalizations have been used (Murphy and Dacin 2011). Executives have argued: (1) Everyone does it—it is a cost of doing business; (2) They didn't think they were hurting anyone (at least when the misreporting began); or (3) They were saving the company and the employees' jobs. Many of them also viewed the misreporting as being temporary in the beginning. They planned to fix the fraud—by issuing future financial statements that corrected the fraud—when economic conditions improved. Unfortunately, conditions don't always improve, which is why cases of fraudulent reporting are more prevalent during tough economic times.

Fraud Triangle Summary

The fraud triangle is useful in identifying conditions within the organization that indicate an increased risk of fraud. For the purposes of our discussion, the presence of these three conditions leads to a higher risk of poor-quality financial reporting.

Top management, specifically the chief executive officer (CEO) and chief financial officer (CFO), are responsible for the organization's financial reporting, before the reports get to the audit committee of the board of directors and the auditors. The CEO and CFO are responsible for ensuring proper incentives for employees—incentives that encourage performance and not unethical behaviour. The CEO and CFO are primarily responsible for the internal controls that ensure that errors or fraud do not become part of the financial statements.

Finally, they are in charge of their own attitudes/rationalizations and they should be aware of the employees' as well. It is important to identify these conditions before a fraud begins, because once someone commits fraud and gets away with it, he or she usually continues it at higher and higher levels.

The Role of Ethical Culture

The ethical culture within the organization deserves more discussion. Earlier in this chapter, reference was made to the control environment, or the "tone at the top" as an important part of strong internal controls. As you recall, internal controls help reduce the opportunity to commit fraud. However, because of the fundamental importance of the culture of the organization, it deserves to have its own dimension in the fraud triangle—perhaps a fraud pyramid—or at least be explicitly considered within each side of the current fraud triangle (Murphy et al. 2011).

Top management is responsible for setting the proper tone within the organization—a tone or culture that encourages ethical behaviour and discourages unethical behaviour. This often starts with being good role models, by acting ethically themselves. But it has to go further. Top management often creates a code of ethical conduct for the organization. It has to go further there as well. Top management has to take action—action witnessed by employees—to show its commitment to ethical behaviour. For example, management often institutes a whistle-blowing system whereby employees can anonymously report unethical or fraudulent behaviour (for more on whistleblowing, see Chapter 13, "The Individual in the Workplace"). As part of that system, management needs to report back to employees on how the process is *actually*, not theoretically, working, so that employees feel they can trust the system. When an employee is caught behaving unethically, other employees need to see that the offender is punished appropriately. In sum, actions speak louder than words. An ethical culture cannot exist solely on paper; it must exist in daily activity.

General Mills, a global food giant, is known for taking codes of conduct seriously.[3] All employees receive a detailed code of conduct and are reminded of it

---

3   See http://www.generalmills.com/Responsibility/ethics_and_integrity/Code_of_conduct.aspx.

with posters and messages. They take training classes in which ethical dilemmas that may occur in their particular jobs are discussed. Periodically, employees receive reports of the outcomes of investigations into questionable behaviour that is reported through their free and anonymous ethical hotline, and sometimes employees are given an award for ethical behaviour. In sum, the company sets clear expectations, rewards ethical behaviour, punishes unethical behaviour, and is transparent about it.

Summary

Financial statements provide valuable information to many individuals and organizations. Fraudulent financial statements can cause devastating losses for investors, creditors, and employees. Corporate governance mechanisms are in place to ensure high-quality financial statements, including internal controls within the organization, a financial statement review by the board of directors, audits by independent auditors, and oversight by regulators. Despite all this, financial statements can still be of lower quality or fraudulent.

The fraud triangle is a helpful tool for analyzing whether an organization's financial statements are fraudulent. The three sides of the fraud triangle are: (1) opportunity, (2) motivation, and (3) attitude or rationalization. The presence of these three conditions leads to a higher risk of poor-quality financial reporting. The fraud triangle can be used not only for detecting financial statement fraud, but also for preventing it. For example, if members of the board of directors notice that economic times are tough and that it will be nearly impossible for the organization to meet earnings targets, they should take action *before* the financial statements are prepared. They should remind the CEO and CFO of the importance of the ethical culture of the organization, which includes issuing accurate financial statements. They could neutralize potential rationalizations that the CEO or CFO might use, for example, by telling them that they would not be viewed as less competent for not meeting earnings targets.

To produce high-quality financial statements, many things are required. First, checks and balances must be in place, including strong internal controls, an active board of directors, and an independent financial statement auditor. Second, executives should instill an ethical culture within the organization. Third, executives and all employees should be aware of the fraud triangle, especially how easy it is to rationalize unethical behaviour, thus dimming their judgment.

DISCUSSION QUESTIONS

1. Is it ethical to manipulate accounting numbers for the sole purpose of meeting a target income, even when such manipulation is within the law and accounting rules?
2. Given the facts of the case, analyze whether each condition of the fraud triangle is present for Jeb and for Hugh. Discuss the specific motives, opportunities, or attitudes/rationalizations each man may have had in this situation.
3. Describe the alternatives available to Hugh at the time Jeb first told him to alter the financial statements. What is the likely outcome of each alternative?
4. What would you have done if you had been Hugh? Why?

SUGGESTED READINGS AND ONLINE RESOURCES

Bakan, J. 2005. *The corporation*. New York: Penguin.

The corporation. 2003. http://www.thecorporation.com/index.cfm?page_id=46.

Enron: The smartest guys in the room. 2005. http://www.imdb.com/title/tt1016268/.

Henderson, S. 2006. Corporate fraud still flourishing. *CA Magazine*. March.

Inside job. 2010. http://www.imdb.com/title/tt1645089/.

Lewis, M. 2010. *The big short: Inside the doomsday machine*. New York: Norton.

McLean, B., and P. Elkind. 2004. *The smartest guys in the room: The amazing rise and scandalous fall of Enron*. New York: Portfolio.

REFERENCES

Committee of Sponsoring Organizations of the Treadway Commission (COSO). 1992. *Internal control-integrated framework*. From http://www.coso.org/IC.htm.

Graham, J.R., C.R. Harvey, and S. Rajgopal. 2005. The economic implications of corporate financial reporting. *Journal of Accounting and Economics* 40 (1–3): 3–73.

Hogan, C.E., Z. Rezaee, R.A. Riley Jr., and U.K. Velury. 2008. Financial statement fraud: Insights from the academic literature. *Auditing: A Journal of Practice & Theory* 27 (2): 231–252.

International Auditing and Assurance Standards Board (IAASB). 2009. *The auditor's responsibilities relating to fraud in an audit of financial statements*. International Standard on Auditing 240. New York: IAASB.

Knechel, W.R., S.E. Salterio, and B. Ballou. 2007. *Auditing assurance and risk*. 3rd ed. Mason, OH: Thomson Higher Education.

Murphy, P.R., and M.T. Dacin. 2011. Psychological pathways to fraud: Understanding and preventing fraud in organizations. *Journal of Business Ethics* 101: 601–618.

Murphy, P.R., C. Free, and C. Branston. 2011. The role of ethical climate in fraud. Working paper. Queen's University.

Marketing Ethics

Case Study: TanzaFooty Soccer Trading Cards in Tanzania*

Introduction

As the summer of 2011 was coming to a close, Nilesh Virani was debating whether to move from his hometown of Vancouver to Tanzania to pursue his business idea of starting TanzaFooty, a line of soccer trading cards featuring players from Tanzania (the term "footy" is short for "football," the common term for soccer in much of the world). Four months earlier, Virani had graduated from a business program at a prominent Canadian university and was keen to start his own business.

In the back of his mind, he wondered whether it was a good idea to invest time and money in TanzaFooty. At school, he had been introduced to Professor C.K. Prahalad's book, *The Fortune at the Bottom of the Pyramid*, and was convinced that the next big opportunity lay in large underserved markets. Was TanzaFooty one of those opportunities? After spending the better part of the summer thinking about whether to launch the business, it was time to decide: go or no go?

Tanzania

Tanzania bordered the Indian Ocean with Kenya to the north and Mozambique to the south and had a population of 42.7 million. The country was relatively

---

* This case was written by Jordan Mitchell to provide discussion only. Some information has been disguised to protect confidentiality. It is not the intention of the author to illustrate effective or ineffective handling of the situation or to comment on any prevailing laws, government policy, or company and industry practices. The author would like to acknowledge Peggy Cunningham and Andrew Quinlan in the development of this case.

young, with 42 percent of the population under 14 years old (9 million male and 8.9 million female). GDP per person was estimated to be US $1,400, with Tanzania ranked 201st out of 227 countries. The minimum monthly government wage was 137,820 TZS (Tanzanian shillings), about US $83 per month (or US $996 per year). Fifty-five percent of households had a modern roof, 35 percent had modern walls, and 13 percent had electricity (CIA 2004; United Republic of Tanzania, National Bureau of Statistics 2010).

Soccer in Tanzania

Soccer was Tanzania's most popular sport. The country's top soccer organization was called the Tanzanian Premier League and had 14 teams. Over the past ten years, nearly all of the championship games had been won by the country's two biggest clubs, both located in the capital, Dar es Salaam: Young Africans (nicknamed "Yanga") and Simba Sports Club.

At a national level, the Tanzanian national football team had yet to qualify for the World Cup finals. Many Tanzanian soccer players were playing for teams in other countries as diverse as Bolivia, Norway, China, the United Kingdom, and Canada.

Idea for TanzaFooty Cards

Nilesh Virani was born in Vancouver in 1988. His parents, both Indian, had lived in India and Tanzania before settling in Canada. As a child, Virani had always been known in his family as the "entrepreneurial one," starting with his lawn-cutting business and later making his own line of T-shirts. After completing business school in May 2011, Virani had taken time off to see his extended family in India and Tanzania. He was keen on developing an entrepreneurial idea that had international reach.

On arriving in India, Virani discovered the popularity of the recently released "Cricket Attax" trading cards made by the US company Topps in cooperation with the Indian Premier League. The cards featured individual player ratings for the cricket skills of batting and bowling. Two children could play the card game; one child would choose his or her favourite offensive player and the other his or her favourite defensive player. Both would flip over their cards to determine which player had the higher score. The children could then keep track of who had the highest number of points. The "Cricket Attax" cards had reportedly sold five million units within their first few months on the market (Ambwani and Bhushan 2011).

When Virani arrived at his extended family's place in Tanzania, he thought about whether the sports card idea might work there:

I know that Tanzania is a much poorer country than India. However, people are soccer crazy here and a big company probably won't make Tanzania a priority in the next couple of years since it's not a big enough market for them. I think the reason why cards like this work so well is because they're universal. Sure, the players might change from cricket to soccer, but they reinforce the same ideas of strategic thinking, competition and trading. It's a fun way to inspire kids and teach kids some of the fundamentals of business.

Virani himself had been inspired to do something in India or Tanzania after reading C.K. Prahalad's book. Prahalad talked about how serving the world's poor was often ignored by big business even though the poor represented tremendous opportunities to develop new markets and alleviate poverty. Virani commented:

> I really like Prahalad's ideas. He said that many multinationals have an outdated view of the world and that they're ignoring the 4 billion people (or 65 percent of the world's population) that make under $2,000 per year. He illustrated that many people living in shantytowns in India had so-called luxury items like televisions, pressure cookers and telephones because they preferred to spend the little money they did have on improving their lives instead of saving for a house, which was far out of their reach (Prahalad and Hammond 2002).
>
> I was reading Prahalad around the time we were also studying the Indian company Infosys. I love how Infosys' co-founder, Narayana Murthy, said: "You cannot distribute poverty" (Murthy 2011).

Operational Details

Although Virani still had yet to confirm all of the operational details of the venture, he had some initial projections and had confirmed some of his assumptions with meetings while he was in Tanzania. He wanted to do a pilot run of 50,000 units (each unit was a package containing five cards). He projected that he could sell 100,000 units in his first full year of operations, 500,000 in his second, and one million in his third year.

For the pilot, Virani figured that he would start by making cards of the 22-player Tanzanian national team. He had already bought photographs of each player from local photographers (each photo was sold to him for US $25 to US $100, with the average being about US $50). If he were to launch as a full business, he would aim to have the top 10 players of all 14 teams and would need to purchase new photos each year.

Virani had used his family's contacts to meet with the president of the Tanzania Football Federation to talk about an official licensing agreement and had secured a verbal agreement for a five percent royalty fee to be paid to the Tanzania Football Federation.

A friend in Vancouver had agreed to design the first set of cards for a flat fee of $500 (for the entire set). Virani figured that, in future years, he would have to pay at least $2,500 per year for design.

While there were some printing houses in Tanzania, Virani decided to print the initial run of cards in Canada. Each pack containing five cards could be produced for a total of US $0.25, including the wrap, if he did an initial run of 50,000 units. At 100,000 units, the price would drop to US $0.24 per pack, at 500,000 to US $0.20, and at one million units, to US $0.15.

Pricing was targeted at US $0.50 per package, which worked out to about 800 Tanzanian shillings (TZS). Virani would be able to carry some of the initial run of cards (although not all 50,000) with him in his luggage on returning to Tanzania. Thereafter, he would either need to find a local printer or incur shipping costs at about US $100 per 5,000 packs. Virani was a bit concerned about the reliability of shipping from Canada to Tanzania and was unfamiliar with the customs requirements.

He was convinced that he would be able to sell out the initial run as long as he rewarded distributors and resellers appropriately. He wanted to distribute the cards through confectionary distributors, who would charge him approximately $0.05 per unit. Shop owners and independent resellers (who would offer the cards to people on the streets) would make $0.10 per unit. Virani estimated marketing costs at $10,000 for the pilot and the first year and $20,000 thereafter.

Reactions to TanzaFooty

Virani had shared his idea with his family as well as former classmates. His uncle in Tanzania had agreed to be his financial backer through a no-interest loan because he was keen to see the venture off the ground and was excited at the prospect of his nephew relocating to work in Tanzania. Virani's uncle was a successful business person whose import–export business had made him quite wealthy. Virani had a standing offer to stay at his uncle's five-bedroom house indefinitely. His family also thought that he was putting his education to good use by applying what he had learned, although both of his parents were a little concerned that the venture might lose money.

Reactions among his former classmates were mixed. One of his classmates pointed Virani to the academic work of Aneel Karnani, who had critiqued aspects of Prahalad's *Fortune at the Bottom of the Pyramid*. Karnani had advised considering the type of product that would be marketed to the poor. He divided products that were beneficial and harmful to the poor into a 2 × 2 matrix known as the "four Cs": cigarettes, colas, cellphones, and condoms. For the beneficial products, Karnani noted where free markets worked well and where subsidies were needed. In the harmful-product categories, he identified the need for constraints on the

Table 15.1   Beneficial and Harmful Products (Aneel Karnani)

	Beneficial for the poor	**Harmful for the poor**
Profitable for companies	Cellphones "Markets at their best."	Cigarettes "Need for constraints on markets."
Unprofitable for companies	Condoms "Need for government or civil society to subsidize."	Colas "Markets penalize business. No need for intervention."

market and where the market could be left alone because it would naturally penalize business (Karnani 2012).

What to Do?

Should Virani move to Tanzania and attempt to launch TanzaFooty? Or should he continue looking at other opportunities? Virani tried to decide:

> You know, I've been thinking about this for a long time and I think I've got a really good idea. I don't want to be pushed into inaction just because I'm nervous something won't work.
>
> At the same time, I'm a bit concerned that I'll be viewed to be exploiting the poor. My intention is quite different—I want to help the poor. I'm just unsure as to whether this is the best idea to begin my career.

Marketing Ethics

Marketing, whether conducted within a single city or internationally, is the most visible function of the various business disciplines (which also include human resources, accounting, finance, operations/manufacturing, and procurement/supply-chain management). Thus, it is often the business discipline that draws the most ethical criticism. Some of this criticism may be justified, but most professional marketers are highly ethical and professional. The primary stakeholder for most marketers is the customer, and ethical marketers work hard to understand the needs and wants of their customers (often termed the *target market*) so that they can serve these needs and wants in an ethical and responsible manner. While this may seem pretty black and white, there are often many shades of grey, as the TanzaFooty case suggests. In particular, marketers must ask themselves an important question—are they responding to pre-existing *needs* or are they creating particular types of *wants* that may or may not benefit the customer and society? The answer to this question often changes the degree of responsibility the marketer has for the outcomes marketing creates and the tactics marketers use. If marketers are creating wants for particular products or services, then they must take full responsibility for the outcomes that result from the sale and use of the product.

Questions of responsibility also vary in terms of the target market being served. For example, some customers are more vulnerable and marketers need to exhibit a higher duty of care toward such customers (Gilligan 1982). Children (usually defined as people under the age of 13) are one such market. People with mental disabilities or the elderly with impaired cognitive functioning are other vulnerable markets. Even in more general markets, however, marketers must consider whether or not they are preying on their target customer's vulnerabilities. For example, marketers are often criticized if they focus on people's fears of things like crime or social rejection. This is why marketers of cosmetics are subject to ethical criticism if they prey on people's fears about social rejection as a result of appearance.

You see marketing in action almost everywhere you look. There are obvious aspects, such as ubiquitous advertising or the huge variety of products offered in a seemingly endless selection of retail stores. There are also less obvious aspects. Marketers establish the prices you pay, and determine how and when products are shipped. Because marketing affects all of us, it is important that you understand this practice and the ethical issues associated with this key business function.

Why Marketing Ethics Is Even More Important Today

While ethical marketing practices have always been important, they are even more important today. Marketing is a highly sophisticated practice that uses advanced tools to understand consumers' every wish. You leave a data footprint with almost every purchase and transaction, and not just online. You also leave a footprint when you use a loyalty card or when a cashier asks you for additional information (such as your phone number and address) to enter into their database when you make a purchase. Marketers analyze this huge collection of data so that they can understand your every whim and want. It is therefore a very powerful discipline. With that power comes the demand that marketers act ethically and responsibly, and be accountable for how they use their power.

With the huge variety of goods and services on offer today, marketers are realizing more than ever before that they need to build customer loyalty. Therefore, they often rely on customers' repeat purchases to do that, a practice called relationship marketing. Without openness, honesty, and trust, there can be no ongoing relationships because customers will flee marketers they don't trust. As noted above, marketers need information about consumers so they can tailor their products and services to meet their needs. If consumers don't trust marketers, they will not divulge that information. Thus, good ethics is at the heart of good relationship marketing.

This is also an era of social media. With the click of a mouse, a firm's most valuable asset, its reputation, can be attacked and perhaps even destroyed. Criticisms of firms, their marketing practices, or their shoddy products are no longer just the subject of headlines in the local newspaper, they can be flashed around the world in an instant over the Internet. The press is also very vigilant, and in the wake of the recent financial crisis and growing distrust of business, unethical practices are often front-page news. Consumers and employees alike are more educated and empowered today than ever before, and less tolerant of unethical practices. It is not surprising, therefore, that marketers are working at being far more ethical than some of the old stereotypes would suggest.

Marketing's Major Stakeholders

A recent book, *Firms of Endearment*, demonstrates how companies that act ethically and responsibly, focusing passionately on their customers and creating value for them and other key stakeholders, outperform less ethical and responsible companies (Sisodia, Wolfe, and Sheth 2007). The book's authors note that it is no longer "share of mind" that matters, but "share of heart." Customers truly love such companies—like Mountain Equipment Co-op, Lululemon, Apple, or Costco—and the products they offer. They purchase from them again and again. To have that share of heart, marketers must be trusted and transparent as well as be value creators.

Firms of Endearment uses the SPICE acronym to help marketers remember key stakeholder groups (see sidebar). Each one is expanded on in more detail below.

SIDEBAR

SPICE

The SPICE acronym is one useful way to remember key stakeholders:

- **S**   Society and the broader community
- **P**   Partners, such as suppliers and retailers
- **I**   Investors or shareholders in the firm
- **C**   Customers
- **E**   Employees

Source: Adapted from Sisodia, Wolfe, and Sheth (2007).

Society and the Broader Community

Directly or indirectly, marketing affects all of the stakeholders in the SPICE model. Criticisms of marketing's impact on society have a long and hotly debated history. Ethical criticisms include the assumption that marketing practice makes society more materialistic, that people judge self-worth by what they own, not by who they are, and that marketing raises anxiety among potential consumers because it places a heightened value on certain physical features, like white skin, a thin physique, or a young appearance.

Other critics focus on issues like cultural pollution—they claim that marketing has caused us to live in a world littered with billboards, bombarded with advertising, harassed by unwanted telemarketing, and subjected to television programs and movies that are full of commercial messages and products.

Marketers are also accused of building demand for unnecessary products or services. Bottled water, for example, is often cited as such a product. Canada has one of the best fresh-water and municipal-water supplies in the world, yet consumers have been convinced to buy water in plastic bottles. Millions of barrels of oil are used to make these bottles, and more is used in their shipping and in their recycling—using a non-renewable resource for an unnecessary product.

More recent criticisms of marketing have taken aim at the fact that marketing may encourage overconsumption, which is not sustainable. Critics who voice this complaint often ask whether marketing is responding to customer needs, or whether it is instead creating those needs. Anne Leonard makes this case very strongly in her "Story of Stuff " (Leonard 2012). She asks why we buy so excessively and why much of what we purchase is never used or used only infrequently. In reaction to this, events like "Buy Nothing Day," which was founded in Vancouver in 1992 by cartoonist Ted Dave, now span the globe. The purpose of Buy Nothing Day is to draw attention to the harmful effects of overconsumption. It not only asks consumers to stop shopping for 24 hours, it also asks them to think about issues such as where their products originate, why they purchase them, and what they do with them after purchase. Buy Nothing Day has been praised for drawing attention to issues such as how many resources consumers use in developed versus developing countries.

In contrast to marketing critics, there are also marketing advocates, who point to the many good things that the marketing discipline has been responsible for. Marketing uncovers consumers' needs and wants and uses this information to drive innovation and the creation of goods and services to meet these needs. Without marketing, consumers would be uninformed about key features of products or how to compare a high-quality product with one of lesser quality. Marketing is responsible for the effective distribution of these products and services, ensuring that they get to consumers at the right time and that they are in the right place. The rivalry between firms that marketing fosters keeps prices competitive. Nonprofits also use marketing techniques to draw attention to their causes and make them more attractive to donors. Social marketing has been used to encourage changes in behaviour in unhealthy practices such as smoking or overeating, or beginning an exercise program, or eating more healthily. Marketing is used to encourage consumers to take advantage of needed but avoided services such as regular visits to dentists or medical tests like breast cancer screening.

Partners

Marketers may be accused of not treating partners fairly. Walmart, for example, has been vilified for pushing its suppliers too hard on the prices they can charge Walmart, the belief being that the constant push to get even lower and lower prices eventually pushes the supplier out of business. Walmart responds that its tactics have improved the efficiency of all firms and marketers. Good relationships between manufacturers and their retail partners are essential to the efficient delivery of goods and services, and most marketers work diligently to ensure that their relationships are ethical and that both parties benefit from the association.

Investors

Marketing is responsible for building and maintaining corporate and product brands. Brands are the most valuable asset of any firm and are critical assets that create a significant portion of the returns desired by a firm's investors. Marketers must avoid being deceptive or overly zealous in painting a rosy picture of a firm and its products and services, or the value of its brands. Such actions may encourage poorly informed investors (shareholders) into making unwise investment choices. Unethical actions in this area of marketing can result in action against the firm by regulators.

Customers

Customers are a critical stakeholder group for marketers. The ethical issues associated with customers will be the focus of the rest of the chapter once the discussion of the SPICE model is complete.

Employees

Marketing also affects current and prospective employees. The same marketing tools that are used to communicate with consumers are also used to attract the best possible people to work for a firm. Internal marketing is used to keep employees informed about the company's strategies and policies, to understand their needs, and to create working conditions essential to keeping employees passionate about knowing and serving customers. Again, good ethical practices are essential, and internal communications are open, honest, and transparent.

One stakeholder group not addressed by the authors of *Firms of Endearment* is regulators. Marketing is subject to many regulations both nationally and provincially, so this group of stakeholders cannot be ignored. For example, marketers must be aware of regulations related to interprovincial trade, labelling in both official languages, advertising to children, and those that are particular to specific product categories such as communications products, banking services, or pharmaceutical products.

A large number of regulators and groups scrutinize marketing practice in Canada to help ensure that it is done legally, ethically, and responsibly. These include Advertising Standards Canada, the Canadian Marketing Association, the Canadian Radio-television and Telecommunications Commission, the Competition Bureau, provincial consumer affairs offices, and the Privacy Commissioner. Federal government departments, such as the Canadian Food Inspection Agency or Health Canada, may regulate marketers depending on the type of products or services sold by the firm.

While marketers have to be aware of and create value for a range of stakeholders, customers are the focus of most marketing tasks. The remainder of this chapter will focus further on the ethical issues of this key stakeholder group.

Ethical Principles Regarding Customers

Before exploring some of the major ethical issues facing marketers, it is important to understand some of the key principles that marketers use in addition to the main ethical theories described earlier in the text. These principles serve as criteria to help marketers ensure that they are acting in an ethical fashion. They arose from the consumerism movement that began in the 1930s and became powerful in the 1950s, receiving widespread attention and adoption after being promoted by US President John Kennedy in the 1960s in what became known as the Consumer Bill of Rights (Kennedy 1962). They are just as important today as they were then.

According to these principles, each consumer has six basic rights. Marketers that ensure that these rights are respected are well along the path of being ethically and legally compliant marketers:

- *The right to safety:* The products and services that marketers sell should not result in injury or harm to the consumer if they are used as prescribed. Marketers have the duty to ensure that products meet safety standards before they are made available to the public. If defects in products emerge after they are launched, marketers have a duty to recall such products, and compensate consumers if required. Because some essential products may not be inherently safe (e.g., some drugs or chemicals), marketers are also required to provide clear warning labels about their dangers and provide directions for safe operation.
- *The right to be informed:* Consumers have the right to clear, accurate, understandable information about the products and services they are thinking of buying. There should be no misleading information in the firm's advertisements, on product packaging or labels, on financing terms, or in warranties.

- *The right to choose*: Our society believes that competitive marketplaces serve customers best. Thus, consumers have the right to choose among competitive offerings and they should not be coerced into purchasing products or services or continuing relationships with companies with whom they no longer wish to do business.
- *The right to be heard*: Consumers have the right to voice complaints about products, services, or marketing practices and companies have a duty to listen openly and empathetically to consumer concerns and input. Such input may help the firm and its marketers to improve their products and increase customer satisfaction.
- *The right to redress*: If consumers have legitimate claims about a faulty product or service, they are entitled to fair compensation or settlement of their claim. If firms do not address consumer concerns, the consumer may seek redress from regulatory bodies such as the Competition Bureau or industry bodies such as the Advertising Standards Association.
- *The right to privacy*: In the current era of advanced consumer research combined with mass and tailored communication technologies, the consumer's right to privacy must be honoured. Privacy is defined as the right to be left alone, to enjoy one's private space, to expect confidentiality, and to control access to personal information. Canada's *Personal Information Protection and Electronic Documents Act* (PIPEDA), provides the regulatory framework to ensure that consumers' privacy is protected online.

We will now explore some of the major ethical issues related to key aspects of marketing practice.

Ethical Issues Associated with Marketing Practice

Every aspect of marketing practice may have an ethical issue embedded within it. Thus, when marketing managers are designing their strategies and their marketing mixes, they must be highly sensitive to these issues and work to avoid or mitigate these ethical concerns. In doing this, marketers must not only consider consumers, but also a wide range of stakeholders and the principles, duties, outcomes, and the potential consequences of their practices.

Marketing Research

Without information, marketers would be unable to tailor their products and services to customers' needs. Research is therefore an essential aspect of marketing practice. Professional marketers may design their own research studies to learn more about competitors, customers, or the marketing environment, or they may employ a research agency to do the work. No matter what vehicle is used, ensuring the study is ethical is as important as its validity and reliability.

Conducting research that involves human subjects requires special vigilance to avoid a number of ethical pitfalls. First, consumers, or other stakeholders, have the right to choose to participate or not participate in a research study. They have the right to be informed about the purpose of the study and the time it will take them to complete the research instrument (such as a survey or an interview). They should not be exposed to risks (i.e., their right to safety) such as psychological stress. They have the right to refuse to reveal personal information, or if they do reveal such information, they have the right to insist that it must be protected and reported only in anonymous formats.

Competitive intelligence gathering is another aspect of market research that must avoid unethical tactics. Marketers certainly need information about their competitors' offerings and practices if they are to create superior offerings for their customers, but there are ethical and unethical means of acquiring such information. The use of publicly available information about competitors is usually considered ethical, and there is a vast quantity of such information. For example, marketers can look at their competitors' websites, their annual reports, their advertisements and product brochures, their press releases, and their regulatory filings, such as those for patents or those with the Securities and Exchange Commission. Marketers can dig through industry directories, observe competitors at conferences and trade shows, or gather profiles and biographies of senior executives. They can gather information about competitors by surveying people who purchase products within a particular category. Ethically questionable means of gathering competitive information include the hiring of competitors' employees with the purpose of learning about their proprietary material or practices, dumpster diving and searching competitors' garbage, or secret observation of competitors' operations. Illegal means of acquiring competitive information includes trespassing on competitors' property, bribing their employees to reveal trade secrets, wiretapping, or stealing proprietary information such as drawings, specifications, or private reports. The Society of Competitive Intelligence Professionals provides standards of ethical intelligence gathering, which guides marketers' practice in this important area.

Segmentation, Target Marketing, and Positioning

These concepts form the heart of marketing strategy. Marketers divide up markets into discrete segments, select key segments that they can best serve (i.e., their target market), and create a position for their products (often called a *value proposition*) that will appeal to the consumers they are targeting.

In undertaking the segmentation task, marketers must guard against inherent bias against particular groups. They must not discriminate against poor or disadvantaged consumers or against people of a particular ethnicity. Banks, for example, have been accused of a type of unethical practice called "redlining," excluding poor neighbourhoods when thinking about where to locate their branches or to whom they want to offer products such as mortgages or loans.

Marketers must be careful to ethically align their target market choices with the products they sell, and how they position these products. For example, a marketer of a diet product should be sensitive to the anxieties of anorexic women, and shouldn't position its products as making people unusually thin. A classic example of ethically poor product–market alignment was the cigarette brand Virginia Slims. It was criticized for its famous marketing slogan "You've come a long way, baby" because the campaign equated smoking an addictive product with women's freedom. Similarly, marketers of violent video games must be careful not to include children in their target market or position the game so that it is appealing to children.

Product-Related Issues

As noted earlier in this chapter, consumers have the right to insist that the products they buy be safe for their intended use. In 2007, Fisher-Price and other toy manufacturers had to recall many products manufactured in China because the paint used in the toys contained lead, making the toys unsafe for children (Canwest News Service 2007).

Safety issues can also include being sure that the directions for operating the product are clear and understandable, so that consumers can learn how to use the product safely. However, ensuring product safety is not always a straightforward task and the processes marketers use to ensure safety have come under ethical scrutiny. For example, there have been ongoing concerns and protests about product testing on animals.

The marketing of socially controversial products such as alcohol, cigarettes, or firearms has drawn ethical criticism for many years, and arguments that these products are inherently unsafe have been at the centre of these criticisms. Nonetheless, the ethical debate is complex. Those who continue to advocate their right to market these products note that they have been deemed legal for sale and also claim that consumers have the right to choose for themselves whether they want to purchase these products or not. Thus, as you can see, making ethical choices may not be straightforward when one consumer right comes into conflict with other customer rights or with the rights of other stakeholders.

More recent ethical issues surrounding the management of product mixes (the range of products a company sells) focus on sustainability issues. The manufacturing and marketing of products may deplete non-renewable resources. The components of computers and cellphones, for example, contain many rare minerals, which cannot be replaced. As product life cycles for these products shorten (often referred to as planned obsolescence), more and more of these resources are consumed. Marketers are also criticized for not thinking about issues such as how to recycle these products, because many of them end up in landfills where harmful materials can leach into water supplies. Responsible marketers have, therefore, expanded their thinking and are working more and more to use recycled materials and are seeking substitutes for non-renewable resources in their manufacturing processes.

Ethical considerations about packaging and labelling must be undertaken when planning for product sales. Marketers have been criticized, for example, if packages are designed so that they appear large, but contain very little product. While it is a legal requirement to have nutritional information on food packaging, ethical issues arise if the serving size is misleading. For example, look at some beverages. You may be surprised to find that a small beverage is labelled as containing two servings, with the nutrition and calorie information you see on the label referring to only half of the liquid contained in the bottle. Few consumers may notice this "fine print" on the label. Their right to be informed has therefore been violated.

Ethical criticisms have also been lodged against marketers because of misleading terms placed on labels. Terms like "lite," "healthy," and "green" have been found to be ambiguous and often mislead consumers. Using excessive packaging to attract attention to a product beyond the need to protect the product is under ethical attack because it uses scarce resources and adds to the waste stream. Many labelling and packaging materials use harmful chemicals in the inks used to print images or information on the packages. This also raises ethical concerns about harm to consumers. In all cases, a marketer's ethical role is to not knowingly do harm to its key stakeholder—consumers.

Many companies today try to market themselves with a "green" message in an attempt to appeal to consumers' desire to buy eco-friendly products, but in many cases there is very little substance behind the claims on their labels.

Source: iStock.

Pricing

Marketers must be aware of the major legal and ethical issues of pricing products and services. The major legal issue is collusion. It is illegal to establish price agreements with competitors, and the Competition Bureau will prosecute marketers suspected of this infraction. Beyond legal issues, there are a number of other ethical issues with pricing. For example, consumers often use price as an indicator of quality. Some marketers, especially those of luxury cosmetics or fashion goods, have been ethically criticized for inflating the prices of these goods to mislead consumers into thinking that their products are of higher quality. Negative option billing—sending unrequested goods to consumers who have not ordered them, and then demanding payment for the goods—has also raised ethical concerns.

Sometimes consumers have to negotiate the prices they pay, and marketers have to guard against stereotypes and prejudice when training the sales staff who are part of these processes. Research has shown that women and visible minorities may be discriminated against and have to pay higher prices in negotiated price situations such as buying a car or negotiating a mortgage. Women have long complained that the cost of basic services such as dry cleaning or haircuts is much more costly for them than it is for men. Again, marketers have to scrutinize their practices and avoid such harm to their key stakeholders.

Advertising and Communications Programs

This aspect of the marketing mix has drawn the most ethical criticism of all marketing practices. Communications programs have three purposes—to inform consumers of the benefits of their products, to remind consumers about the need to restock products, and to persuade consumers to buy products. It is the latter aspect that has drawn the most fire. In particular, marketing and communications programs have been accused of creating "false" needs, and encouraging people to buy excessively. Some activists see food advertising, especially of unhealthy products and fast food chains, as a root cause of the recent obesity epidemic. Other critics blame excessive advertising as the reason behind the growing materialism in society (Pollay 1986).

Sex-role stereotyping in advertising has also drawn considerable ethical criticism and complaints. Showing sexually explicit images or showing women only in domestic roles are typical examples of advertising deemed to be unethical. The use of overly thin models whose images are altered so that they appear flawless has been shown to cause stress and dissatisfaction among women. Marketers at Unilever Canada did a lot of the research and work behind the worldwide Dove Campaign for Real Beauty that first launched in 2004, a campaign that did a lot to challenge such stereotypes.

Men may be under similar pressure: advertising shows slim, highly muscular men in many advertisements. For many years, sex-role stereotyping has been the number one complaint about advertising investigated by the Canadian Advertising Standards Commission. Lack of accuracy and misleading advertising has been the second-highest category of complaints, and showing products in advertisements used in an unsafe manner (e.g., showing cars or recreational vehicles speeding) has been the third-highest complaint category. The use of violent imagery in advertising in such areas as video games or music videos has been deemed to have a particularly harmful effect on children and is a growing area of concern.

When designing their communications programs, marketers can avoid some of these pitfalls by ensuring that the claims they make in their advertisements are true and that they are not misleading. The Canadian Advertising Standards code provides helpful guidelines that marketers can follow to avoid many ethical pitfalls. For example, the code notes that "Advertising should strive to provide an equal representation of women and men in roles of authority and in decision-making roles," and "Advertising should avoid the exploitation of sexuality of both women and men."

Sales and Channel Management

Marketers are responsible for the flow of goods and services from their organization (the organization that produces the good or service) to the end consumer. They must ensure that the right products are made available in the right places for the right consumers. Two particularly important players in channel management are sales personnel and retailers. High-pressure sales tactics, especially those directed at consumers, have been deemed harmful in that they encourage consumers to buy products they do not want need or want. Telephone and email sales tactics have been ethically criticized because they violate consumers' right to privacy. There are many regulations that control the relationships between manufacturers and retailers, and marketers must be aware of these to avoid legal as well as ethical pitfalls.

Canadian Marketing Association's Code of Ethics and Standards of Practice

Canadian marketers have an excellent resource in the form of a comprehensive code of ethics published and maintained by the Canadian Marketing Association. The code stresses that marketers are required to maintain a high standard of practice. Ethical marketing practices are essential to winning and holding public confidence, and they are the foundation of a successful and independent information-based marketing industry in Canada. The code contains a special and comprehensive section on marketing to children, noting "Marketing to children imposes a special responsibility on marketers. Marketers must recognize that children are not adults and that not all marketing techniques are appropriate for children." The code also cautions that, in many cases, marketers must get consent from the child's parent or guardian before collecting any research information from children (Canadian Marketing Association 2012).

SIDEBAR

CMA Code of Ethics

The Canadian Marketing Association Code of Ethics and Standards of Practice

The CMA Code of Ethics and Standards of Practice is designed to establish and maintain standards for the conduct of marketing in Canada.

Marketers acknowledge that the establishment and maintenance of high standards of practice are a fundamental responsibility to the public, essential to winning and holding consumer confidence, and the foundation of a successful and independent marketing industry in Canada.

Members of the Canadian Marketing Association recognize an obligation—to the consumers and businesses they serve, to the integrity of the discipline in which they operate, and to each other—to practise to the highest standards of honesty, truth, accuracy, fairness, and professionalism.

The CMA Code of Ethics and Standards of Practice is the foundation of the marketing community's self-regulation. Unlike many other codes that are only guidelines, the CMA's code is compulsory for members and as such is a comprehensive regulatory framework governing members' conduct. Organizations selling abroad are governed by this code unless doing so contravenes the laws of foreign jurisdictions.

Some specific provisions of the code note:

1. Marketers must not misrepresent a product, service, or marketing program and must not mislead by statement or manner of demonstration or comparison.
2. Marketing communications must be clear and truthful. Marketers must not knowingly make a representation to a consumer or business that is false or misleading.
3. Marketing to children imposes a special responsibility on marketers. Marketers must recognize that children are not adults and that not all marketing techniques are appropriate for children.
4. All consumer marketers must abide by the *Personal Information Protection and Electronics Documents Act* (PIPEDA) and/or applicable provincial privacy laws, and the ten privacy principles from the National Standard of Canada and five additional requirements outlined in the code.
5. Terms such as "regular price," "suggested retail value," "manufacturer's list price," and "fair market value" must represent prices at which the item has been sold in the relevant marketplace in substantial quantity or for a substantial period of time.
6. Marketers must establish and communicate fair, effective, and timely procedures to handle complaints from consumers or businesses.
7. Marketers recognize and acknowledge a continuing responsibility to manage their businesses to minimize environmental impact.

Source: Canadian Marketing Association, Code of Ethics and Standards of Practice. www.the-cma.org.

Conclusion

Marketing is an important and essential function that touches everyone in Canadian society. Done well, it drives innovation and consumer well-being. Done unethically, it can exploit, rather than serve and create value for key stakeholders—customers, society, partners, investors, employees, and regulators. Marketers must be scrupulous about the ethics of their practices if they are to develop and maintain the relationships that are essential to their ongoing success. Ethical marketing practice builds consumer trust, and is essential to the reputation of a firm and its brands. Respecting consumer rights is at the heart of ethical marketing, but making ethical decisions is a complex task that requires the same rigour and analysis as all good marketing.

DISCUSSION QUESTIONS

1. Some marketers claim that they only respond to the needs and wants of their customers, so they are not responsible for any harm caused by the products or services they sell to meet such needs. Do you agree or disagree with this thinking? Provide clear examples to illustrate your answer.
2. Do you think it is ethical or unethical to market discretionary products (like football cards) to the children of poor families in developing country markets?
3. Advertising is the most visible aspect of marketing. Look through a magazine that you read regularly. Select an advertisement that you believe to be an ethical or unethical example of marketing practice. Explain the reasoning behind your decision.
4. Sales people must serve a number of stakeholders when doing their jobs. Put yourself in the role of a salesperson selling a car to a first-time buyer, a student like you. List the stakeholders the salesperson must serve. Describe an ethical dilemma the sales person might face when dealing with one of these stakeholders.

SUGGESTED READINGS AND ONLINE RESOURCES

Badaracco Jr., J.L. 1997. *Defining moments: When managers must choose between right and right*. Boston: Harvard Business School Press.

Brenkert, G.G. 2008. *Marketing ethics*. New York: Wiley-Blackwell.

Leonard, A. 2012. The story of stuff. Free Range Studios. http://www.storyofstuff.org/about/credits/story-of-stuff-credits/.

Sisodia, R., D.B. Wolfe, and J.N. Sheth. 2007. *Firms of endearment: How world-class companies profit from passion and purpose*. Upper Saddle River, NJ: Wharton School Publishing.

REFERENCES

Ambwani, M.V., and R. Bhushan. 2011. IPL mania: Topps sells 5 million trading cards. *Economic Times*, August 25. http://articles.economictimes.indiatimes.com/ 2011-08-25/news/29927076_1_trading-cards-ipl-teams-indian-premier-league.

Canadian Marketing Association. 2012. Code of ethics and standards of practice. http://www.the-cma.org/regulatory/code-of-ethics.

Canwest News Service. 2007. Fisher-Price recall affects nearly one million toys. August 2. http://www.canada.com/topics/news/story.html?id=d56d740b-7b42-438d -b7c5-599db1d9e807&k=22300.

CIA World Factbook. 2004. Tanzania. https://www.cia.gov/library/publications/ the-world-factbook/rankorder/2004rank.html?countryName=Tanzania& countryCode=tz&regionCode=afr&rank=201#tz.

Gilligan, C. 1982. *In a different voice*. Boston: Harvard University Press.

Karnani, A. 2012. Selling to the poor. http://www.worldfinancialreview.com/?p=215.

Kennedy, J.F. 1962. Special message to the Congress on protecting the consumer interest. March 15. http://www.presidency.ucsb.edu/ws/?pid=9108#axzz1ntDd84De.

Leonard, A. 2012. The story of stuff. Free Range Studios. http://www.storyofstuff.org/ about/credits/story-of-stuff-credits/.

Murthy, N. 2011. Interview with co-founder of Infosys. Interview conducted by Donald and Jean Johnson, Asia Society. http://asiasociety.org/business/finance/ corporate-values.

Pollay, R.W. 1986. The distorted mirror: Reflections on the unintended consequences of advertising. *Journal of Marketing* (April): 18–36.

Prahalad, C.K., and A. Hammond. 2002. Serving the world's poor, profitably. *Harvard Business Review* (September).

Sisodia, R., D.B. Wolfe, and J.N. Sheth. 2007. *Firms of endearment: How world-class companies profit from passion and purpose*. Upper Saddle River, NJ: Wharton School Publishing.

United Republic of Tanzania. National Bureau of Statistics. 2010. *Tanzania in figures 2010*. http://www.tanzania.go.tz/nbsf.html.

Privacy, Ethics, and Technology

I am deeply concerned about the egregious inadequacy of Sony's efforts thus far to notify its customers of these breaches or to provide adequate protections for users whose personal and financial information may have been compromised.

Richard Blumenthal, United States Senator (IBTimes, 2011)

Once the network is back up and secure, and once people calm down and realize they didn't lose anything, the damage will largely be repaired.

Michael Pachter, Wedbush Securities (IBTimes, 2011)

Introduction

What exactly is information technology (IT)? Merriam-Webster's online dictionary defines it as "the technology involving the development, maintenance, and use of computer systems, software, and networks for the processing and distribution of data" (Merriam-Webster 2011). Over the last few decades, IT has come to be both an essential and major component of business activity. Because technology allows for the collection, storage, and use of vast amounts of information, ethical issues arise in a variety of ways in the context of IT.

Of particular significance is personal information collected by businesses. Businesses collect and store both customers' and employees' personal information. This is not particularly new, but the extent of the personal infor-

mation collected, and the extent to which the information can be exploited (e.g., customer information can be used for targeted marketing, data mining, and outright sale) has grown significantly, alongside the ability of businesses to exploit their IT. In a bricks and mortar environment, someone attempting to obtain personal information had to physically access where it was stored, perhaps acting illicitly and illegally to do so. Further, the potentially smaller amount of information collected (or stored in hardcopy at a given location) provided less of an incentive to take the risk. While the threat could come from both outside and within an organization, in a traditional bricks and mortar environment collecting personal information typically remained a challenging high-risk venture regardless of who attempted it.

With computers and the development of data warehousing, such personal information can be accessed by people who never even have to set foot on the business premises. Such information is also subject to unauthorized access and use by people (particularly, but not solely, IT professionals) within the business organization. Without appropriate safeguards and controls, businesses can be particularly vulnerable to such incidents. This does not imply that it is necessarily easy to access personal information stored on business computers/servers, but it is clear that there can be distinct advantages to being able to take the time to perpetrate an information theft from the comfort of one's own controlled premises as opposed to illicitly entering onto someone else's property to obtain such information. It is evident that there are a variety of ways that the security of an IT system can be compromised, along with the personal information stored therein. A particularly notable and recent example of a breach of a company's IT network involved Sony Computer Entertainment (a subsidiary company of Sony Corporation). Do privacy breaches automatically raise ethical issues, or constitute a breach of ethical standards? Using the example of Sony's experience, it will be argued that although they can raise ethical concerns, privacy breaches do not, contrary to what many may think, automatically amount to an ethical failure.

Case Study: Sony PlayStation Network Security Breach

In April 2011, Sony surprised its customers and the general public with news of a major privacy breach to its Sony PlayStation (PSN) and Qriocity networks (Paronen 2011), the result of a major cyber attack directed at the company and one of the most significant privacy breaches (in terms of potentially affected consumers) of a large multinational company in recent memory (Reuters 2011). What was particularly notable about the PSN privacy breach was the wide-ranging response by consumers, the industry, and even the media (both industry-related and general media). The two opening quotes show the contrasting views expressed about Sony's response as well as the underlying ethical ambivalence that exists with respect to matters of privacy. Before discussing the ethical issues involved with this matter, it is helpful to understand what the PSN is and how the cyber attack occurred.

The PSN has direct links to Sony's earlier-generation gaming consoles. Before the commercialization of the Internet, gaming consoles operated on a stand-alone basis. Multiple players had to play using a single console and separate games were bought and inserted into the console. As gaming technology entered the new millennium, it was recognized that linking gaming consoles to the Internet represented a significant business opportunity. For customers, this represented another level of gaming that could be achieved in accessing and using electronic games. Games could be downloaded from a website and users could interact with other players from around the world. As the distinctions between gaming and entertainment continued to blur, it was apparent that gaming consoles could represent another platform upon which to obtain and consume additional types of media beyond electronic games.

The Sony PSN and the related Qriocity network are Internet-based networks that capitalize on the linkages between gaming consoles and the Internet. The networks allow owners of Sony gaming consoles (e.g., PlayStation 3, PlayStation Portable, etc.) to download various types of media and, in the case of PSN, to participate in games online or download games for use on the Sony console. PSN was launched in 2006 to coincide with the release of a new Sony gaming console. By early 2011, PSN had approximately 77 million created user accounts worldwide. Sony thus had a significant amount of personal information in its possession (Flickr 2011).

Consumer information presents a significant business opportunity and to be able to use the PSN, individuals had to provide personal information to establish an account. A typical user provided their full name, home address, date of birth, and email account, and created a password. For most users, this probably represented a fairly benign request, the same request made by the vast majority of websites who provide a service the user wants to access. However, because games can be purchased and downloaded online, it is also possible to provide credit card information for payment. By early 2011, almost 18 million account holders had provided credit card information to Sony for use on the PSN (Flickr 2011).

A typical priority for most users of a website is that, whatever service it provides, it should be efficient and dependable. On April 20, 2011, to the considerable surprise of users attempting to access the PSN, the system was shut down. No immediate reason was given. On April 22, Sony acknowledged that there had been an "external intrusion," although little additional information was provided to the public at that time (Seybold 2011a). For the next several days there was significant industry chatter about what had happened that could cause an entire gaming network to be taken offline, for multiple consecutive days, without any advance warning whatsoever.

On April 26, Sony finally released a media statement saying that the PSN had suffered an "illegal and unauthorized intrusion." This was the acknowledged reason why Sony had taken the PSN offline. The release went on to state that

> an unauthorized person has obtained the following information that you provided: name, address (city, state, zip), country, email address, birthdate, PlayStation Network/Qriocity password and login, and handle/PSN online ID. It is also

possible that your profile data, including purchase history and billing address (city, state, zip), and your PlayStation Network/Qriocity password security answers may have been obtained. If you have authorized a sub-account for your dependent, the same data with respect to your dependent may have been obtained. While there is no evidence at this time that credit card data was taken, we cannot rule out the possibility. If you have provided your credit card data through PlayStation Network or Qriocity, out of an abundance of caution we are advising you that your credit card number (excluding security code) and expiration date may have been obtained. (Seybold 2011b)

People quickly identified the discrepancy between the date of the media release (April 26) and the dates identified in the release as to when the cyber attack had occurred (April 17–April 19). For them, Sony's release was an implicit acknowledgment that the security of personal information had been compromised for over one week and an explicit acknowledgment that Sony could not guarantee that financial information was not included in the compromised information.

The collective breach was described by one Canadian commentator as one of the largest of the previous decade (*Globe and Mail* 2011a). It not only made headlines in gaming-related media, which was to be expected, but, following the Sony news release, it became a regular news item in mainstream media for days, and even weeks, as additional information about the cyber attack and its consequences surfaced. Post-breach, Sony acknowledged that more than 1 million Canadian customers had been affected (*Globe and Mail* 2011b).

Reactions to Breach Vary

Reaction to the breach by Canadian and American governmental authorities was also fast and significant. Within a few days of Sony's first media release about the cyber attack, Canada's federal privacy commissioner, Jennifer Stoddart, expressed disappointment that she had not been directly and quickly notified by Sony about the breach (*Globe and Mail* 2011b). In the United States, the House of Representatives Subcommittee on Commerce, Manufacturing, and Trade directed specific questions to Sony for immediate response. The subcommittee wanted to understand the scale of the attack and what Sony had done, and was planning on doing, to address it (IT News 2011). In its response to the subcommittee, the chair of the board of directors of Sony Computer Entertainment (in a letter the company also publicly released by posting to Flickr.com) acknowledged that early indications were that some personal information from all 77 million accounts had been compromised (Flickr 2011).

In contrast to governmental reactions, and the reaction of much of the media, the public reaction varied. In the weeks following the breach, the stock price of Sony declined while the Dow Jones Industrial Average generally increased (Infosecisland 2011). This certainly suggested an ongoing concern by a segment of the investing public that the security issues would be harmful to Sony's business success. However, this does not necessarily suggest that Sony had been "at fault," only that the market appeared concerned about the impact of the event on Sony's future business prospects.

At a more individual level, a 21-year-old Mississauga woman, whose personal information might have been compromised, was motivated enough to retain legal counsel and start a class action lawsuit on behalf of all potentially affected Canadian account holders. The claim made was over 1 billion dollars on behalf of the more than 1 million PSN users living in Canada. In a press release accompanying the announcement of the lawsuit, the plaintiff stated that, "If you can't trust a huge multi-national corporation like Sony to protect your private information, who can you trust?" (McPhadden 2011).

Contrast the above reactions, and their expressions of considerable concern over what occurred, with the response of Sony account holders following the privacy breaches. The PSN remained offline for 28 days and when it did resume, Sony attempted to entice account holders to return by offering two free games for download in addition to some other free offers. By the end of June 2011, it was reported that approximately 90 percent of account holders had returned to the PSN system, in spite of additional interruptions in service, albeit much shorter ones, that resulted from follow-up cyber attacks in the weeks following the initial attack (Businessweek 2011). While some might argue that this figure represented the loss of millions of account holders, conversely it can be pointed out that almost 9 out of 10 account holders either did not care about what had happened, may have cared but concluded it was unlikely to occur again, or if they did care, were sufficiently attracted by Sony's offer to continue to use the PSN despite the interruptions. As can be seen, the reaction was wide-ranging, with much of the reaction of the general public deviating from the reaction of major societal institutions, such as government and media.

Considering the different reactions, can it be easily concluded that the collection and use of personal information, and the related concept of privacy, even raises ethical issues? After all, it could be argued that Sony itself was the victim of an intentional malicious action and that it did everything in its power to address the matter as soon as it could. What could be unethical about that? To better understand privacy as a potential matter of ethics, it is helpful to have a basic understanding of the concept of privacy, and why governments, to varying degrees, have opted to try and regulate it. From there, it is easier to understand how it can be perceived as an ethical matter.

Privacy as an Ethical Concept

Historical Underpinnings of Privacy and Its Regulation

Privacy makes allowance for the desire of individuals to have a personal sphere and control over what is disclosed by them, or known about them by others. It has long existed as a concept in many, though not necessarily all, cultures to varying degrees. However, it has been little more than a century since it was first advocated to be an inherent human right. It is generally agreed that a late-19th-century article by two American legal academics was the first attempt to define what the private sphere is and to espouse some type of basic human entitlement for privacy in law. However, conceptions of what should be included within the sphere of the private have been fluid and expanding since first being acknowledged (Charters 2002, 246–249).

Concern about personal information entering into the possession of government entities came to be part of the discussion about privacy in the mid-20th century (Boatright 2007, 149). This was driven both by the recognition that various social institutions (particularly state entities) had used personal information about citizens to harmful effect (particularly in Europe) and a developing theoretical discussion about the importance of privacy as a necessary democratic foundation (Privacy International 2011). The United Nations (UN) explicitly referenced an expectation of privacy in its 1948 Universal Declaration of Human Rights (OHCHR 2011). Unlike the UN's explicit statement, Canada did not identify (and has never identified) a clear constitutional right to privacy. Throughout the mid-20th century, the collection and use of personal information by private businesses was not identified as a notable privacy matter. That changed with the adoption and use of computers in business, and the subsequent exponential increase in computing power. By the 1990s, governments were starting to consider regulating when and how the private sector could collect and use personal information. In some cases, they were already passing such legislation.

Approaches to regulating the collection of personal information in the private sector have varied significantly. At one end of the legislative continuum is the European Union (EU). The EU took a comprehensive approach to regulating the collection of personal information by businesses based in EU member countries. While it does not prohibit collection, the EU places significant obligations on businesses that collect, retain, and use personal information. At the other end of the spectrum is the United States, which has opted to selectively regulate the collection of personal information, with the legislation tending to focus on specific types of economic activity. For example, the financial services sector, health services industry, and online web entities that cater to minors are all subject to individual and distinct pieces of legislation that govern the collection of information (Privacy International 2011). The Canadian approach to private sector privacy

Personal Information

Canada's *Personal Information Protection and Electronic Documents Act* (PIPEDA) defines personal information as information about an identifiable individual. This phrasing requires some consideration to fully appreciate its application. Presumably, information that is *related to* an individual but not *about* them might fall outside the purview of the legislation. Further, if, for some reason, information could not be connected to an individual in a way that makes them identifiable, then, arguably, it would fall beyond the legislative terminology and a business would not be legally required to comply with the legislation's parameters in the collection of such information. Finally, the information does not have to already be clearly connected for PIPEDA to apply it but it does have to be capable of being connected to an identifiable individual. For example, if a company had an IT system with multiple databases, simply making someone anonymous (or personally un-identifiable) would not suffice to remove the application of the Act if one or more other databases could be cross-referenced or synched to render the information personally identifiable. Such situations would dictate that the requirements of the legislation be followed even if initially it appears that there is anonymity.

Realistically, most information is still going to qualify as information that, pursuant to PIPEDA, should only be collected in compliance with the legislation's requirements. However, one explicit exception applies to employees. Currently, PIPEDA explicitly states that the personal information of an employee of an organization (name, title, business address, telephone number) is not considered personal information for PIPEDA's purposes. This long-standing exclusion of employee information will be removed once a recently introduced federal bill is passed. Organizations found to have violated PIPEDA requirements can potentially face audits of information management practices and mandatory orders to change deficient practices, as well as potential (but generally nominal) fines for deemed offences within the Act. In addition, legislative amendments will soon make it mandatory to notify the privacy commissioner's office when information breaches occur as well as notifying affected individuals, provided those individuals face a real risk of harm.

Source: iStock.

SIDEBAR

Identity Theft

Identity theft is a particular type of information theft. It generally involves not just obtaining personal information and using it on a limited basis (e.g., an online credit card transaction), but adopting the innocent victim's identity based on personal information in the perpetrator's possession. The perpetrator may use the alternate identity for limited specific purposes (e.g., to rent a car they might not otherwise be able to rent because of age, licensing, or other constraints) or on a wide-ranging basis (e.g., using personal information to obtain government-issued identification that is then used to engage in further fraudulent/illegal activity). Taken to extremes, identity theft can involve the perpetrator passing themselves off as the victim in actual interactions with people who would not otherwise be able to know the difference. It can cause significant problems for third-party businesses that may be innocently harmed by the fraud, but even more so for victims, who are forced to deal with the consequences. It may take months, and even years, for victims whose identities were stolen to fully resolve the damage done by an identity-theft perpetrator.

---

legislation falls closer to the EU end of the continuum. The legislation is comprehensive in terms of what is included as personal information. Further, it applies across the country, with allowance for substantially equivalent provincial legislation, and across all types of for-profit economic activity (OPCC 2011). Government regulation in and of itself does not inevitably lead to the conclusion that management of customer (and employee) personal information and personal privacy raises ethical issues. However, it does, arguably, potentially heighten public perception that it is an ethical issue.

Notwithstanding significant legislation, public perceptions about the importance of controlling personal information tend to vary widely. Numerous studies have identified broad categories of how people view the importance of personal information. The studies consistently show that a small minority of people have no concerns whatsoever, a larger but still small minority are at the other end of the spectrum and have substantial concerns, but a majority of people are pragmatic about it. Such people only become concerned about their privacy in particular situations (Ponnurangam and Cranor 2005). In many respects, this spectrum is reflected in the reaction to the Sony PSN information breach. If one looked only at the reaction of media and government bodies, one would assume a common reaction of uniform concern. However, that reaction did not mirror the restrained response of the general public.

Ethical Underpinnings of Privacy and Its Regulation

Knowing the foregoing, it is now reasonable to consider how privacy, and Sony's particular cyber attack and response, can raise ethical considerations. The ethical underpinnings of the privacy issue arise in at least a couple of respects. A fundamental issue is the concern about harm to individuals when their personal information is compromised and then used in a way that has a negative outcome for them (Boatright 2007, 154). A tangible example in the context of the PSN situation would be if a hacker obtained credit card information and proceeded to put charges on it, responsibility for which the owner of the credit card would have had to assume. Another example might be a hacker who uses personal information to engage in identity theft, leaving the individual whose identity has been stolen to deal with the consequences of the act. In the latter case, other third parties might be harmed as a result of the identity theft. (Imagine someone using another's identity to apply to a university program. The admitting university faces a cost in addressing the matter and, quite possibly, there is an unnamed, unidentified individual who may not have had the opportunity to pursue an academic opportunity as a result of being denied admission.) In any event, the focus is on harm, which places the issue within the utilitarian ethical framework. In the utilitarian framework, harm is only one part of the equation. It is also necessary to evaluate the harms against the benefits of an activity. Collecting personal information may be necessary to allow basic access, or enhanced service, each of which can provide enjoyment and psychological benefit to a wide range of people. Someone attempting to argue that there is an overall ethical outcome might try to argue that the benefit of the activity across a wide range of people exceeds any negative outcome, in this case, from occasional, albeit significant, compromises of personal information.

There is also a second basis for considering privacy, and the management of personal information, to be an ethical issue. A second foundational approach is to be found within the context of Kantianism, an ethical theory developed by Immanuel Kant (see Chapter 2, "Theories of Ethics"). Kantianism as an ethical framework focuses not on outcomes to evaluate the ethics of an action, but on certain basic imperatives and whether the imperatives are violated as a result of certain actions. The violation of the imperative creates the ethical concern. One of Kant's imperatives (his second categorical imperative) dictates that individuals should not be used for selfish ends. All humans possess inherent value as autonomous beings, which should be recognized. Every individual represents an end in themselves and should not be used by others as a means to an end. The imperative recognizes that people are individuals who are capable of rational choice (Boatright 2007, 155). A cynic might argue that collecting information from people for the ultimate purpose of earning a profit is, by its very nature, an affront to a Kantian approach to ethics. However, in the context of individuals providing personal information about themselves to a third party, if such information is provided freely, and with knowledge of the collector's ultimate intention (and the related attendant risks of giving a third party personal information) personal autonomy is, arguably, respected. The choices of customers to provide such information are presumably made on the basis that their personal information is going to be secure and that the third party will only use it for the purposes indicated. A failure by the third party to live up to either of those considerations arguably undermines the autonomous consent premise, thus raising an ethical concern.

How might government legislative initiatives reflect the ethical underpinnings discussed above, if at all? A reading of the EU provision that established private sector privacy requirements makes clear that it is premised much more on the belief that personal privacy is akin to a human right, something that is far more reflective of Kant's categorical imperative. While it might be to a lesser degree, Canada's legislative approach is similar. The legislation in the US is premised to a far greater degree on an ethically utilitarian approach to the issue—that is, there is a willingness to allow businesses to collect and use personal information without significant government limitations on how it is done, unless there is a concern that the potential for harm is considerable. This is not to suggest that a full-scale utilitarian analysis actually takes place, but utilitarian concepts at play are certainly discernible. The result is a legislative framework that is probably more utilitarian in its foundational ethical justification. Ultimately, while the existence of legislation can contribute to an expectation that information management is an ethical matter, it is essential to push beyond the mere presence of legislation to consider whether the matter truly raises ethical concerns, and whether a party has failed to meet certain expectations of ethical conduct.

Sony PlayStation Network: An Ethical Failing?

When one looks at the overall context of the PSN privacy breach, and has a fuller understanding of the related ethical considerations, it is easier to understand how there can be a deep ambivalence about whether the privacy breach also amounted to an ethical breach. It is possible to conclude that such an incident is an ethical failure on Sony's part, but that should not be the automatic conclusion.

It must be recognized that the type of personal information that was compromised would be characterized by many people as fairly benign. That is not irrelevant to an ethical assessment. The Sony breach involved specific objects of information that were provided to a third party that the third party ultimately failed to properly secure. While certain objects of personal information (e.g., credit cards, and various government-issued documents and related identifiers) are obviously sensitive, much personal information would not, in the estimation of many, rise to the same level of sensitivity. Many people do not consider their name to be private information nor would many think the same of an address (which tends to be readily accessible). Still others think little of disclosing their age or an email address.

If or when people fully grasped the extent to which online activities can be tracked and retained, many would have a greater concern about appropriate privacy limits. Would someone want their Internet usage history tracked and disclosed? Would someone want all their online purchases disclosed (some possibly done online specifically to avoid completing such a purchase in a public space)? Of the information involved in the Sony breach, many people (albeit not all) would only identify credit card information as a particularly sensitive category of information. Because it did not appear that credit card information, if compromised, was acted on, this significantly reduced the ethical implications from a utilitarian perspective. The actual harm resulting from the incident for users appeared quite minimal.

From a Kantian perspective, many would not see a failure like this as a matter of failing to recognize their inherent value and autonomy, at least not when considering Sony's conduct toward PSN users. As noted, failing to meet expectations about maintaining appropriate security might raise concerns for some. However, apparently it was not the result of a shoddy security system but the result of a very intentional and dedicated effort by an aggressor party, so it does not really imply that Sony was cavalier or callous toward its users. One of the other fundamental criticisms of Sony was that it failed to notify customers as soon as possible after the breach. Yet, taking Sony's responses to the congressional subcommittee at face value, it seems that taking the time necessary to understand what was occurring, assessing what had happened, then notifying customers with a reasonably detailed response within a few days was all quite reasonable. Very arguably, they acted in a timely and transparent way with regard to their user base throughout the situation.

Also, the mere presence of a legislative requirement for handling personal information does not automatically justify a conclusion that there has been some type of ethical breach. The nature of the information involved in the breach, the fact that it appeared to be a third-party intentional act of sabotage, and Sony's subsequent steps and conduct are all quite relevant to making any determination in this respect. Much of the general public's concern about information control seems to rest primarily on a more utilitarian basis—that is, unless given a specific reason to fear that harm has occurred, or is imminent, most people have a reasonably high tolerance for the collection and use of their personal information. To this an element of Kantianism can be added. People are also presumably more comfortable and satisfied when they conclude they are being dealt with in a reasonably direct and transparent way.

Conclusion

Despite significant challenges over a number of weeks, Sony appeared to overcome the ethical allegations that permeated the discussion. Perhaps this is because, ultimately, the general public was actually more nuanced in its collective consideration of whether the cyber attack amounted to a breach of an ethical expectation than much of the media. There was no significant public outcry about Sony's conduct during the event and most PSN users returned to the network post-incident. In this respect, Michael Pachter's statement proved to be largely accurate and the senator's somewhat overblown. However, the incident did have the potential to be not just a massive IT failure, but also a significant ethical one. To that end, it remains a cautionary example of the potential ethical issues that companies can face in managing the IT function of a business.

DISCUSSION QUESTIONS

1. If Sony did not act in an unethical manner, should an automatic conclusion be that the cyber-attack perpetrators acted unethically? What if the attack was premised on socially conscious considerations (e.g., Sony was exploiting third-world child labour)?
2. Do you agree that if a hacker obtained sensitive information (e.g., credit card numbers), but chose not to use it in a harmful way, that this should play a determining role in whether the "victim" company acted ethically from a utilitarian perspective?
3. If the majority of Canadian citizens are really not that concerned about how companies use their personal information, has the federal government overreacted by creating such comprehensive private sector privacy legislation?

SUGGESTED READING AND ONLINE RESOURCES

Phukan, S. 2002. IT ethics in the Internet age: New dimensions. InformingScience.org.
Stanford Encyclopedia of Philosophy. Computer & information ethics.
    http://plato.stanford.edu/entries/ethics-computer/.
Wright, D. 2011. A framework for the ethical impact assessment of information
    technology. *Ethics and Information Technology* 13. http://www.springerlink.com/
    content/1388-1957 (or other articles in this journal).

REFERENCES

Boatright, J. 2007. *Ethics and the conduct of business.* 5th ed. New Jersey: Pearson Prentice Hall.

Businessweek. 2011. Sony to focus on online services even after hacker attacks. http://www.businessweek.com/news/2011-06-28/sony-to-focus-on-online -services-even-after-hacker-attacks.html.

Charters, D. 2002. Electronic monitoring and privacy issues in business marketing: The ethics of the doubleclick experience. *Journal of Business Ethics* 35: 243–254.

Flickr. 2011. Sony letter to Bono Mack and Butterfield. May 4. http://www.flickr.com/ photos/playstationblog/5686965323/in/set-72157626521862165/.

Globe and Mail. 2011a. Sony data breach fuels privacy concerns. April 27. http://www.theglobeandmail.com/news/technology/tech-news/ sony-data-breach-fuels-privacy-concerns/article2001228/.

Globe and Mail. 2011b. Privacy czar joins critics of Sony security breach. May 5. http://www.theglobeandmail.com/news/technology/tech-news/ privacy-czar-joins-critics-of-sony-security-breach/article2010404/.

Infosecisland. 2011. Sony stock hammered in wake of security breaches. June 6. https://www.infosecisland.com/blogview/14224-Sony-Stock-Hammered-in -Wake-of-Security-Breaches.html.

IT News. 2011. US Congress wants answers from Sony on PlayStation hack. April 29. http://www.itnews.com/regulation/31794/us-congress-wants-answers -sony-playstation-hack.

McPhadden, S.T. 2011. Canadian Sony PlayStation network class action. May 2. http://www.mcst.ca/LinkClick.aspx?fileticket=RlXFlfrf51k%3d&tabid=463.

Merriam-Webster Dictionary. 2011. Information technology. http://www.merriam -webster.com/dictionary/information%20technology.

Office of the High Commissioner for Human Rights (OHCHR). 2011. Universal declaration of human rights. http://www.ohchr.org/en/udhr/pages/introduction.aspx.

Office of the Privacy Commissioner of Canada (OPCC). 2011. *A guide for businesses and organizations—Your privacy responsibilities.* http://www.priv.gc.ca/information/ guide_e.cfm.

Ponnurangam, K., and L.F. Cranor. 2005. Privacy indexes: A survey of Westin's studies. School of Computer Science Technical Report Collection Carnegie Mellon University (CMU-ISRI-5-138).

Paronen, L. 2011. Tech wrap: Sony admits PlayStation Network privacy breach. April 26. http://blogs.reuters.com/mediafile/2011/04/26/tech-wrap-sony-admits -playstation-network-privacy-breach/.

Privacy International. 2011. Overview of privacy. https://www.privacyinternational.org/ article/overview-privacy.

Reuters. 2011. Sony PlayStation suffers massive data breach. April 26. http://www.reuters .com/article/2011/04/26/us-sony-stoldendata-idUSTRE73P6WB20110426.

Seybold, P. 2011a. Update on PlayStation network/Qriocity services. April 22.
http://blog.us.playstation.com/2011/04/22/update-on-playstation-network
-qriocity-services/.

Seybold, P. 2011b. Update on PlayStation network/Qriocity. April 26.
http://blog.us.playstation.com/2011/04/22/update-on-playstation-network-qriocity/.

Energy and Ethics

This chapter examines two aspects of energy and ethics: first, the question of energy sustainability and environmental concerns, and second, the ethics of business dealings in the energy sector. It begins with one of the most widely discussed and hotly debated ethical topics in Canada today: the development of the Alberta oil sands. Following an analysis of the various ethical issues raised by that topic, the chapter concludes with a second case study that explores questions of ethical conduct in one Canadian energy company's dealings with foreign government officials.

Case Study: Alberta's Oil Sands

Ethical Oil Versus Dirty Oil: An Overview of the Debate

Canada is a country awash in energy resources. We have abundant resources in all forms of energy, including hydrocarbons and renewables. Our reserves of crude oil, mostly in Alberta's oil sands, place us third globally. Only Saudi Arabia and Venezuela have larger reserves (US Energy Information Administration 2011).

Some of the statistics surrounding the oil sands development are staggering:

- The oil sands represent 12 percent of the world's global oil reserves.
- Commercial production began in 1967; since then, less than 5 percent has been produced.
- Since 2001, nearly $300 billion has been invested in Alberta's oil and gas sector, with over 40 percent of it in the oil sands. In 2011, the value of bitumen and synthetic crude oil from oil sands production amounted to nearly $60 billion.
- It should be noted that while some believe that the oil sands represent one of the world's single biggest sources of greenhouse gases, they rank far below sources such as US coal-fired power plants, which produce 6 percent of global emissions, compared with 0.12 percent from the oil sands.

Canada is the only non-OPEC country among the top five oil reserves in the world and the third largest net exporter of natural gas. Canada is also third globally in hydroelectricity production. Nearly 60 percent of all electricity generated in Canada comes from hydropower. And while we produce a lot of energy, Canadians also rank alongside the Americans as the world's biggest per capita consumers of energy. In part, this is because Canada is a very large country with a small, widely dispersed population; a lot of energy is used to transport ourselves, as well as to get our goods to market. Canada is also a northern country that requires a lot of heating during the winter.

In Canada today, there is a debate about how to describe oil from Alberta's oil sands. The two dominant descriptions are often portrayed as being at odds with one another. On the one hand is the description offered by Ezra Levant in his book *Ethical Oil: The Case for Canada's Oil Sands. Ethical Oil* is asking that, when purchasing oil, a company's ethics, demonstrated, for example, in the human rights record of a country or company, be considered along with its environmental record. Thus, oil from Canada's oil sands should be viewed as more ethical than, for example, oil from Saudi Arabia. Many opponents object to this line of thinking. A common form of this objection is that the ethical oil position is just a smokescreen to allow Canada to sell oil that is environmentally harmful (*Edmonton Journal* 2011).

On the dirty-oil side of the debate, the argument is made that oil from what its opponents call the "tar sands" is more harmful to the environment than other forms of energy and thus its development should be reduced or abandoned. (Note that the term "tar sands," with its negative connotations, is not used by supporters of developing Alberta's reserves, who use the term "oil sands." For the sake of expediency, this chapter will in most cases employ the term "oil sands.") The media focuses a lot of attention on this issue. For example, much has been written about the emissions coming from oil sands production. Advocates of oil sands development object to this criticism by reframing the amount of emissions in a global context, by stating, for example, that, according to Canadian government figures, the oil sands contribute 6 percent of Canada's total emissions and Canada's total emissions, according to the United Nations, account for about 2 percent of global emissions.

Students of business ethics should recognize that both sides are employing consequential ethics in its simplest form (see Chapter 2, "Theories of Ethics"). This type of ethics says that the rightness of an action is determined by the outcome resulting from the action. Thus, the formula for dirty oil goes something like this: "Don't buy Alberta oil because it harms the environment." And for ethical oil: "Don't buy Saudi oil because it harms human rights." The consequence or outcome of buying a certain kind of oil will produce results that harm someone or something, so it is considered unethical to do so. For our purposes in analyzing the ethics of the two positions, it is not too hard to see that they are really the same formula. If the issues were not so serious, some of the proponents debating the two positions might sound, to an outside observer, like young children fighting over who is right or wrong. Both sides often dismiss one another with various arguments that challenge the credibility of the other side. For example, we hear that the ethical oil issue is just an attempt to misrepresent the real issue: environmental concerns about the oil sands. However, given that both have the same ethical formula and both can be substantiated, the two positions are then either both right or both wrong. That either side discounts the other only diminishes the credibility of their arguments, especially to those who value *both* human rights and the environment.

From an energy economics perspective, proponents of both ethical and dirty oil are concerned about access to the market.[1] On the one hand, the environmental side of the debate would like to limit oil sands access to the market, while the ethical side of the debate would like to limit conflict oil's access to the market, or at least make what is deemed ethical oil a first choice of buyers in the market. Interestingly, when access to the market issues are debated from an ethical point of view, they are often framed in consequential-ethical formulas. This is particularly true of iconic environmental campaigns by environmental non-government organizations (ENGOs). For example, 35 years ago, Greenpeace ran a campaign directed against killing Canadian harp seals for their fur. Using a consequential ethical formula, the campaign sharply reduced this Canadian export (Greenpeace 2012). However, the campaign did not reduce the output of European fur farms, which continue to dominate the market.

The Importance of Energy in Today's World

What do you think about the energy you use when you fill up your car with fuel, or plug in your cellphone for a charge, or heat your home with natural gas? Where does the energy come from? Does it matter? Will the energy be available tomorrow? Are there costs to the energy you use besides what you pay at the end of the month? Do the ethics of the people who produce energy matter? Is there anything in ethics that refers to the production, distribution, and consumption of energy? Is any type of energy more ethical than others?

---

1   The access to market is one of four economic concepts important to the energy industry and is discussed later in the chapter.

These are some of the questions in today's debate about energy. No longer are just the economics of energy being considered, but also the ethical issues surrounding energy and its use.

So why is all of this important? It's about our quality of life. From life expectancy to material well-being to basic needs such as clean water, clean air, food, and sanitation, there is an increasing demand for a better quality of life. For example, look around your own home. Have you increased the number of small home entertainment devices over the years? It is estimated that such devices account for 10 to 15 percent of all electricity used in the home today (ACEEE 2012).

SIDEBAR

Energy Junkies

When it comes to energy consumption, Peter Tertzakian, a Canadian author on energy issues, compares human beings to junk food junkies—we are hooked on cheap energy calories. In fact, in the last hundred years or so we have gotten obese on them. Globally, the human desire for an ever-increasing quality of life and our current appetite for energy to meet that need is the greatest challenge facing the world in the 21st century.

Tertzakian writes about the *first principle of energy consumption*. This principle states that the more energy you consume, the higher your standard of living. The reverse is also part of the principle: the higher your standard of living, the more energy you consume. So the punch line is: it's all about energy. But there is a catch. The type and amount of energy we consume may be neither sustainable nor healthy for us or our planet.

And we are not alone in our desire for an improved quality of life. With the world population passing seven billion people in October 2011, there are more people than ever asking for that better life. The International Energy Agency (2011) points out that on a percentage basis, the consumption of energy is increasing faster than the population. This trend is expected to continue.

Ethics and Energy

At the heart of the ethical challenges we face with our use of energy and the types of energy we choose to use are the consequences, dangers, and harm that may result from those energy choices. Nowhere is this clearer than in the emissions that our energy use produces. For years, eastern Canada suffered from acid rain, which destroyed lakes, rivers, fisheries, and forests. The rain, mixed with the sulphur dioxide emissions from coal-fired plants that generated electricity, created a sulphuric acid that was destroying habitats. But these are not the only emissions we need to be concerned about. Scientists have been warning about the changes that global carbon emissions are causing and will continue to cause on our planet. Even today, early warning climate change impacts can be seen. For example, cold snaps in winter have long controlled the mountain pine beetle in western Canada. Today, however, the beetle has destroyed vast tracts of pine forests well over the size of England, and is progressing eastward. Natural outbreaks in the past, as in the 1940s, are no longer controlled by cold snaps winter after winter.

Sir Nicholas Stern, a British economist, is one of the most respected voices in the world on climate change. In 2006, Stern led a team that produced the *Stern Review: The Economics of Climate Change*, which summarized the potential economic harms of climate change and raised the issue that our energy use is not only an economics issue but also an ethical one.

> The nature of the problem [climate change] in terms of its causes and effects implies that a broad range of ethical perspectives are likely to be involved, including issues of consequentialism, equity, fairness, justice, freedom, rights, sustainability and stewardship. There are fundamental ethical differences among these approaches, but each would point towards a focus on similar measurable outcomes such as incomes, forms of capital and wealth, including the environment, health, education and ways of life. (Stern 2006)

Stern went on to state that the cause of climate change is market failure. Market failure occurs when the price for something, in this case energy, does not include the full costs of that energy (climate change).

> Climate change is a result of the greatest market failure the world has seen. The evidence on the seriousness of the risks from inaction or delayed action is now overwhelming. The problem of climate change involves a fundamental failure of markets: those who damage others by emitting greenhouse gases generally do not pay. (Benjamin 2007)

Do our personal choices about energy contribute to climate change? Except for residents of Alberta and British Columbia, which have some form of carbon tax, Canadians do not pay for the greenhouse gases we emit. This is evident in transportation. We are a big country and we depend on personal transportation a lot. A large amount of emissions comes from transportation, particularly personal transportation. The choice we make for transportation does have consequences. (See Exercise 17.1: Our Personal Energy Choices, later this chapter, which examines a few trends in Canada.)

Future Key Energy Issues and What They Mean for Sustainability

The Three Hard Truths

So what are the key issues in the energy sector? And are there ethical considerations behind those issues? One way of discovering and understanding the issues is by using possible scenarios. Since the 1970s, Shell has used scenarios to help them with these issues and in 2008, it published *Shell Energy Scenarios to 2050*, which included the scenarios "Blueprint" and "Scramble." These scenarios talk about what Shell calls "the three hard truths" for this century. In a nutshell, these truths that the world must confront are: *no more easy oil, increasing demand for energy,* and *it's a carbon-constrained world.*

The first truth means that although there is enough oil to meet our needs for the 21st century, it will be harder to find and more expensive to develop and its development will have greater impact on the environment. It also means that other energy technologies will need to be developed and that these too will be expensive.

The second truth refers to the growing demand for energy. An important part of this truth is that, for the time being, hydrocarbons will play a major part in supplying that energy demand, particularly in rapidly developing economies such as China and India. The International Energy Agency (IEA) is projecting that global primary energy demand will grow by 1.6 percent per year on average between 2006 and 2030—an increase of 45 percent. Demand for oil will rise from 85 million barrels per day to 106 million barrels per day by 2030, in spite of sharp increases in other sources of energy, including wind, solar, and geothermal (IEA 2011).

In the third truth, global CO_2 emissions are set to rise as the world uses more energy, resulting in an increasing awareness and concern over climate change and the effects it will have on places and people.

These three truths speak about sustainability. Traditionally, the three pillars of sustainability are the economy, society, and the environment. We need to reconcile the demands of all three to be sustainable. So, for example, the first truth, no more easy oil, means that energy is more likely to be more expensive in the future. However, economies need affordable energy to grow and develop. Energy producers thus look at developing more efficient technologies in whatever type of energy they are producing. For example, wind turbines have grown in capacity and efficiency to generate more energy and can produce electricity more cheaply than older and smaller models. Likewise, in the social arena no more easy oil means that that people must make hard choices about the kind of energy they wish to see developed and how it affects their communities. For example, First Nations peoples struggle with balancing their traditional ways of life with the development of

Alberta's oil sands. (See Exercise 17.2: Sustainability Implications, later in this chapter.)

The Four Accesses of Energy

At this point, as we look at the various ethical issues concerning the energy sector, it is important to understand a bit more about how it operates. To be sustainable, the energy industry depends on four key accesses: access to the market, access to various types of capital, access to technology, and access to social licence. It must achieve success in all four of these continuously; to ignore even one is to invite failure. Looking at the energy sector this way helps us understand what is important to the industry and why it is important. This framework can also help us in our investigation of the key ethical issues in energy today by reframing the debate and demonstrating key interconnections. For example, the "ethical oil" debate currently happening in Canada is really a debate about gaining a social licence to operate, a recognition that is critical for the industry to maintain its access to the market. Finally, the framework gives voice to where the risks for the industry are and what they must be concerned about for sustainability.

Access to the Market

Any energy form must have access to a market to be successful and useful. For example, Canada is the largest single supplier of hydrocarbons to the United States. Access to this market means that infrastructure, relationships, international agreements, contracts, foreign policies, and regulatory systems must be in place. To maintain market access, the energy industry must offer a product whose environmental footprint is continually being reduced, understand the trade relations that support the strategic objectives of partners, and have a solid understanding of the economics and structures of markets.

Access to Various Types of Capital

Energy companies know the importance of attracting and retaining human, financial, and natural capital. Having the right people with the right skills at the right price is critical. Companies need access to their skills and training. They also need access to financing. For example, over $100 billion is currently invested in the oil sands. Part of the reason that the oil sands is so heavily invested in is that international oil companies like Shell or Exxon simply have fewer choices about where to invest because approximately 75 percent of world reserves are held by national oil companies, whose majority owner is the national government of their country. Finally, accessing the resource involves a practical and working knowledge of land rights, First Nations treaty rights, royalties, and sustainable practices, in addition to government policies and regulations.

Access to Technology

Accessing technology includes investment, research, development, and deployment. Many technology decisions are long term and the economics must be done right. The basic concepts and implications of the global shift from conventional to unconventional and renewable energy sources are not generally well understood. In many ways, the various energy forms currently at our disposal (e.g., hydrocarbons, nuclear, wind, solar, etc.) are competing on their technology. That technology must deliver the energy in an accessible and usable form, at an affordable price when it is needed, and with the least impact on the environment. For example, while wind power has one of the least impacts on the environment, it cannot be delivered reliably because it is hampered by the very nature of wind—its inconsistency and unpredictability.

Access to Social Licence

Corporate activities need society's acceptance—all societies, from local to global communities. Society wants energy to be developed, transported, and used in efficient and environmentally responsible ways. While society recognizes that the production and consumption of fuels produces emissions, it also wants effective strategies to manage environmental impacts such as greenhouse gas emissions and water usage. Companies need to gain and maintain their social licences to be sustainable.

And just as we have seen in other chapters, energy companies need to consider not only the interests of their shareholders, employees, and governments, but also the competing interests of legitimate stakeholders such as energy consumers and environmentalists.

Summary

Our world faces significant challenges in meeting its energy needs in an environmentally, ethically, and socially responsible manner. New and different energy sources will need to be developed. New and advanced technologies will need to be created, economically evaluated, and marketed. Governments will need to introduce innovative policies and regulatory tools to manage greenhouse gas emissions, water, and other resources and environmental challenges. Industry will need to capture efficiencies and meet evolving market demands. Challenges such as climate change require a deeper understanding of their ethical implications to generate sustainable solutions for the sake of our planet.

Exercises

Exercise 17.1: Our Personal Energy Choices

Our first exercise on energy and ethics starts with the choices Canadians make for their personal transportation. What do these trends tell us is happening?

1. Analyze the total amount of energy for passenger transportation in Canada by type of vehicle. What are the significant trends from 1990 to 2008 in the six subsectors? During that same period there was a trend to larger and heavier vehicles (SUVs). Industry argues that heavy and bigger is safer. Is this true? What does this say about how our personal choices affect the environment? Do they matter?

   http://bit.ly/A7I1en; http://iopscience.iop.org/1748-9326/2/1/014003/fulltext/

2. What fuel economy does Christopher Knittel's recent study show was in the average vehicle from 1980 to 2006 (Knittel 2011)? What about the average weight? Is it ethical that we are driving heavier, more powerful vehicles that contribute to climate change?

   http://pubs.aeaweb.org/doi/pdfplus/10.1257/aer.101.7.3368

Exercise 17.2: Sustainability Implications of the Three Hard Truths

After reading the accompanying section about Shell, above, discuss the sustainability implications of the three hard truths.

For the first truth of no more easy oil, consider the environmental costs of hydrocarbon development and production. Do renewables like wind power also have environmental costs?

For the second truth of increasing energy, demand begins first with a discussion of its social implications. Do China and India have the right to increase the quality of life for their populations by using more hydrocarbon energy sources? On the economic side of sustainability, while the increase in energy demand will increase prices, this demand is uneven, and sometimes it is very difficult to switch from one energy source to another. Discuss. On the environmental question, discuss the concept of externalities in the marketplace.

For the third truth of carbon constraints, discuss the types of economic measures that can be put in place to resolve this, including carbon taxation or carbon trading. How is climate change different from weather change? And, socially, how might carbon taxation affect the poorer segments of society more than the wealthier ones?

Exercise 17.3: The Environmental Debate

Debate the following statement:

> The environmental debate about the oil sands is important because it is challenging people to think about where their energy comes from, the kinds of energy they consume, and the impact that their energy consumption has. Given that most of the emissions from transportation fuels comes not from their production but from their actual use, a real measure of success is people choosing smaller, lighter, more efficient vehicles or cycling more.

Exercise 17.4: The Ethical Debate

Debate the following statement:

> Imagine a world where regimes and corporations are held accountable for their human rights violations. Where effective economic pressures are brought to bear for violations. Where companies see a significant reduction in market share for supporting, directly or indirectly, places where human rights don't matter. Such a world, where human rights are highly valued, is important. It does matter that my running shoes are not made by child labour, it does matter that my food comes from workers receiving a decent wage, it does matter that our energy companies don't bribe foreign officials, and yes, it does matter where my energy comes from.

Corruption and the Energy Industry

An increasingly important issue in the energy sector is corruption and bribery. Here, corruption is defined as the abuse of entrusted power for personal gain, economic or otherwise while bribery is the offering, promising, giving, accepting, or soliciting of an action that is illegal or a breach of trust. In the mid-1970s, during the US Securities and Exchange Commission investigations, over 400 US companies admitted to paying off foreign government officials and politicians in the course of their international work. In 1977, in response, the United States passed the *Foreign Corrupt Practices Act*, which was intended to affect the way American firms do business in non-US countries (US Department of Justice 1998). In the next decade, the US Congress became concerned that US companies were operating at a disadvantage compared with their foreign competitors. At the time, their competitors were not operating with the same restrictions, so were free to use bribes. In fact, in some countries, bribes could be deducted as a legitimate business expense. To create a level playing field, the Congress directed the US Department of Justice to work with the Organisation of Economic Co-operation and Development (OECD) to have major trading partners enact similar legislation to the FCPA. In 1997, almost ten years later, 34 countries signed the OECD Convention on Combating Bribery of Foreign Public Officials in International Business Transactions. This convention committed the signing countries to holding their companies to account for their behaviour abroad.

In a separate and broader initiative, the United Nations Convention Against Corruption (UNCAC) came into force in December 2005. This convention recognizes that corruption threatens the stability and security of societies, jeopardizes sustainable development and the rule of law, and undermines the institutions and values of democracy, ethical values, and justice. The key actions of this convention focus on prevention, criminalization, international cooperation, and asset recovery. The convention is seen by many as part of an international trend, along with the OECD action, to stem the tide of corruption practices. Transparency International sees it as an important step in dealing with one of the major causes of poverty (Transparency International 2010; United Nations 2004). As David Nussbaum, former Transparency International CEO, has stated, "Corruption isn't a natural disaster: it is the cold, calculated theft of opportunity from the men, women and children who are least able to protect themselves."

Transparency International also issues a Corruption Perceptions Index (see Figure 17.1) that illustrates the perceptions of the degree of public sector corruption as seen by business people and country analysts.

Notice that, except for Canada, the United States, and northern European countries, all the other major energy-producing countries are perceived to be more corrupt (as shown by the darker shades on the map). This connection between the energy sector and corruption will be touched upon later in this section.

In 1999, the *Corruption of Foreign Public Officials Act* (CFPOA) came into effect in Canada, followed one day later by the OECD convention. The Canadian legislation carries with it a maximum imprisonment term of five years for individuals but with no limit to the fines for corporations (Canada 1999).

In 2007, Canada ratified the UNCAC and also formed RCMP units to begin investigating corruption of foreign officials by Canadians and Canadian companies. Of particular note is that half of the 24-member unit is located in Calgary.

Before these events, Canada had come under international criticism for its lack of legislation and lack of capacity to enforce its anti-corruption commitments.

SIDEBAR

"Ethical Hollowness"

In January 2012, ARC Resources gifted the Haskayne Business School at the University of Calgary $9.5 million to create the Canadian Centre for Advanced Leadership to embed ethical leadership in its curriculum, research, and culture. The key driver for the donation was ARC's chairman Mac Van Wielingen's dismay over the 2008 financial crisis and his perception of "ethical hollowness" in many executive teams. "I was appalled by the inability of business leaders to look at the root cause of the business failures," Van Wielingen said.

What do you think Mr. Van Wielingen was referring to when he spoke of "ethical hollowness"?

What are the root causes of business failures that leaders do not have the ability to look at?

Did you think an energy company would make such a donation?

FIGURE 17.1 Corruption Perceptions Index 2011

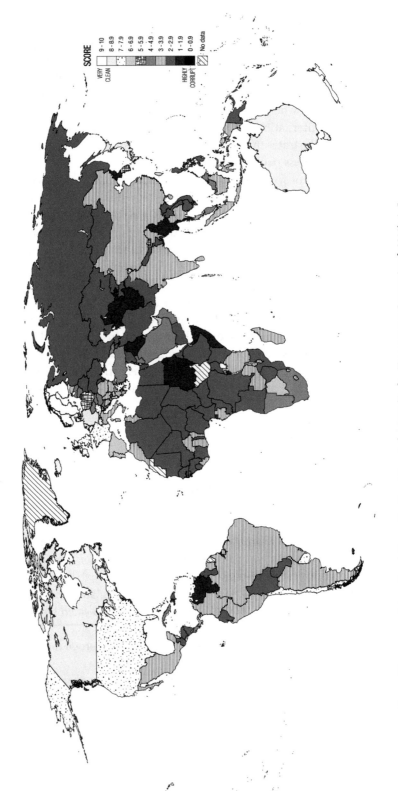

Source: Transparency International, *Corruption Perceptions Index 2011* (Berlin: Transparency International, 2011), 4–5.

So why is corruption against foreign public officials an energy issue in Canada? While Canada's energy products account for about 22 percent of our exports (Statistics Canada 2011), it is important to realize that we are also involved in the exploration and development of the world's hydrocarbon energy resources. Oil is the world's single largest energy traded commodity (IEA 2011). When you realize that the world produces and consumes over 87,000,000 barrels of oil each day, you can understand that the immense size of this market and its value can create temptation and, therefore, opportunity for corruption.

Case Study: Niko Resources

In May 2005, the subsidiary of a Canadian corporation with head offices in Calgary provided the use of a new Toyota Land Cruiser costing over $190,000 to the Bangladesh State Minister for Energy and Mineral Resources. Niko Canada, through its subsidiary company, Niko Bangladesh, gave this gift with the purpose of influencing the minister in his dealings with Niko. In addition, Niko Canada paid all the expenses for the minister, A.K.M. Mosharraf Hossain, to travel from Bangladesh to Calgary to attend an oil and gas exposition, then on to New York and Chicago, where he could visit his family who lived there. The trip cost approximately $5,000. The next month, Minister Hossain resigned from his position. Five years later, to the month, Niko Canada would pay the single largest fine under the new Canadian legislation on anti-corruption (Court of Queen's Bench of Alberta 2011).

Niko Canada and Niko Bangladesh

Niko Canada is an oil and natural gas exploration and production company. Initially, its operations were in Alberta and Saskatchewan, but after 1993 the company focused on international opportunities in exploration and development. Since then, it has operated in several eastern countries. Niko Bangladesh was financed by its parent company. In Canada, Edward Sampson was in charge of Niko while Qasim Sharif, who assisted in setting up the new Bangladesh company as Niko's in-country agent, became its first president in 2003. Mr. Sharif was expected to provide the necessary expertise to navigate the complex relationships of business and government in one of the most corrupt countries in the world.

The Joint Venture

In October 2003, Niko Bangladesh signed a joint venture agreement (JVA) with Bangladesh's state-owned gas company, BAPEX, to conduct exploration in natural gas fields in Bangladesh. Under the agreement, Niko would only recoup its investment after the sale of gas that it produced. Interestingly, a common industry

practice of signing a Gas Purchase and Sales Agreement (GPSA) was not concluded with the JVA at that time. This meant that Niko had taken on significant
price risk, not knowing the value of gas it would produce. The GPSA would eventually be signed on December 27, 2006.

The First Blowout

On New Year's Eve, 2004, Niko began drilling operations in northeastern Bangladesh. Seven days later, an explosion at the well site did significant damage to the
surrounding village. While no one was killed, the ensuing gas fire burned for
weeks, causing widespread evacuation. Another result of this explosion was the
negative press for Niko and the Bangladesh government. It was also at this time
that rumours began to circulate about how Niko had received the JVA award. At
this point, the Canadian government, through its diplomatic corps, became
interested.

The SUV

In February 2005, Niko Bangladesh made the first of three payments for a Toyota
Land Cruiser. Although the vehicle was registered to BAPEX, it was delivered instead to Minister Hossain. Mr. Sharif said that he had directly advised Mr. Sampson
of the delivery to the Minister. Mr. Sampson denied ever being told that the SUV
was being delivered to the minister.

The agreed statement of facts goes on:

> According to a letter dated May 16, 2005, written by Brian Adolph (vice presi-
> dent and country manager of Niko Bangladesh) to the managing director of
> BAPEX, Niko had turned over the Toyota Land Cruiser to "the offices of the
> Hon'ble State Minister for Energy & Mineral Resources Division." The letter was
> signed with the following salutation: "I take this opportunity on behalf of Niko
> Management to thank you all for the support you have given us in the past and
> hope to receive the same in the coming days for the mutual benefit of NIKO and
> BAPEX joint venture."

Niko Canada acknowledges it would be deemed for criminal law purposes
to know of this letter.

> On May 23, 2005 the Toyota Land Cruiser was delivered to the home of
> Energy Minister Hossain in Dhaka, Bangladesh. The driver of the vehicle
> also made note of the delivery on a Niko Bangladesh letter. Present at the
> time of the delivery were Qasim Sharif and Sayed Kabir, both representing
> Niko Bangladesh.

On June 15, 2005, the Bangladeshi newspaper *The Daily Star* broke the story
with, "Niko gifts minister luxurious car." In part, the article noted, "The energy

and mineral resources ministry on Monday denied that the state minister has received any gift from the Canadian oil company." Later the ministry's senior information office went on record saying that the Toyota was a replacement vehicle and had nothing to do with the Tengratila explosion and damage.

On June 18, 2005, Minister Hossain was summoned to the Bangladeshi prime minister's office, where he offered his resignation. Canadian media suggested that the resignation had come as a result of allegations that Hossain had accepted a bribe from Niko. The media also alleged that Hossain had delayed Niko Bangladesh's payment of compensation for the first blowout. On June 20th, BAPEX took back the SUV.

SIDEBAR

The Role of the Canadian Government in Foreign Countries

Part of the role of the Canadian missions in foreign countries is to make representations on behalf of Canadian companies. Indeed, it is not unusual for a Canadian mission to go as far as intervening on behalf of a Canadian company. The mission can also assist a company by identifying and even introducing the company to key government decision makers. At the same time, it can provide the company with information as to the mission's assessment of the issues involved when the company does business in a foreign country. The Canadian government is clear that when it introduces company officials to foreign government decision makers, it is not for the purpose of offering bribes.

The Second Blowout

On June 24, 2005, while Niko was bypass-drilling a relief well to seal off the gas leak caused during the January blowout, a second explosion occurred. *The Daily Star* reports that thousands of people had to leave as the huge fireball leapt 46 metres (150 feet). It took over two months for the flames to die down (*The Daily Star* 2009).

The RCMP

The Niko Resources case was one of the first under the new Canadian legislation and was seen by many as a true test for the new *Corruption of Foreign Public Officials Act*. The first conviction under the Act was the case of another Alberta energy company, Hydro Kleen, which resulted in a fine of $25,000. Canada was seen by many as a laggard when it came to enforcing its own crime legislation. It took nearly ten years after passing the CFPO legislation for the government to dedicate any RCMP resources to actually enforcing it. The Canadian government simply did not take its international commitments under the United Nations and the OECD seriously. As *The Globe and Mail* reported:

> Milos Barutciski, a regulatory expert who advised the government on the drafting of the law, quickly arranged a professional conference concerning the new prohibition. Afterward, over a meal with a senior lawyer from the Department of Justice and several other colleagues, Barutciski pressed the federal official, whom Barutciski declines to identify by name. How many police officers and prosecutors was Ottawa going to devote to this new international effort?
>
> "We're not dedicating any resources," he says he was told.
>
> "It was disheartening," says Barutciski, now a partner at Bennett Jones. "At the same time the government was issuing press releases out of Foreign Affairs about how Canada was doing the right thing…these guys were saying, 'That's it. We're not doing anything more.'
>
> "I was blown away. If you're not dedicating resources to it, then you effectively have no law."
>
> Canadian officials have never explained why Ottawa did not take the convention more seriously in its early days. In an interview, one federal government lawyer theorized, "It was an international political convention and it probably sailed through cabinet without skin off anyone's nose. … Why did it take so long [to enforce]? If you're suggesting that there wasn't enough attention put to it, I can't argue with that."
>
> But if the federal government believed it could shirk its obligations, it underestimated the will of the OECD and the power of public shaming.
>
> While other member nations were dedicating investigators and prosecutors to the anti-bribery cause, and racking up staggering fines against major corporations along the way, Canada largely did nothing. In 2007, at a Washington, D.C., conference of anti-corruption lawyers, Canada was included in a list of countries dubbed the "coalition of the unwilling." Transparency International, the anti-corruption group, routinely ranks Canada alongside countries like Bulgaria and Greece for its poor performance. As part of the OECD convention, each member country is graded on its efforts, and Canada's reviewers have repeatedly expressed dismay about how a country that is home to so many international mining and oil giants has garnered only one conviction.
>
> As recently as May 2011, the chair of the OECD anti-bribery group was still chastising Canada. "It's quite astonishing that, having so many operations in such difficult areas, one has not more cases," said Mark Pieth, a Swiss lawyer who has overseen the OECD group since its inception in 1990. "What I have to say to Canada is, wake up to your responsibilities. And be what you're actually assuming to be, and that's an economic superpower—a G7 superpower. That brings obligations with it."

The message had in fact resonated, even if it had yet to produce results. By April 2008, the RCMP had hand-picked 15 officers, at a cost of $3.1 million annually, to exclusively investigate cases of foreign bribery by Canadian companies. (McArthur 2011; RCMP 2011)

The Niko Resources case cost the RCMP about $870,000 and involved the cooperation of several other law enforcement agencies, including the Bangladeshi Anti Corruption Commission, the United States Department of Justice, the FBI, and enforcement agencies in Japan, the United Kingdom, Switzerland, and Barbados.

Niko Resources

Upon learning of the investigation by the RCMP, Niko Canada took a proactive approach. For example, it sent a notice to all Niko employees in whatever country they were in, instructing them to preserve documents and electronic information that might be relevant to the investigation. An audit committee comprising un-related, independent directors convened its first meeting within 48 hours of knowing about the investigation. At the same time, independent legal counsel was brought in and asked to oversee an independent forensic investigation. The RCMP was given unfettered access to people and documents, including all electronic information.

In moving forward, Niko implemented several anti-corruption measures prior to the issuing of the courts probation order. Finally, when the issue came to court, Niko pleaded guilty to breaching section 3(1)(b) of the *Corruption of Foreign Officials Act*. In other words, it pleaded guilty to bribing a foreign public official.

Sentencing and Probation Order

On June 24, 2011, Mr. Justice Brooker of the Court of Queen's Bench in Calgary, Alberta sentenced Niko to pay a fine of $9.5 million and to be subject to a probation period of three years. The probation order has some seven pages of requirements that Niko must demonstrate and be in compliance with the Court order and Canada's anti-corruption laws. It was noted by the court that Niko did not actually benefit from the bribes offered to the minister of energy.

DISCUSSION QUESTIONS

1. Compare the probation order with the actions that Niko had taken to rectify and prevent the situation occurring again. What is different? Were these actions important? What more could Niko be doing? Compare Niko's actions with Transparency International guidelines for Canadian companies. What more might be added?

2. What else might Niko Resources do to clear its name of the conviction?

3. What concerns might you have in working in an overseas branch of a Canadian energy company?

4. Why did the Canadian government delay international anti-corruption investigations for nearly a decade? Do you think this was right?

5. How has the impact on Niko's access to natural capital and financial capital been affected by its access to social licence issues?

SUGGESTED READINGS AND ONLINE RESOURCES

Levant, E. 2010. *Ethical oil: The case for Canada's oil sands*. Toronto: McClelland & Stewart.

McArthur, G. 2011. Niko Resources: Ottawa's corruption test case. *The Globe and Mail, Report on Business*. August 25. http://www.theglobeandmail.com/report-on-business/rob-magazine/niko-resources-ottawas-corruption-test-case/article2140358/.

Shell International BV. 2008. *Shell energy scenarios to 2050*. http://www-static.shell.com/static/public/downloads/brochures/corporate_pkg/scenarios/shell_energy_scenarios_2050.pdf.

Stern, N., et al. 2006. *Stern review on the economics of climate change*. Cambridge: Cambridge University Press.

Tertzakian, P. 2009. *The end of energy obesity*. New York: John Wiley & Sons.

Transparency International Canada. 2011. *Anti-corruption compliance checklist*. 1st ed. Toronto: TI-Canada.

REFERENCES

American Council for an Energy-Efficient Economy. 2012. Home electronics. http://www.aceee.org/consumer/home-electronics.

Benjamin, A. 2007. Stern: Climate change a "market failure." *The Guardian*. November 29. http://www.guardian.co.uk/environment/2007/nov/29/climatechange.carbonemissions.

Canada. Department of Justice. 1999. *Corruption of Foreign Public Officials Act: A guide*. May. http://www.justice.gc.ca/eng/dept-min/pub/cfpoa-lcape/guide.pdf.

Canada. Foreign Affairs and International Trade. 2011. *Corporate social responsibility—bribery and corruption, twelfth annual report to Parliament*. October 17. http://www.international.gc.ca/trade-agreements-accords-commerciaux/ds/12-report-rapport.aspx?view=d#iii.

Corruption of Foreign Public Officials Act. S.C. 1998, c. 34. http://laws.justice.gc.ca/eng/acts/C-45.2.

Court of Queen's Bench of Alberta, Judicial District of Calgary. 2011. *Agreed statement of facts: Her Majesty the Queen and Niko Resources Ltd.* http://www.osler.com/uploadedFiles/Agreed%20statement%20of%20facts.pdf.

Daily Star. 2009. Tengratila blow-out victims demand full compensation. June 24. http://www.thedailystar.net/newDesign/news-details.php?nid=93899.

Edmonton Journal. 2011. Ethical oil idea misses the point of oilsands debate. http://www.edmontonjournal.com/business/Ethical+idea+misses+point+oilsands+debate/5781774/story.html. November 29.

Greenpeace. 2012. Canadian seal hunt. http://archive.greenpeace.org/comms/vrml/rw/text/z04.html.

International Energy Association (IEA). 2011. Oil market report. May 12. http://omrpublic.iea.org/omrarchive/12may11sup.pdf.

Knittel, C. 2011. Automobiles on steroids: Product attribute trade-offs and technological progress in the automobile sector. *American Economic Review* 101 (7): 3368–3399. http://www.aeaweb.org/articles.php?doi=10.1257/aer.101.7.3368.

McArthur, G. 2011. Niko Resources: Ottawa's corruption test case. *The Globe and Mail Report on Business,* August 25. http://www.theglobeandmail.com/report-on-business/rob-magazine/niko-resources-ottawas-corruption-test-case/article2140358/.

Royal Canadian Mounted Police (RCMP). 2011. Corruption charge laid against Niko Resources. June 24. http://www.rcmp-grc.gc.ca/ab/news-nouvelles/2011/110624-niko-eng.htm.

Statistics Canada. 2011. Exports of goods on a balance-of-payments basis, by product. http://www40.statcan.gc.ca/l01/cst01/gblec04-eng.htm.

Stern, N. 2006. What is the economics of climate change? *World Economics* 7 (2) (April–June). http://www.enjoy.eans.net/Presse/PMitt/2006/061030c76.pdf.

Tertzakian, P. 2009. *The end of energy obesity.* New York: John Wiley & Sons.

Transparency International. 2010. *Corruption perceptions index 2010.* Berlin: Transparency International. http://www.transparency.org/policy_research/surveys_indices/cpi/2010/results.

Transparency International. 2011. *Corruption perceptions index 2011.* Berlin: Transparency International. http://cpi.transparency.org/cpi2011/results.

United Nations Office on Drugs and Crime. 2004. United Nations Convention Against Corruption. New York: United Nations. http://www.unodc.org/documents/treaties/UNCAC/Publications/Convention/08-50026_E.pdf.

United States. Department of Justice. 1998. *Foreign Corrupt Practices Act: A lay person's guide.* http://www.justice.gov/criminal/fraud/fcpa/docs/lay-persons-guide.pdf.

US Energy Information Administration. 2011. Canada: Background. http://www.eia.gov/countries/cab.cfm?fips=CA.

Business Ethics in Health Care

Case Study: MedLabs Inc.

Jim Pierce looked up from the papers on his desk and pushed his chair back. Why was this decision so difficult? He ran his hands through his hair and decided to take a short break. He swivelled his chair around to look out the window of his third-storey office.

Jim was the vice-president of diagnostics for MedLabs Inc., a large multinational health-care company involved in a number of health-care businesses, including diagnostic medical testing. Jim was responsible for all of MedLabs' diagnostic testing businesses, the largest division within the company. It had hundreds of millions of dollars in revenue, thousands of employees, and completed the testing every day for millions of patients across Canada. MedLabs' basic diagnostic business consisted of providing medical testing for out-patients (patients not currently admitted to a hospi-

tal) by collecting samples (blood, urine, or stool) from them at collection sites run by MedLabs, transporting the samples to a laboratory for testing, and then reporting the results to the physician who ordered the test.

Jim's gaze settled on the golf course across the street. Two golfers were standing over their balls in the middle of the 18th fairway, looking across the large pond in front of them to the green, and, from their body language, obviously discussing their options. Jim chuckled to himself because he had been in their position many times before. Golfing was his thing. The players had both driven good drives off the tee and their balls were lying in the middle of the fairway, but the hole was designed to present the players with a difficult choice at this point. The safe choice was to lay up short on the left-hand side of the fairway and then chip onto the green. The riskier choice was to try to hit across the pond. It was a long distance to travel and the landing area was small, but it was possible and the rewards were great. Jim continued to watch, curious to see which choice each golfer would make.

It was somewhat like the choice that he had to make for his diagnostic business: a safe option with a known payback, or a riskier option with a potentially higher payback. The decision he had to make concerned what to do with MedLabs' executive health business. The executive health business serviced the needs of insurance companies that provided insurance policies for senior corporate executives. To qualify for a policy, all executives were required to undergo full physicals to determine their state of health at the time the policy was issued. The service also included ongoing check-ups to ensure that the executives stayed in good health. The executive health business had two clinics, one in Toronto and one in Montreal, staffed with highly qualified doctors, specialists, and nurses. They also had all the latest diagnostic equipment, including some rare and in-demand instruments such as MRI machines.

Given the incomes of senior corporate executives, these types of insurance policies could be worth millions of dollars, so the insurance companies were willing to pay for the best testing to get the best information possible. Because the clinics were private and the insurance companies were paying the costs, clients could normally be seen within a couple of weeks of requesting an appointment, and most of their diagnostic procedures could be completed during their first appointment. MedLabs had owned the business for about 10 years and while the financial performance had been inconsistent at first, the clinics now had a stable set of customers and consistent financial returns.

The issue with the business was not financial or service-oriented—it was reputational. Jim thought back to MedLabs' senior executive meeting three weeks before and the words of MedLabs' CEO, Brian Avery, echoed in his mind:

> Given the recent events, I would like each of you to go back and look at your businesses with a critical eye and determine whether we are engaged in anything else that has the potential to damage our reputation like this incident did. The board of directors would prefer not to have any more surprises. I would like to discuss any of these businesses at our meeting next month and please come prepared with action plans for how to deal with them.

The incident that the CEO had been referring to was an incident in MedLabs' water-testing business, in which *E. coli* had gotten into the water supply in a small town and a number of people had died. MedLabs was not responsible in any way for the incident but because it was the laboratory that had done the testing and reported the *E. coli* contamination, it was featured prominently on a number of newspaper front pages and in a few lawsuits. Jim had been the executive responsible for the water-testing business at the time, and after the incident he had decided to sell it because he believed that the reputational risk had outweighed the financial gains. The sale of the water business was closing next week. The decision he was facing was whether the executive health business held the same kinds of risks. He did not want to relive the past few months again.

The main issue with the executive clinics was that they were private diagnostic clinics operating within the public health-care system in Canada (sometimes referred to as medicare). The Canadian health-care system is based on principles that are enshrined in federal legislation called the *Canada Health Act*. These principles include universal access and government funding, which mean that everyone who needs a procedure should have access to it and that the costs of the testing are borne by the government, not the individual. One outcome of this system was long waiting lists for a number of crucial and expensive high-tech tests, including MRIs and CAT scans. The waiting lists were managed based on need, and in some cases patients had to wait months to get their necessary tests. In Canada, there was no way to move ahead on the waiting list—even if you were prepared to pay for the procedure. In Ontario, this principle was enshrined in section 17(1) of the *Commitment to the Future of Medicare Act* as the anti-"queue-jumping" provision, which states that "no person ... shall, pay or confer a benefit ... in exchange for conferring upon [a patient] a preference in obtaining access to [medical services]." For most people, this provision was not a problem because it applied only to cases of bribery or paying a medical professional to move up in the queue. However, the provision created an interesting problem when taken in the context of the executive clinics because there was no waiting list at the clinics and the government did not pay for the testing—the insurance companies did. The executive clinics were allowed to exist because there was an exception to the queue-jumping provision that allowed someone to jump the queue when the testing or procedures were required to qualify for an insurance policy.[1] After the meeting last month, Jim had contacted MedLabs' in-house lawyers to confirm this interpretation and they had verified that the executive clinics were in technical compliance with the exemptions of the medicare system in Canada.

---

1 The actual exemption was found in section 24(1)8.2(iv) of Regulation 552 under the *Health Insurance Act* (R.R.O. 1990, Reg. 552). It is referred to as the "Third-Party Exemption" and it exempts from medicare non-medically necessary services rendered in response to the request of a third party (such as an insurance company, employer, or university). The exemption reads: "The following services ... are not insured services .... The production or completion of a document, or the transmission of information to any person other than the insured person, if the document or the transmission of the information relates to an entitlement to benefits, including insurance benefits or benefits under a pension plan."

Jim's rational side believed the compliance argument but his emotional side found it a little uncomfortable. All he had to do was think back to the dinner party he and his wife had hosted the week before to feel doubtful. His brother, Bob, a surgeon in a public hospital, had been at the party, and Jim had asked his opinion on the dilemma with the executive clinics. His brother's response had surprised him:

> Jim, you know I respect you a lot, but honestly, if you are worried about reputation, do you really think people who read on the front page of the paper that corporate executives can get an MRI within a few days, while the rest of us have to wait over three months, are going to care at all that there is a technical exemption buried in some regulation? What you are talking about is a two-tiered system where some people can pay to get access to health care that other people cannot get. In Canada, that is a threat to the whole health-care system. It's a slippery slope and who decides when or where it stops?

Jim had brought up his brother's comments at the next weekly meeting with his senior diagnostic managers. Some of them had agreed with his brother, but just as many were comfortable with the status quo: the clinics were within the exemption; therefore, there were no ethical issues. Bob Paterson, Jim's manager of patient services, had voiced this opinion during the managers' meeting:

> Jim, I am not sure what you are worried about. This isn't the water business. No one is going to die. The services we offer are clearly exempt from medicare, the government knows we are providing them, and the clinics are a model organization for health-care delivery. We are all proud of them and I know you are too. The clinics make everyone happy: the patients are happy; the insurance companies are happy; the doctors are happy; the employees are happy; we are happy; and we think the government is happy. My vote is to keep business as usual.

Did MedLabs have an obligation to go beyond technical compliance? Was the government really comfortable with the clinics? If it was not, then as the clinics grew, the reputational risk would grow. MedLabs was already talking about plans to broaden its services, and hoped to expand to Calgary and Vancouver. After his managers' meeting, Jim had decided to check what the government's position on the executive clinics was. He had made some informal inquiries with the Ministry of Health and although no one would confirm that they were legal, they did confirm that the clinics operated in a "grey area"; the government knew they existed and chose not to do anything about them.

Jim's attention focused back onto the golf course just as the first golfer hit his shot. He had chosen the safe option and his shot landed safely on the fairway as expected, a short chip shot away from the green. Jim's immediate reaction was to conclude that he also needed to make the safe choice and sell or exit the executive health business. The reputational risk was just too great.

As his mind began planning what it would look like to exit the business, the second golfer began lining up his shot. He was going to take the risk and hit over the pond. What would that option look like for the executive clinics? MedLabs could keep the clinics and continue to run them. They were profitable and Jim and the other MedLabs managers had an obligation to the shareholders to provide them with a reasonable return. Jim was sure they would find a buyer for the business—they were always being approached—but he was also sure that MedLabs would not receive as much financial compensation from a sale as it would from continuing to run the clinics. The margins were good (but not *too* good) because MedLabs had always run the clinics the right way: It had charged reasonable fees for its services, and invested most of the revenue back into having the best medical professionals, equipment, and facilities possible. This was not a business that was making money at the expense of providing excellent services to its clients, or paying fair wages to its employees.

Jim also had to consider the other groups of people that were involved in the clinics. The clinics were really a model organization for health-care delivery. The physicians who worked there were given the latitude to prescribe any medical diagnostics that they felt were necessary, they had access to all the latest equipment and medical technologies, and they were compensated well for their services. The patients were also treated extremely well and received whatever diagnostics they required within a reasonable time. In fact, the patients of the clinic were almost always satisfied. Jim remembered what he had heard just the week before from a patient who had stopped him in the reception area of the clinic during a visit: "This is the best medical service I have ever received. This is what health care should be like for everyone—all the time." Finally, there were the insurance companies and the corporations that had requested the testing in the first place. Issuing these kinds of insurance policies was a legitimate business concern and the government had validated the business by legislating the exemption. So, if MedLabs was not offering the service, someone else would, and, as far as Jim knew, the insurance and corporate customers were extremely happy with the service they received. Maybe they should keep the clinics.

This was a tougher decision than he had thought. Jim slumped his shoulders dejectedly and looked back out the window. The second player was lining up to take his shot. As the golfer started to wind up, Jim abruptly turned his chair back to face his desk. He needed to make this decision and he did not want to be influenced by the outcome of the shot. He ran his hands through his hair again and committed to making the decision before he left the office today. He had all the information he was going to get and he had collected the opinions of everyone he felt was important. His team needed to know his decision by tomorrow so that they could prepare plans for the follow-up meeting with the CEO next week.

What should Jim do?

Key Definitions for Health-Care Business Ethics

Health care is an interesting business because it is the place where business ethics meet medical ethics. First, there are a few important key terms and concepts that anyone studying this topic needs to be familiar with.

Medical ethics are the ethics that apply in the care and treatment of patients and in medical research (Weber 2001, xi). They are often regulated by professional bodies of medical practitioners—for example, the Canadian Medical Association—which have a code of ethics. *Health-care business ethics* are broader and refer to the combination of medical ethics with the business interests of the health-care organization (Weber 2001, xiii).

There is a debate in health-care business ethics about whether organizations are required to simply comply with laws and regulations or whether, because of medical ethics, there is an obligation to go "beyond" compliance. The *strict compliance* view argues that as long as the organization is not doing anything illegal, all ethical issues have been addressed (Weber 2001, xi). The *beyond compliance* view argues that simple compliance with laws and regulations is not enough in health care and that attending to ethics in a health-care organization requires the development of an informed, sensitive, and practical understanding of the organization's responsibilities to patients, staff, the organization, and the community (Weber 2001, 8). In relation to the executive clinics case, is it enough for Jim to have satisfied himself that the clinics were in compliance with the law or does he need to consider the wider consequences to the Canadian health-care system?

Key Debates About the Health-Care System

Three interesting and related debates about the health-care system illustrate the different underlying assumptions that people have about health care.

The first debate is how to resolve situations that occur when medical ethics and business ethics come into conflict. What happens when a doctor is ethically bound to prescribe a treatment or procedure for the health of a patient and the health-care organization deems that treatment too expensive? Or what if a doctor wants to try a new experimental treatment that may save a patient's life but the health-care organization is only obligated to pay for treatments that are proven to be effective? On one side of this debate are people (such as medical professionals) who would argue that in health care, the ethics of the profession are more important than business concerns. On the other side are people who would argue that there is a limited amount of money and resources available for health care and thus an obligation to ensure that those resources are being used in the most cost-effective way. Health-care ethics are where these two positions meet, the main question being: how should health care be delivered in accordance with business principles?

The second debate takes the first debate a step further and is focused on whether health care is a business or a humanitarian activity. On one side of this debate are the people who argue that health care is not a business, has never been a business, and should not be operated as a business (Gilmartin and Freeman 2002, 53). They believe that for-profit entities, corporations, free markets, and efficiency are concepts that should not apply to health care. On the other side of the debate are the people who argue that health care was always a business and was always concerned with providing the best possible care for the amount of money that was available (Gilmartin and Freeman 2002, 54).

The third debate is whether or not health care has the same ethical standards as other businesses. On one side of this debate is the argument that health care operates at a higher ethical standard than other businesses because the services provided relate to life, death, health, and illness. This argument is often put forward by health-care professionals (Gilmartin and Freeman 2002, 54). On the other side of the debate is the argument that all businesses share similar ethical dilemmas involving people, when they take into account their employees and their customers. For example, Collins and Porras have shown that many traditional for-profit businesses have corporate values that are similar to the values of medical ethics, including respect for individual and personal growth, work that benefits society, and respect and opportunity for people (Collins and Porras 1994).

Stakeholder Analysis of the Health-Care System and the Case Study

There are two useful ways to conceptualize the stakeholders involved in the health-care system.

The first is based on who they are: an individual, an organization, or society as a whole. *Individuals* can be patients, doctors, employees, managers, and government officials. *Organizations* can be public organizations (e.g., the Ontario Ministry of Health, OHIP, hospitals), non-governmental organizations (e.g., the Canadian Medical Association), or private organizations (including private diagnostic companies and clinics). *Society* can be conceived of as patients at large—the populace, or the taxpayers—depending on the situation.

The second way is based on what role each stakeholder plays in the health-care system: patient, provider, or payer. The *patient* is the person who receives the medical treatment, whose main concerns are access and quality. Access refers to the ability to receive every treatment that is medically required within a reasonable time-frame as determined by medical needs. Quality ensures that all of the medical services patients receive are of adequate quality. In Canada, patients do not have to pay directly for most of their medical treatments, so cost is not necessarily a concern.

The *provider* is the person or entity that provides the treatment to the patient. In most cases, the primary provider is a doctor, physician, surgeon, or other medical professional. The main concerns of the provider are to be able to provide high-quality medical services and to be paid a fair compensation for their services. Medical professionals, and especially doctors, are bound by the ethical codes of their profession, but at the same time most medical professionals are also part of a larger health-care organization such as a hospital or clinic. In some cases in Canada, the provider is a private organization or even a publicly traded corporation or income trust. In any case where the medical professional is part of a larger organization, that person's medical ethics could come into conflict with the economic pressures, limits, or profit targets of the organization, with negative consequences for access to or the quality of medical services. Medical professionals who work in these organizations have to balance their medical, ethical, and professional obligations with their obligations to the organizations in which they work.

The *payer* is the person or entity that pays for the medical services. In Canada, this is almost always the government, although there are examples where it could be an individual—for an allowed test that is not covered by medicare—or an organization such as a corporation or an insurance company, as in the case study at the beginning of this chapter. The person who pays for the service is primarily concerned with how much it costs, and is less concerned with access or quality. In Canada, this has at times led to scenarios where waiting lists are longer than, medically, they should be because the government is cost-constrained or cost-conscious. In contrast, in the United States, individuals usually pay for medical services themselves, unless they are insured, so in those cases, the patient is the payer. It is also possible in the United States for individuals to purchase or be provided with health insurance. However, when health insurance companies get involved, disputes between patients and insurance companies can also arise over access to expensive medical treatments.

One way to gauge which of these many stakeholders is relevant to a particular health-care issue is to use the stakeholder methodology presented in this book in Chapter 4 to determine the legitimacy, power, and urgency of each stakeholder. In the case of the executive clinics, the potential stakeholders whose interests Jim should consider are:

- the patients (of the clinic);
- the employees (doctors and other medical professionals);
- the customers (insurance companies);
- the government (the Ontario Ministry of Health and other government agencies);
- the shareholders (of MedLabs); and

- the public as a whole (the Canadian health-care system principles against queue jumping and all the other patients who are on the waiting lists).

Using the chart provided on the following page, take a moment to complete the stakeholder analysis in the manner described in Chapter 4, by gauging each stakeholder's *legitimacy*, *power*, and *urgency* using a 5- or a 10-point scale. Remember, in this context, *legitimacy* means an objectively clear entitlement to a desired outcome or the risk the stakeholder is exposed to; *power* means the relative influence the stakeholder has over MedLabs (the decision-maker); and *urgency* considers how soon the stakeholder needs or wants its stakes to be met. Your rankings of each stakeholder on the scale you choose should be relative to the other stakeholders in the problem. For example, you could rate patients' *urgency* needs for treatment as a 4 or 5 out of 5 because the people on the wait list for procedures have medical reasons for being on the list. This rating would be relative to an *urgency* need for treatment for the customers (the insurance companies) at a lower 2 or 3 out of 5—because the *urgency* to get a test to issue an insurance policy where there is no pre-existing medical need is much less urgent. Or is it? After completing the analysis, what decision would you make in this case, using the stakeholder analysis framework suggested in Chapter 4?

While we do not have space to explore this set of priorities in detail in this chapter, does each priority pair outlined above make sense to you? Would you change any of the priorities?

Conclusion

Recommendation

When applied to the case of the executive clinics, Weber's priorities would show that the public good is more important than the clinic's patients' interests, or the interests of the insurance companies. Therefore, the public good and the prohibition against "queue jumping" are of higher ethical importance. In other words, protecting the spirit of the Canadian health-care system is more important than allowing insurance companies to get timely access to diagnostic information so they can quickly price insurance policies. Using Weber's framework, Jim should decide to exit the executive clinic business. Does this seem like the right conclusion to you? Why or why not?

The Reputational Risk Materialized

The fictional case study presented in this chapter was loosely based on a real situation. In the actual situation, MedLabs decided to sell the executive clinics to another large Canadian health-care company in 2005. The new owner expanded its services to provide lifestyle assessments, annual check-ups, and a medical concierge

Complete the Following Stakeholder Analysis Summary

	Patients	Employees	Customers	Government	Shareholders	Public
Legitimacy						
Power						
Urgency						

Weber has suggested another way of prioritizing stakeholder interests in health-care issues: by ordering the ethical interests of the stakeholders, using a set of principles that rank the four major interests that can be at play in any ethical decision (Weber 2001, 16–17). Those four interests are:

1. **Basic individual rights**—in this case, every patient's right to access medical treatment equally;

2. **Individual self-interest**—in this case, the ability of the clinic's patients to get services ahead of other patients;

3. **The interests of the organization**—in this case, the needs of the insurance companies and corporations to get medical information to issue insurance policies;

4. The **public good**—in this case, the law against queue-jumping and the protection of the idea of universal access to health care in Canada (Weber 2001, 16–17).

The set of priorities Weber suggests applying is:

- The **organization's interest** (#3) takes priority over an **individual's self-interest** (#2)
- **Individual rights** (#1) take priority over the **organization's interests** (#3)
- **The public good** (#4) takes priority over **the organization's interests** (#3)
- **The public good** (#4) takes priority over an **individual's self-interest** (#2)
- **Individual rights** (#1) take priority over **individual self-interest** (#2)

service. It also opened new clinics in Vancouver, Calgary, Ottawa, and Quebec City. The potential reputational risk of the clinics materialized in 2011 over allegations of queue-jumping in Alberta. The headline on 660News in Calgary on June 11th was: "Alleged healthcare queue-jumping could be government's downfall." The clinics are being investigated to determine whether they are complying with the law.

DISCUSSION QUESTIONS

1. Is health care a business or a humanitarian activity?
2. Does health care have different ethical standards from other businesses?
3. Can you envision a health-care business that effectively balances the needs of all of its legitimate stakeholders, including patients, customers, employees, shareholders, government, and the public? What would it look like?
4. In what order would you personally prioritize Weber's four interests: basic individual rights, individual self-interest, organizational interests, and the public good? Try to match each interest up as a pair with each other interest and prioritize which is more important to you.

SUGGESTED READINGS AND ONLINE RESOURCES

Gilmartin, M.J., and R.E. Freeman. 2002. Business ethics and health care: A stakeholder perspective. *Health Care Management Review* 27 (2): 52–65.

Thompson, D. 2005. *Restoring responsibility: Ethics in government, business & health care.* Cambridge: Cambridge University Press.

Weber, L. 2001. *Business ethics in health care: Beyond compliance.* Bloomington: Indiana University Press.

REFERENCES

660News (Calgary). 2011. Alleged healthcare queue jumping could be government's downfall. June 11. http://www.660news.com/news/local/article/239096--alleged-healthcare-cue-jumping-could-be-goverment-s-downfall.

Canada Health Act. R.S.C. 1985, c. C-6.

Commitment to the Future of Medicare Act. S.O. 2004, c. 5.

Canadian Medical Association. 1996. *Code of ethics of the Canadian Medical Association.*

Collins, J., and J. Porras. 1994. *Built to last: Successful habits of visionary companies.* New York: Harper Books.

Gilmartin, M.J., and R.E. Freeman. 2002. Business ethics and health care: A stakeholder perspective. *Health Care Management Review* 27 (2): 52–65.

Ontario Health Insurance Act. R.S.O. 1990, c. H.6.

Weber, L. 2001. *Business ethics in health care: Beyond compliance.* Bloomington: Indiana University Press.

Additional Case Exercises

---

* Cases 7, 11, and 12 written by W. Peter Kissick.

Case 1: The Glass Ceiling

You are a human resources manager for an insurance company with 2,000 employees. Both the working conditions and the pay at this company are above industry standards. For the most part, employees like working for this company. Women are well represented in departments such as sales, claims adjustments, and accounting, where they work in clerical capacities as well as in supervisory positions. However, women are poorly represented in senior management positions and on the board. A task force has just gathered information on the numbers of women in these positions. The task force calls for something to be done to address this problem. You have been asked to develop a plan of action. What will you recommend?

As you think about this problem, you decide that it is important to explore its causes. Are women not applying for senior positions? Are there really fewer women with the qualifications and competencies required for these positions? Are otherwise qualified women being discriminated against? Or does the problem result from procedures that, in unintentional and overlooked ways, produce these consequences?

On the basis of preliminary inquiries, you come across several interesting pieces of information. One, in making promotion decisions at the most senior level, executives often weigh their judgments about others in terms of whom they think they can work with productively—and getting to know others informally seems to matter. Two, at the supervisor, and lower-management levels, women often scored higher in their formal performance appraisals than men. Three, many men complain that women with children seem less willing to assume extra work because of family obligations. Four, a number of female middle managers objected to being treated differently precisely because they were women. They felt that more was expected of them, not only as co-workers but as "representative" women. Investigations showed that few women had in fact applied for senior positions; they argued that it would make it hard for them if others felt that they were promoted primarily because they were women. At the same time as when the results of the initial task force survey became known, a number of female employees voiced complaints about the way women seemed to be excluded from positions of significant authority and influence. However, you can identify no clear case in which a woman was not promoted to a senior position because of bias.

Questions: What should the company's plan of action be? Are there injustices in this situation? Are some ways of addressing this issue more fair and just than others? Are there ways of proceeding that are likely to have greater impact? What steps would you take first? What steps would you take later on?

Case 2: Homeless Men at City Bus Depot

An increasing number of homeless men have begun sitting and sleeping on the benches in the waiting room of City Bus Depot. They wear ragged, dirty clothes. They occupy seats that regular passengers would like to use. Sometimes they gather together and tell stories and jokes. They make the waiting room seem overcrowded. From time to time, they become a nuisance. Both regular passengers and staff members have begun to complain. Some kind of action has to be taken.

You have been asked by your superiors at City Bus Depot to devise a strategy to deal effectively with the homeless men problem. City Bus Depot is a public corporation. You do some research and discover several pieces of information. For example, the number of homeless people in the area has grown steadily in recent years. Many of these people have at one time or another received some form of treatment for mental illness or emotional distress. Almost all of them have had no contact with family members or relatives for several years. Every year, several homeless people die of exposure during the winter. Although the waiting room of the bus depot is the private property of the City Bus Depot corporation, you know that the waiting room is regarded as a semi-public space where people arrange to meet each other and greet and bid farewell to travellers. Some executives have proposed hiring private police to chase off vagrants and homeless people. City Bus Depot certainly has the legal right to pursue this kind of policy. But then what would become of these homeless men? Others argue that this kind of tactic might backfire: it might cause public disturbances that would be upsetting to customers and staff and adversely affect the image of a people-first organization that the corporation is trying to cultivate. Does the corporation have a responsibility to act on behalf of these men in some way, either by itself or in conjunction with other local businesses and agencies?

Questions: What do you propose and why? What steps would you take? Whom would you involve?

Case 3: Off-Budget Payments in International Business

Consider how managers in international businesses should respond to the following situations. Are there some basic principles that might help those involved determine how best to act?

(a) An international business firm, AA, contracted to help construct a natural gas pipeline in a country in South America. Local police informed the firm that a protection ring had been threatening residents in a middle-class neighbourhood in the large city where the firm had located its project headquarters. The firm has helped to find housing for most of its expatriate managers, engineers, technicians, and other professionals in this neighbourhood. The police informed the firm that they would be able to spend the extra hours needed to control the protection gang. However, they would expect to be paid for this extra time.

Question: Should the firm, like other international firms, hire the police for this extra duty? Or should the firm adopt a different strategy?

(b) The same firm, AA, has been informed by the managers of the warehouse at the docks that they required extra payments to arrange to release the equipment that it had shipped to the port. The warehouse managers explained that they were understaffed and that if the firm wanted to obtain its shipments in a timely manner, it would help if the firm made extra payments to facilitate the efforts to release the goods.

Question: Should this firm, like many other international firms using this warehouse, make these extra payments?

(c) Another firm, CC, has been conducting business in East Asia for several decades. When the firm as a whole adopted fairly strict guidelines with respect to gifts and off-budget payments, officials of the firm in East Asia successfully asked for an exception. They explained that executives of local firms with whom they had been, or hoped to be, doing business expected to receive lavish gifts for the weddings and funerals of family members. The CC officials in East Asia argued that it would be impossible to arrange business transactions with local firms unless they were prepared to make these unsolicited gifts.

Question: As with AA above, should CC make these payments, as an acknowledgment of the cultural practices in that country?

(d) Another international firm, DD, put in a bid to help construct a power grid in a South Asian country. The government official in charge of selecting which bids would be considered demanded an extra payment from all applicants who wanted their bids to be judged as having met the minimal specifications. The bids were indeed complicated. This public official and his staff had to screen these bids carefully. Other firms competing for this project offered the official even more than he requested. They explained that all of these officials were underpaid.

Questions: Should DD make these payments as well? What other alternatives might it pursue?

(e) Another Canadian-based international firm, EE, has been selling high-tech equipment in developing countries. Because it was unfamiliar with local customs and lacked contacts with officials, it was using local agents to help develop contracts. It required these agents to sign statements that they would abide by local laws and not offer payoffs in order to secure contracts. However, several agents submitted bills for their services that seemed excessive. Some of the firm's employees working in these areas worried that EE was indirectly implicated in making questionable payments. Other employees felt that what the agents were doing was no different from what lobbyists do in Canada.

Questions: What actions might the firm take regarding its relationship with these agents? Why?

Case 4: Barama Forestry Company in Guyana*

Barama is a forestry company headquartered in Malaysia that harvests lumber and wood products from a number of other developing countries. Barama has worked hard to become an environmentally responsible firm. It avoids clear-cut harvesting. It contracts with local firms to plant trees in the areas it has lumbered. Recently, it received an award from the Forestry Stewardship Council for its environmental policies. It won this award in part for its environmental practices in Guyana. However, its social experiences in Guyana were very mixed. It developed the contract with the government of the country, which legally owned title to the lands that Barama lumbered in a remote area in the northwest part of Guyana. There had been no roads into the area, which was accessible primarily by river. Trace amounts of gold had been discovered in the rivers in other parts of Guyana. In several areas, these led to significant gold finds. There were several mostly illiterate indigenous peoples who had been living in these remote areas for centuries. The indigenous people lived in and off the forests. They thought of the lands as theirs on the basis of use. Of course, they did not use all of the forest; they would pass through to hunt and fish and gather fruit, berries, and edible wild plants. Barama generally respected the traditions of these people and their ways of life. An environmental consulting group had cautioned the firm that greater sensitivity was called for in their relations with the indigenous groups.

Barama built roads into this area in area in order to move in equipment and workers and to bring out the lumber that they harvested. Several unexpected things began to happen. Large numbers of men living along the coast travelled along these newly developed lumber roads and began small mining operations along the river in this remote area. They were unruly both when they failed to find gold and when they did. A number did find gold, although mostly in small amounts. They ignored the customs and implicit land claims of the indigenous peoples. In some areas, the men abducted teenage girls from among the indigenous villages and forced them to become prostitutes. They burned houses in some villages where people protested.

---

* This case is based on research originally undertaken by Gail Whiteman. Another version of this case appears in Frederick Bird and Stewart Herman, eds., *International Businesses and the Challenges of Poverty in the Developing World* (Houndmills, UK: Palgrave Macmillan, 2004).

Questions: What responsibilities does Barama have with respect to this situation? To what degree is it responsible for the ugly situation that developed? Barama has now finished logging. Are there any steps it should now take? Are there actions it should have undertaken previously? Are there ways that it might have limited access to its lumber roads or closed them down after it ceased operations? Could it have used its own legal expertise to help the indigenous peoples legalize their traditional land rights? Could it have managed its operations in different ways to avoid or reduce the harm subsequently experienced by the indigenous population?

Case 5: Paying Taxes in Italy*

In the late 1950s, a new manager was appointed as the director of an American bank that was recently established in Italy. The former manager had been recalled to the United States because of how he managed the way that the bank paid its Italian taxes. At that time in Italy, firms prepared tax forms in which they understated their earning by at least 30 percent (it should be noted that the historical situation described in this case is different today). The government in turn initially levied tax assessments in which it assumed that firms exceeded their recorded last year's earnings by at least 30 percent. The firm then hired a *commercialista*, who negotiated with government officials until they reached an agreement. They were more likely to reach an agreement based on an assessment of earnings that was closer to what the firm initially announced if the *commercialista* offered a cash payment, a *bustarella*, to the government agent.

The former bank manager refused to hire a *commercialista*. He cited the firm's earnings accurately and paid taxes that he judged the firm actually owed. The government responded by charging the firm a much higher tax, based on the government's assumption that the firm's initial statement of earnings understated its actual earnings by at least 30 percent. The firm protested and refused to pay any additional taxes. The government then reviewed the firm's tax form and disallowed as a legitimate expense the interest that the firm had paid its customers on their deposits. This was a basic expense and should have been allowed. When the bank manager inquired about this matter, he was told that the government was just trying to get his attention. They urged him to hire a knowledgeable *commercialista* so that they could begin the negotiations that should have started months ago. The bank manager hired a *commercialista* but instructed this agent not to make any kind of *busterella* payments, because these seemed to him both unethical and in violation of American law. In the end, the bank was charged a tax less than the government's initial statement but still considerably larger than the amount the firm felt that it ought to have paid based on accurate estimates of its earnings. The bank manager was replaced, and the new manager was instructed to find a better solution.

How should the new bank manager deal with the tax problem? The new manager was also a man of conscience. He knew that the situation was complex. It should be noted that while the practices described above have been widespread, there was also considerable public outcry about corruption in Italy. Several governments were voted out of power because of public concerns about corruption. Nonetheless, the practice of tax negotiation, which was not fully transparent,

---

* This case is based on a longer version originally written by Tom Donaldson.

worked similarly for all concerned. The new manager wondered: Are these practices much different from the practices of large firms in the United States that hire clever accountants to use the intricacies of generally accepted accounting principles to reduce their apparent earnings, and hire smart lawyers to find loopholes in the tax law?

Questions: In such a situation, should one just pay taxes in the same way that the other Italian firms do, and then send back alternative books about expenses and earnings to the head offices in the United States? Were there alternatives? Might it have been possible to collaborate with other firms to develop alternative approaches to the tax problem that involved fewer questionable practices? What was just in this situation? What was practical? What are the costs involved in violating one's own conscience? What would you recommend?

Case 6: Child Labour in South Asia

The clothing firm Gladrags has been purchasing much of the clothing it sells from various suppliers in the developing world. Gladrags has been doing quite well. Its clothes are stylish, popular, and well made. It has intentionally sought to work with manufacturers in developing countries not only to save on labour costs but also to foster the economic development of these areas. For the most part, design ideas have originated at Gladrags' headquarters in North America. The company developed overall policies regarding pay and working conditions. It has succeeded in getting all of its suppliers to pay going wages or better and to ensure that working conditions are safe, healthy, and pleasant. Additionally, the company requires that all suppliers provide adequate maternity leave, offer opportunities for workers to increase their skills, and allow workers both adequate vacation and sick leave. As a result of these policies, the suppliers and partners helping to manufacture products for Gladrags enjoy very good reputations in their communities. People like to work for these firms.

After a close inspection of a number of the supplier/partner firms in South Asia, Gladrags executives became aware of a problem that they had previously overlooked: in a number of these plants, young teenagers were working alongside their mothers. The company had publicly stated its opposition to child labour. Yet its own suppliers seemed to be employing teenagers. Company executives formally wrote to the managers of these South Asian firms and expressed their concern. These managers replied that the practice of employing young teenagers was generally acceptable in the local culture and that the mothers and children involved had sought to work together when the plants opened. In fact, the managers noted that they thought it was good to keep family members together in this manner. Younger children often played in corners of the factories and sometimes helped with errands. This allowed families to eat lunch together. Older children helped younger children with reading and other useful activities. The managers pointed out that the local schools were not very good and that many of the students would either perform poorly or receive an inferior education. The managers argued that two adverse consequences were likely to result if they were to prohibit the children from working. One, the children would instead probably end up working in shops and factories that were dangerous and unhealthy, paid lower wages, and separated children from their mothers. Two, both the mothers and children would stop working and the families would become more impoverished.

Questions: What should the executives at Gladrags do about this situation? They are concerned about the fact that the employment of children may both obstruct educational opportunities and also be unhealthy. It clearly violates company standards. However, the suppliers are not legally part of their company. What is fair and just in this situation? Are there different standards for different cultures and communities? Are there useful historical examples of how to handle this situation? What strategies proved most successful in reducing child labour during the periods when developed countries were initially industrializing? Is there a possible compromise? Can their suppliers offer any helpful suggestions?

Case 7: Islington Chemical and the Civil War in Malbodia

Islington Chemical Corp. (ICC) is a Toronto-based manufacturing company that produces, among other products, compounds used in the making of carpeting and synthetic flooring. While ICC has conducted extensive research into producing non-carbon-based material from which to make carpeting (such as hemp and various strong grasses), its primary product is a synthetic material called "nylene," which is made from petrochemicals. ICC prides itself on limiting, to the extent that it can, its environmental footprint. It has tried to adopt some of the environmental techniques adopted by market innovator Interface Carpets to keep both pollution and carbon emissions to a minimum at ICC plants.

ICC sells its products, including nylene, throughout the world (into markets where carpet makers are located, primarily Mexico, the United States, and Southeast Asia). It operates six manufacturing plants: three in Canada, two in the United States, and one in Mexico. All of the manufacturing plants are operated by ICC in accordance with consistent, if not identical, environmental, operational, and employment policies created by the head office in Toronto.[1] In 25 years of operation, ICC has had no major environmental issues at any of its plants. Its employment record is enviable, and ICC is considered one of the best employers in Canada in the chemical manufacturing sector.

Three years ago, ICC recognized that it was selling more and more of its nylene to carpet makers in Southeast Asia—especially to buyers in Vietnam and Thailand. At about the same time, Robert Smythe, ICC's president, received a visit from representatives of the trade commission of a small Southeast Asian country called Malbodia. The Malbodian officials were keen on attracting well-established Western companies—especially manufacturing companies—to set up operations in their island country.

Malbodia[2] is located in the South China Sea at the mouth of the Gulf of Thailand. It is an island country approximately the size of New Brunswick, with a population of 1,800,000 people. Historically, its economy was based on agriculture and fishing, until 30 years ago, when tin was discovered in minable quantities. For 20 years while the tin mines were developed, the country's abysmal standard of living increased substantially; however, with increased prosperity came political unrest to the country. In 2002, General Mahat, with the support of the military, established himself as leader of the country (by force, without any democratic

---

1   "Consistent, if not identical" because ICC has made allowances in its policies for cultural variations among the locations for employees and to take into account varying employment and environmental laws.

2   To be clear, Malbodia does not exist and is not based on any specific country, government, or people. The geography of the country, however, is meant to be somewhat realistic.

election). Clamping down on any opposition, Mahat used brutal means to retain his power. Mahat also argued that foreign corporations were "raping" the Malbodian land and "stealing" its resources, such as tin. Malbodia "purchased" tin mines from foreign mining companies (allegedly for fair value, but the mining companies suggested otherwise) and the mines were nationalized. Between 2002 and 2009, Mahat ruled as a dictator, and the two elections that were held were a sham. Given the existence of the tin reserves, the country's economy did not suffer, but its GDP was still about 25 percent the size of neighbouring countries.[3]

When ICC received the visit from the Malbodian Trade Commission (Mahat's people), Mahat and his advisers had decided that the country's economy needed diversification—including the establishment of a manufacturing sector. They had already been successful in attracting some large Western manufacturers to set up in Malbodia, and they were anxious to have ICC set up a plant there as well. The Malbodians impressed Smythe with their knowledge of the carpet-manufacturing industry in Southeast Asia. They offered tempting incentives for ICC to set up operations in Malbodia, but indicated that any plant opened in Malbodia would have to be operated as a 50–50 joint venture between the Malbodian government and ICC. (The country's officials told Smythe that Mahat did not want a repeat of the country's experience with what he thought were the unethical practices of the foreign tin-mining companies. In truth, Mahat felt entitled to a "cut" of any product that would be sold outside of Malbodia.)

Smythe discussed this proposal at length with the ICC board of directors; he was hesitant to enter into a relationship with the Malbodian government and worried that ICC might not be able to operate a plant in the "ICC way." The board, however, believed this to be a tremendous financial opportunity for ICC in light of the company's growing presence in the region, and the board felt that the Malbodians really wouldn't want to interfere with the ICC model.

In August 2008, ICC signed a joint venture agreement with the Malbodian government, with the nylene plant to open in Malbodia in April 2009. In March 2009, Mahat's officials contacted the ICC people in Malbodia and advised that "security personnel" must be hired to protect the plant. The ICC employees in Malbodia were surprised because they had not seen any evidence of vandalism or antagonism from the local people. But the Malbodian officials applied pressure and the "security personnel" were hired. (In fact, it was discovered a year later that the security personnel were a paramilitary group controlled by General Mahat, and the fees for the security went directly to Mahat.)

---

3   To put Malbodia's GDP in context, in 2007 Thailand's GDP per capita was US$8,000, Cambodia's was $1,900, Canada's was $38,600, and the United States' was $45,800.

To an extent, the ICC board was correct; ICC was permitted to set up the nylene plant in the image of its other plants, implementing both rigorous environmental standards and a generous (by Malbodian standards) employment environment. Noting that many in the workforce had had only minimal levels of schooling, ICC offered (and paid for) the equivalent of high school classes for its employees. The plant was a financial success, shipping its product to existing and even new customers in Thailand. The Malbodian government left the plant alone, except for the "security personnel" and, of course, the 50 percent cut of the revenue it took as joint venture partner. The ICC employees had expected government health and safety and environmental examiners to visit the plant (as was customary in North America), but the plant was never visited by a regulator.

In February 2011, the political climate in Malbodia changed dramatically. The Malbodian people, historically peaceful and passive, began demonstrating against their despotic government and the dictator General Mahat. Initially peaceful demonstrations were repressed brutally by Mahat—in one demonstration, a dozen protesting students were shot to death by the army. This incident spurred the repressed Malbodian people into action against an intolerable and undemocratic government. There were more protests, widespread strikes, and armed conflict.

Smythe heard about this on radio one morning and raised it at the monthly board meeting held a day later. The board was concerned about ICC's Malbodian operation. They asked the general manager of the ICC plant in Malbodia (a Canadian named Stewart Keith) to speak to the board to explain the situation so that the board could consider the situation and decide what, if any, action should be taken. At the meeting, Keith explained that he feared for the safety of his workers and the plant, noting that both the Malbodian government (the army) and the rebels have attacked and destroyed buildings in the uprisings. This worried him because of the nature of the product being manufactured at the ICC plant—a highly flammable and potentially environmentally poisonous chemical. Keith pointed out that the ICC plant was perceived as being aligned with the government, although it was clear to him that the employees were sympathetic to the rebels. He mentioned the background of the security personnel and their allegiance to Mahat. After Keith left the meeting, the board members began discussing the Malbodian operation.

Question: What should Smythe recommend to the board that ICC do about its Malbodian plant?

Case 8: Aboriginal Hiring Initiative

PC was a large manufacturing corporation with plants at eight sites employing 2,000 people. PC had developed a special initiative to hire Aboriginals, and had developed several complementary policies and programs. One, it made special effort to recruit Aboriginals. PC sent recruitment teams to areas where Aboriginals lived in order to inform them of employment opportunities. As part of its recruitment program, PC worked with local secondary schools both to let students know about employment opportunities and to offer special courses, which taught skills that were regularly used by its employees. Two, PC initiated a special apprenticeship/training program for Aboriginal youth so that they could develop the employable skills needed to work in diverse parts of the company. The company provided scholarships for those Aboriginals who qualified for this program. Three, as the business expanded over the past decade, the company was able to hire more than 70 Aboriginal employees, in a form of affirmative action. Four, the company went out of its way to contract with Aboriginal-run businesses for certain services and supplies. In some cases, PC actually helped Aboriginal entrepreneurs establish these small companies. Finally, PC established a special office within the Human Resources department whose goal was to help integrate individual Aboriginals within the larger non-Aboriginal workforce.

In spite of good intentions and much planning, after the first several years the attrition rate among the Aboriginal employees became fairly high. At present, only half as many Aboriginals worked at PC as were working there during the first two years of the program. A few Aboriginals had used their experiences at PC as a basis for seeking better jobs elsewhere. Several were dismissed because of irregular attendance and the tendency to show up late for work too often. Others drifted away. When inquiries were made, Aboriginals complained that they felt they were often subtly discriminated against. Others spoke of cultural differences. In hopes of making their Aboriginal policies work better, several executives championed the idea of developing more flexible work standards for Aboriginal employees. Almost none of the Aboriginals had succeeded in gaining any promotions. However, one Aboriginal woman, who had been promoted to a supervisory position, took the opposite position. She felt that the policies at PC were condescending and provided too many special considerations for Aboriginals.

Questions: You have been asked to develop some practical steps to address these issues. What problems seem to be of concern in this case? What injustices or conflicts seem to be at stake? What steps might you take to increase the numbers of Aboriginals who stay with PC? Alternatively, should PC view the high attrition rate as something that it ought to have expected? What should be done? Why? How would you proceed? Whom would you involve?

Case 9: Executive Compensation

You have recently been appointed to the board of directors of Large Corporation (LC). LC is a sizable business of 10,000 employees. You have been named to the board because of the active role you played in local community organizations, including a shelter program for the homeless, and because you have a growing reputation as a promising corporate lawyer. You have become aware of the increasing inequalities in society, and you have uneasy feelings about these trends. You wonder about the extent to which the policies of LC contribute to these inequalities. The compensation levels of senior executives have been raised several times over the past few years. These raises have far exceeded the normal cost-of-living increases. Not only have their salaries risen sharply, but executives have also been offered various stock options, perks, and benefits. The overall increases in executive compensation have been much greater than the increases in LC's return on investments. Twenty-five years ago, senior executives received overall compensations that were 15 times greater than the compensation for the lowest level of regular full-time employees. Today, compensations for senior executives are often more than 50 times higher. Because a large part of compensation for executives is in the form of shares in the firms they manage, the higher levels of compensation in large part reflect the tremendous increase in the value of the firm's shares during the two decades prior to 2007.

What should be done? You wonder how the level and forms of executive compensation affect workplace morale. In the face of public outcry exhibited in the recent Occupy demonstrations, you think current practices and rationales for executive compensation need to be re-examined. Arguments have been made that senior executives deserve these compensation packages because of their leadership, because they work proportionately longer hours, because otherwise they might look for employment elsewhere, and because other corporations are providing similar compensation packages. And yet, you wonder about the validity of these arguments. To what extent have boards, often constituted in large part by executives from other firms, become complicit not only in creating an inflated market in executive compensation but also indirectly in fostering and remaining uncritical with respect to possibly inflated markets in share values?

Questions: What policies with respect to compensation packages would you recommend? How would you raise this question with other board members? As you decide how to proceed, you may wish to consider the following questions: What are the most important criteria for determining levels of compensation for any workers? To what degree is it legitimate—and/or realistic—to simply set remuneration levels in terms of market forces and trends? To what degree should compensation levels be determined by years of education, background preparation, seniority, risks that workers are exposed to, skill level, hours of work, and/or actual contributions (however these may be measured) to the economic well-being of the organization in question? Note also: if employees receive what they regard as unfair compensation, the quality of their work may suffer, they may be absent more often, and they may seek employment elsewhere.

Case 10: Sustainable Development and the Oil Industry

Since the publication in 1987 of the report by the World Commission on Environment and Development (known as the Brundtland report, which introduced the phrase "sustainable development" to our lexicon), many governments, businesses, and environmental groups have argued that economic development can only be ethical if it is sustainable and ensures that future generations are no worse off as a result of the way finite natural resources are being used today. Many enterprises have begun to modify their operations in order to meet this standard. But the question arises: How can the petroleum industry meet such standards when it involves using up a non-renewable natural resource that is linked to potentially devastating climate change? It should be noted that a widely reported study in the February 2012 issue of the journal *Nature* ("The Alberta Oil Sands and Climate" by Canadian professors Andrew Weaver and Neil Swart) pointed to coal as the greatest threat to climate stability, a finding that was quickly interpreted by many as a confirmation that the oil sands were "not so bad after all." However, Weaver and Swart's study made clear that this was a matter of degree; though less damaging than coal, the oil sands were still a significant contributor to the larger problem of climate change.

One traditional way of addressing—some would say putting off—the problem of sustainable development has been to step up efforts to develop biofuels and to explore for and extract energy from sources of oil and gas in offshore deposits and in shale and tar sands (this option has become more difficult to pursue because the number of oil and gas deposits that are easily accessible is dwindling, and most newly discovered sources are increasingly expensive to exploit). Others have argued that the petroleum industry needs to work much harder to conserve the oil and gas it extracts from the earth. It can stop flaring (the controlled burning of natural gas) and find uses for otherwise unused associated gases. It can work to make sure that its products are used efficiently. It can champion the use of smaller motors, lighter cars, and more efficient furnaces. It can explore more efficient ways of utilizing petroleum byproducts in the chemical and plastic industries, including more accessible and more easily operated recycling centres for plastics. It can improve its efforts to reduce the amount of petroleum wasted during extraction, transmission, and refining.

Questions: What else can and should the petroleum industry do? To what extent should it be exploring and promoting alternative sources of energy? Petroleum firms are increasingly becoming involved in alternative energy sources, and are now identifying themselves more broadly as "energy companies." But are they doing enough?

To the degree that it is exhausting a non-renewable source of wealth in particular areas, should the oil industry be obligated to help create and protect other sources of wealth (in the forms of human and social capital)? What actions seem just and fair? What would you recommend? Why?

The following questions will require some additional research:

To what extent has the use of biofuels adversely affected food prices, and how will this affect consumers? Should the oil industry encourage and/or accept rigorous carbon taxes, designed both to reduce consumption and foster greater efficiency in the use of this non-renewable resource?

Case 11: The Accounting Error

Sue is a corporate lawyer working at a private law firm and Rex is an accountant working at a private firm of chartered accountants (CAs). They are working on a prospectus for an initial public offering (IPO) of a mutual corporate client. As a lawyer, Sue owes a duty of "utmost good faith" to her client, which includes looking out for her client's best interests, and a duty not to disclose her client's confidential information to third parties.

When a company wishes to raise capital by issuing securities—most commonly, shares of company stock—it must comply with securities laws. These laws include the requirement that an issuer provide full disclosure to its prospective investors of its management and affairs. This is typically done in a document know as a "prospectus." The prospectus must be approved by the securities commission of any province into which the issuer will sell its shares. Given these requirements, companies usually retain lawyers and accountants to help prepare the prospectus, and a CA must audit the company's financial statements that appear in the prospectus.

The prospectus that Sue and Rex worked on has been approved by the Ontario Securities Commission (OSC), and the client is in the midst of launching the IPO and "selling its stock." The subscription rate for the stock is very high. At this time, Rex confides to Sue that there is an error in the financial statements that have been included in the client's prospectus, which his firm audited. Rex refuses to tell the client. Sue knows that under the Ontario *Securities Act*, there is potential civil and criminal liability for making a misleading statement in a prospectus, or, in essence, for not correcting a misleading statement (in the words of the Act, one must "make a statement that is necessary to make the statement not misleading"). The OSC also has the power to revoke the prospectus and order all of the shares purchased to be reversed where it determines that a prospectus contains an error.

Questions: Should Sue disclose to her client the fact that the financial statements contain an error? Should Sue do anything else? Suppose that Sue tells the client about the error, but the client refuses to do anything further. Should Sue tell the OSC about the error?

Case 12: The Good Coffee Company Goes Public*

Jane closed the door to her office after her meeting with Albert Chin ended and Albert had returned to his office. Jane, the vice-president, operations of Good Coffee Company (GCC), had just learned from Albert some rather unsettling news about GCC's coffee supply situation in Central America. She needed to decide what to say to her boss, GCC president John Good, given that this news would certainly have some effect on GCC's initial public offering (IPO).

GCC is a small but growing chain of coffee houses that was started as a single outlet by John Good ten years earlier in Kingston, Ontario. John, a Kingston native who had grown disenchanted with a consulting career in Toronto, decided to move back to his hometown to, as he put it, "regroup." With money that he had saved from his consulting career, John purchased a local café at a reasonable price. He rebranded it "Good Coffee Company," both as a play on his name and to indicate the social mission that he wanted it to have.

John was personally committed to issues such as fair-trade coffee (having spent a summer in South America where he saw first-hand the agricultural conditions in countries such as Ecuador), and he also felt that a socially conscious message would work well in a café located close to a university campus. Immediately, John began to work on supply agreements, so that when he reopened the café, 50 percent of the coffee and chocolate products he sold would be fair-trade certified.

His Kingston café was wildly successful. Within three years, he had opened three more cafés, all in small Ontario cities with university campuses. John operated all of the outlets under the GCC brand and corporate name; he was the sole shareholder and the controlling force behind GCC. He wanted to make sure that in each location, the social and environmental programs of his Kingston store were replicated. Among these programs were:

- a comprehensive recycling program;
- a commitment to hiring university students (whom John felt often needed the additional income);
- a supplier policy that included very stringent requirements for fair payment of agricultural workers and producers (a very comprehensive notion of fair trade); and
- a commitment to donating 5 percent of after-tax profits to community poverty organizations (chosen by the employees at each location).

---

* The company and the country described in this case are both entirely fictitious.

By fall 2010, John operated 27 GCC outlets across Canada. He was no longer the sole shareholder, having taken on a small number of additional investors, but he still controlled the company—both operationally, as the president, and legally, as the owner of 55 percent of the GCC shares. Even with this level of corporate growth, all GCC locations practised the same principles that John had introduced at the first few locations. John was more or less content with his financial reward (substantial but not huge), but he was especially proud of the social footprint of GCC—which had a very positive community and ethically minded public image in the various locations in which it operated.

It was against this backdrop that a former classmate currently employed at a Toronto investment house suggested to John that it would be advantageous for GCC to "go public," or offer its shares to the public so as to raise capital to double its operations. John was hesitant—not so much because he would no longer be the majority shareholder—but because he worried about what rapid growth might do to GCC's social principles. The investment adviser assured John that the attraction for investors to this share issue would be the "big picture business model" GCC presented.

Jane was quite familiar with GCC's history—indeed, she too had been attracted by GCC's principled operations when she joined the company five years ago. But Albert Chin, her acquisitions manager, had just told her about what was happening in San Filipe, the Central American country from which GCC purchased 70 percent of its coffee (strictly adhering to fair-trade supplier policies). Albert reported that the recent political instability in San Filipe had worsened, and that a violent organized-crime ring had effectively taken over much of the coffee production in the country, including the producers that GCC bought from. Albert and Jane knew that San Filipe was particularly important to John Good, because he had increased the amount of coffee purchased by GCC from that country after he visited the country and several of its poorest coffee growers (where workers had been paid about $3 a day for their labour). San Filipe was considered the poorest Central American country, and agreements with North American companies such as GCC were seen as essential to its economic development and to enhancing the living conditions of its agricultural workers. Jane's position made her responsible for all coffee supply arrangements, including the contracts with producers in San Filipe. She knew that it would take weeks, or even months, to replace the supply of coffee from San Filipe. And she also knew that the IPO was scheduled to close in two weeks.

Question: What should Jane tell John Good?

Index